METHODISTS AND PAPISTS

David Butler

METHODISTS AND PAPISTS

*John Wesley and the
Catholic Church
in the Eighteenth Century*

DARTON · LONGMAN + TODD

First published in 1995 by
Darton, Longman and Todd Ltd
1 Spencer Court, 140–142 Wandsworth High Street
London SW18 4JJ

ISBN 0–232–52110–7

A catalogue record for this book is available
from the British Library.

Phototypeset in 10½/12¾ pt Garamond
by Intype, London
Printed and bound in Great Britain by Page Bros, Norwich

To Fionna, Jonathan, Michael
and my mother Alice

Contents

Abbreviations

JWJ	*John Wesley's Journals* Vols 1–8, ed. Curnock, London 1909.
JWL	*John Wesley's Letters* Vols 1–8, ed. Telford, London 1931.
NNT	*Explanatory Notes upon the New Testament*, 2 Vols, London 1831.
WJW	*Works of John Wesley*, Abingdon edn. Various editors. Nashville 1984ff.
Works	*The Works of Rev. John Wesley* A.M., Vols I-XIV, ed. Jackson. London 1829ff.

Preface

Some books are a long period in gestation and this one has been
no exception. It probably began in 1968 when my wife Fionna
and I, newly married, spent a year in Rome while I was on the
Finch Travelling Scholarship from Wesley House, Cambridge.
It felt then like a daring act to go into the centre of the Catholic
Church in the wake of Vatican II and *Humanae Vitae* and do
some study on the effect of the two Vatican Councils. We lived
in a small flat at the Methodist Church at the Ponte Sant'Angelo
kindly put at our disposal by the minister, the Revd Alan Keigh-
ley. Rome was then not as open as it has since become to
Protestant students but the English College proved to be as
hospitable to us then as it has been since. My long honeymoon
with Roman Catholicism began then in 1968 and it has continued ever since. Since 1984 I have had the privilege of being
the convener of the British Roman Catholic/Methodist Committee and was for five years on the Roman Catholic/Methodist
International Commission that produced the 1991 report *Sharing in the Apostolic Tradition*.

My thanks are therefore mainly to people from the Roman
Catholic tradition for their help in this work though also to
several Methodists. I am grateful for the hospitality of the rector,
staff and students of the English College in Rome with whom
I spent a sabbatical term in 1991. My particular thanks are due
to Father Jim Sullivan who made several helpful suggestions.
The rector, staff and students of St Mary's College, Oscott have
been equally welcoming to me as to all our Queen's staff and
students, and my thanks go especially to George Every who not
only seems to know everything about this period but also seems

able to find it in the Recusant Library at Oscott. My grateful thanks go also to the Revd Ian Dickie at the Westminster Diocesan Archive, to Gerald Hort, and to the Bodleian Library at Oxford. On the Methodist side, I owe my largest debt to the Revd Raymond George who not only chaired the Roman Catholic/Methodist Committee for many years, but was kind enough to read the first draft and suggest many corrections. His wisdom has been a vital component in our Roman Catholic/ Methodist conversations from their beginnings until his recent retirement in 1993. My thanks must also go to the historian of Wesley's Chapel and Museum at City Road, London, who allowed me to be a part-time curator for a few years and then gave me access to Wesley's library. My debt to the excellent library at our own Queen's College in Birmingham and to the skill of Sheila Russell its librarian will I hope be obvious throughout this work.

The major typing was done by Joanna Vialls to whom I owe a huge debt for her patience and ability to understand the Catholic parts of the book that others could not reach. I am grateful to the principal's secretary at the Queen's College, Jenny Hutton, who typed the chapter on Catholic Spirituality. No note of thanks can miss out Fionna, Jonathan and Michael who gave me leave of absence from home to get the work started. A final thanks to the editors at Darton, Longman and Todd, Helen Porter, Mary Jean Pritchard and Jane Williams. Without them this book would never have seen the light of day.

DAVID BUTLER

Introduction

Some years ago at the request of David Murphy, the General Secretary, I wrote a small pamphlet on John Wesley for the Catholic Truth Society. While it was impossible to put everything within sixteen pages, it was clear that I had to make choices concerning which model of Wesley to offer to what would probably be a predominantly Roman Catholic readership. Clearly I had to choose the eirenical and ecumenical Wesley, the one of the *Letter to a Roman Catholic*, rather than the one of *Popery Calmly Considered*. As a result, the polemical Wesley was ignored; Dr John Vickers was rightly critical of the pamphlet and was kind enough to let me have his comments.

This book is an attempt to set the record a little straighter and to show Wesley 'warts and all' in his relationships with Roman Catholics, as for example in this reference to Roman Catholics in his sermon *A Caution Against Bigotry*:

> But in a far stronger sense 'he followeth not us' who is not only of a different Church, but of such a Church as we account to be in many respects anti-scriptural and anti-Christian: a Church which we believe to be utterly false and erroneous in her doctrines, as well as dangerously wrong in her practice, guilty of gross superstition as well as idolatry; a Church that has added many articles to the faith that was once delivered to the saints; that has dropped one whole commandment of God, and made void several of the rest by her traditions; and that pretending the highest veneration for, and strictest conformity to, the ancient Church, has nevertheless brought

in numberless innovations without any warrant either from antiquity or Scripture. (WJW Vol. 2, p. 71)

On the whole, an attempt has been made to use primary sources and I have gone to Wesley's work for the bulk of my information. It seemed important to begin with a chapter on the Catholic Church in England in the eighteenth century, mainly because this would provide a context for Wesley's meetings with Catholics and with Catholic thought, but also because the sources of information are still somewhat scarce; a history of the Roman Catholics in England in the eighteenth century would be very welcome. In Appendix A will be found a list of penal laws in operation against Catholics taken from an eighteenth century manuscript in the archive of the English College in Rome. Two chapters follow on the practical outworkings of 'Popery' in the time of Wesley, the contacts with Catholics indicated in his works and the curious accusations of Popery made against his movement.

The Cork Riots of 1749 were the background for the most temperate of his works concerning Catholics: the *Letter to a Roman Catholic*, which in our ecumenical times has often been reprinted. This is reproduced in full at Appendix B. One of the other famous riots of the eighteenth century, the Gordon Riots of 1780, shows the leader of Methodism in a less favourable light. This chapter shows Wesley as a leader who was prone to be sympathetic with the aspirations of the Protestant Association led by Gordon. A constant question in the writings of Wesley to Catholics is whether faith should be kept with heretics; the Council of Constance had seemed in 1415 to utter a definite negative to the question with its burning of the heretic Hus. Wesley had a lengthy correspondence with Father O'Leary, an Irish Capuchin, over this.

A comparison of John Wesley and Richard Challoner, Vicar-Apostolic of the London District for much of this period, is then offered in short compass although the parallels really demand a small book. That Challoner and Wesley never met is one of the misfortunes of history for one is convinced that they would have been at one in their discussions concerning the essence of

Christianity. The argument of Challoner's *A Caveat Against the Methodists* of 1760 follows this. It is regrettable that Wesley did not reply fully to Challoner in 1761 as his comments would have been fascinating. That they were very close to each other on the doctrine of Justification I have tried to indicate for those who thought there was a time gulf between Regensburg 1541 and *Salvation and the Church* in 1987.

Wesley reproduced the main parts of Bishop John Williams' reply to the Roman Catechism, without acknowledgement, in 1756. In the chapter on Popish Doctrines there is an attempt to pull together material from the Wesley corpus while relying largely on the outline of *A Roman Catechism* and on the themes of *Popery Calmly Considered*. It seemed appropriate to include short replies to Wesley's work and his misrepresentations, although they belong to the decades just after Wesley. The strictures of Wesley against the Papacy follow since it was clear to the founder of Methodism that the main distinguishing article of the faith of Catholics was adherence to the primacy of the Pope.

Eirenical passages occur in Wesley's writings on Catholic Saints and Catholic Spirituality, although he is as free in his criticisms of some aspects of the lives of the saints as his father Samuel had been. While Wesley's use of Catholic spirituality is perhaps unusual for his time, principally in his *Christian Library* begun in 1749, his selection of works often shows his desire to filter out the extravagant and idolatrous practices of the Catholic spiritual writers. Idolatry indeed is almost the main reason for his severe strictness on Catholic Practices considered in the following chapter.

The final chapters are an attempt to fill in gaps in the rest of the book with a chapter on Wesley's other writings, and then one on contacts between other Methodists and Catholics. The themes in the latter chapter follow those in the book so that it is possible to see what Wesley's contemporaries said about Popish doctrines or about the Papacy. At the end of this introduction one is tempted to speculate on a hypothetical meeting between Wesley and Challoner. Whether they would have done for Catholic/Methodist relations what has been done since by the

International Commissions which have been meeting since 1967 is of course doubtful. But if these two men had been introduced and allowed to discuss the essentials of the faith, who knows whether Catholics and Methodists, far on as they are today in ecumenical dialogue, might not be further on still, perhaps within sight of visible unity. It is of course to further this latter end that this book has been written.

Finally, a word needs to be added concerning the use of the word 'catholic'. The Methodist Church claims its place within the Church Catholic and would not dissent from the use of that word to describe its own tradition of faith. However, it seemed best in this book to use the word 'Catholic' in the narrower sense of referring to the Roman Catholic Church. It is of importance that the English Catholics have been advised recently to avoid the use of the term 'non-Catholic' in describing other Christians.

1

The Roman Catholic Church in England in the Eighteenth Century

On the walls of Oscott College in Birmingham, there is an unfinished oil painting. It depicts the scene on 13 July 1852 at the first Provincial Synod after the restoration of the Catholic hierarchy to England in 1850. Among the dignitaries are Wiseman, Manning and Newman, all three to be cardinals but only one already elevated to that office. The picture breathes a new triumphal spirit abroad at the time; a new type of Catholicism has been born. The sermon, *The Second Spring*, preached by Newman at the Synod, contains this purple passage:

> The English Church was, and the English Church was not, and the English Church is once again. This is the portent, worthy of a cry. It is the coming in of a Second Spring; it is a restoration in the moral world, such as that which yearly takes place in the physical.[1]*

Later in the sermon, Newman reminds his hearers of the dark age through which they have come to this new spring:

> No longer the Catholic Church in the country; nay, no longer, I may say, a Catholic community; – but a few adherents of the Old Religion, moving silently and sorrowfully about, as memorials of what had been. 'The Roman Catholics'; – not a sect, not even an interest, as men conceived of it, – not a body, however small, representative of the Great Communion abroad, – but a mere handful of individuals, who might be counted like the pebbles and *detritus* of the great deluge, and who, forsooth, merely happened to retain a creed which, in

* For Notes see pages 217 ff.

its day indeed, was the profession of a Church. Here a set of poor Irishmen, coming and going at harvest time, or a colony of them lodged in a miserable quarter of the vast metropolis. There, perhaps, an elderly person, seen walking in the streets, grave and solitary, and strange, though noble in bearing, and said to be of good family, and a Roman Catholic.

... there was this difference between the Roman Catholics of England and the Roman Catholics of Ireland, that the latter had bishops, and the former were governed by four officials, called Vicars-Apostolic.[2]

This passage has been quoted in full because it shows, perhaps better than any other, the pejorative evaluation by the new Catholicism of the work of the eighteenth century. At the end of the section, Newman talks of Vicars-Apostolic as if they were an item of detail which did not need consideration. Until just two years before this date, Catholic England had been governed by Vicars-Apostolic. The 'few adherents' of the Old Religion have been shown to be reasonably large in number, reaching a figure by the death of Wesley in 1791 of some twenty thousand more than the new Methodist movement. 'A set of poor Irishmen, coming and going at harvest time', while true to the facts, cannot hide a considerable number of communicant Mass-goers who were as English as Newman. The 'handful of individuals' was kept together as a considerable body not only by regular Mass attendance but by polemical literature, by catechisms and by devotional literature which, if a little derivative and dull, was able to maintain its users in communion with the thinking of the 'Great Communion abroad', indeed it usually contained more wholesome food than the gilded baroque devotions that became the diet of the Catholic faithful in the mid-nineteenth century.

If John Henry Newman's view is too prone to see a Catholic Church in England newly emerged from a dark age, helpful light on the period of the eighteenth century has been shed by the work of recent historians who contradict the views of Newman. Burton, however, in his two-volume *The Life and*

Times of Bishop Challoner 1691–1781 seems to concur with the thoughts of Newman:

> In the history of the Catholic Church in England there is a dark and depressing epoch, the duration of which can only be defined as lasting from the Revolution of 1688 to the Catholic Relief Acts which put an end to the penal laws at the close of the eighteenth century. There is no period of which less has been recorded. It forms the Dark Ages of our later history. The practice of the Catholic faith was proscribed by law and the Church was again in the catacombs.[3]

Dr Burton presumably knew that the catacombs were burial places rather than hiding places for pursued Christians, though he seems to be using the image for a Church in a state of siege which can only batten down its defences and wait for the mid-nineteenth century. Burton accuses Challoner's Church of unproductiveness in the eighteenth century, there having been no new religious houses and seminaries founded on the Continent to continue the work no longer possible in England. Part of the need of the period, as Challoner himself discovered, was to maintain what already existed and even to rationalize what was in excess. To this end three of the continental seminaries were amalgamated at Valladolid, in 1767, to make better use of limited resources.[4] That Challoner did open three schools in England should be noted positively, too; at least one of these was soon well known as a source for the continental seminaries.[5] That he gave them good solid spiritual fare as a Vicar-Apostolic is perhaps his greatest claim to be venerated by the Catholics of England. It certainly does not look quite such a dark age as Dr Burton wants to make it.

That many blows fell on the English Catholics is certainly true. In 1700, the Statute 11 and 12 William III c 4 introduced the penalty of perpetual imprisonment for any priest informed upon and convicted for the saying of Mass. This, as we shall see, was invoked only upon Maloney who received a sentence of perpetual imprisonment in 1767 that was commuted to banishment after four years.[6] The Statute of 1700 also meant that Catholics were unable to purchase land or send their children abroad to be educated without a fine. Another stipulation of 1700 was that Catholic estates would pass preferentially to Protestant next of kin. This was usually observed in the breach and legal loopholes to avoid it were found by many of the richer Catholic families of the eighteenth century. In the first year of the reign of George I, 1714, an Act was passed appointing government agents to investigate the financial state of lands and superstitious adjuncts belonging to Catholic recusants in order to raise money for public use when needed. When the Jacobite rising failed in 1715, it was well known that Catholics had been widely sympathetic and many Catholic estates suffered forfeiture of parts devoted to what were considered to be superstitious uses, including chapels, shrines etc.

There is an interesting extract in Wesley's *Journal* for 14 August 1741 where Wesley indicates an increase in Popery in the area around Grosvenor Square, to which is added an indication that there are few Papists around the Foundery, his preaching house in Moorfields:

> Calling on a person near Grosvenor Square, I found there was but too much reason here for crying out of the increase of Popery; many converts to it being continually made by the gentleman who preaches in Swallow Street three days in every week. Now why do not the champions who are continually crying out, 'Popery, Popery!' in Moorfields, come hither that they may not always be fighting 'as one that beateth the air'? Plainly, because they have no mind to fight at all, but to show their valour without an opponent. And they well know they may defy Popery at the Foundery without any danger of contradiction.[7]

The above passage reminds us that the history of eighteenth century Catholicism in England is not only about decline in numbers but was also the story of conversions to the Catholic faith. During the precautionary measures taken against Papists in February 1744, Wesley was in a house in Spitalfields when a Justice of the Peace arrived with parish officers looking for Papists. Wesley was able to reassure the men of his principles and practice but afterwards had to run the gauntlet of an unfriendly mob on the lookout for Papists. This is one of several references in Wesley's works to the contemporary anxiety of the government in Britain in the face of the possible invasion by the forces of the Young Pretender. Like the previous extract, it shows too the easy assumption that the new movement begun by Wesley was papistical in its pretensions.[8]

The Rebellion of 1745 was by no means as welcome to the majority of English Catholics as the 1715 rising had been and the records indicate that most took the view of the Duchess of Norfolk that any Catholic rising in favour of Charles Edward would merely hurt the Catholics generally. Bishop Challoner is recorded as having dissuaded a Catholic gentleman from joining the rebellion and from taking a considerable number of his tenants with him to assist the Young Pretender. Challoner and other influential leaders may have been instrumental in deflecting several well-born Catholics from the disastrous consequences of 1745. The interesting point to note however is that there is a different feel when 1715 is compared with 1745 for the Catholics of England.

In Rome the Papacy was never as well disposed to the Young Pretender as it had been to his father James. Charles Edward lived a notoriously profligate life in Rome, had abjured the Catholic faith, and clearly had no chance of regaining the throne for the Stuarts. On the death of James in 1766 several British communities in Rome celebrated 'Charles III' with a Te Deum, at one of which Charles was 'crowned'. The Pope reacted vigorously by removing the four rectors of the English College, the Scots College, the Irish Dominicans and the Irish Franciscans.[9] It was the logical political step and the end of a process that had been recognized as long over by the Vicars-Apostolic of the English mission. By 1745 the majority of English Catholics seem to have accepted the Hanoverian dynasty.

This subtle movement within the Catholic community towards acceptance of the Hanoverians made the oath attached to the first Relief Act of 1778 possible for Catholics to accept.[10] The oath declared that *AB* would be faithful and bear allegiance to His Majesty George III, disclose treasonable conspiracies against him and abjure obedience to the self-styled Charles III.

That the oath went on to denounce the views that faith need not be kept with heretics, that princes deposed by the Pope might be lawfully murdered, and that the Pope had no jurisdiction in England, should not really surprise us. These issues had been abroad between Catholics and Protestants since the sixteenth century and needed to be resolved as soon as possible. It is clear that John Wesley did not know about the clauses of the oath when he wrote to the *Public Advertiser* early in 1780, otherwise he would have added one less arrow to the quiver of the Protestant Association (see Chapters 5 and 6).[11]

Before the Catholics of England could obtain further relief, they had to meet head on the fury of the Gordon Riots in 1780. The story will be told below in more detail (see Chapter 5) but the effects were devastating for the Catholics in London. Elsewhere, the extent of the damage was limited, but the effects on Richard Challoner in his ninetieth year can be imagined. Ten years after the death of Challoner and in the year of Wesley's death, the second Catholic Relief Act was passed. Its main interest is perhaps less for what relief was obtained than for the schism between the laity and the hierarchy that was manifested in the events that led up to it.[12] Eventually the passage of the Act of 1791 allowed Catholics to worship openly in officially registered churches, abolished the registration of wills and the dreadful double land tax. If Catholics had not yet reached the Second Spring, it was at least the end of a difficult winter for them.

The Catholic episcopate in England came to an end in jurisdictional terms in 1558 with the accession of Elizabeth, although the last old Catholic bishop of England, Thomas Goldwell of St Asaph's, did not die until 1585 in Rome. In 1598, Pope Clement VIII appointed George Blackwell as Archpriest of the English mission. Such an office had never been held before and produced new problems, being neither episcopal fish nor presbyteral fowl. The Archpriest Controversy dragged on for several years and was settled only by the appointment of a Vicar-Apostolic in 1623.[13] The Vicar-Apostolic was under the jurisdiction of Propaganda (the organization set up in Rome in 1622 that was responsible for foreign missions) but in episcopal orders, with a see *'in partibus infidelium'*.[14] The first Vicar-Apostolic, William Bishop, appointed a chapter to help him in the administration of the mission. After the death in 1655 of the second Vicar-Apostolic, Richard Smith, who had been forced to spend his last 24 years in exile in Paris, Rome refused to appoint another bishop and left the administration of the mission to the dean and chapter. In 1685, at the beginning of James II's reign, another Vicar-Apostolic, John Leyburn, was appointed.[15] In April 1688, another Vicar-Apostolic, Bonaventure Giffard, was openly consecrated in the Banqueting Hall in Whitehall. By the end of James II's reign, four Vicars-Apostolic had been appointed for the London, Western Midland and Northern Districts, Ellis and Smith like Giffard having been openly consecrated in London.

Among the notable Vicars-Apostolic of the century should be recorded Bonaventure Giffard (c. 1643–1734) who spent at least four periods of his life in prison for his profession when Vicar-Apostolic of the London District, and Benjamin Petre (1622–1758) his successor, generously described by Burton as 'a devout and retiring man' whose inactivity put enormous burdens on the shoulders of Richard Challoner when he became Petre's co-adjutor in 1741. Other significant Vicars-Apostolic were Robert Walmesley (1723–97) of the Western District, John Stonor (1678–1756) of the Midland District who in his later years largely took the initiative with the bishops, and the Talbot brothers, James (1726–90) co-adjutor of the London District under Challoner and then Vicar-Apostolic, and Thomas (1727–95) Vicar-Apostolic of the Midland District.

If Richard Challoner (1691–1781) was the greatest of them that should not be taken to disparage the enormous contribution that these others made to the continuity of the Catholic community in England. That contribution had to be made at times with extreme care and although the impression is that the situation eased as the century went on, there were times when heads needed to drop below the barricades. The arrival of a Payne or a Gordon could make life extremely difficult for the hierarchy. There are times when Challoner and his colleagues seem extremely cautious in their correspondence with Propa-

ganda in Rome. The Pope becomes 'Mr Abraham', Bishop Petre
is 'Mr White', the Prefect for the Congregation of Rites is Mr
L. . . . (Mgr Lercari).[16] Some of this habitual caution extended
to Bishop Challoner's publications which during his lifetime
were written and published by 'RC'. After the death of Challoner, RC was revealed as not being 'Roman Catholic', as might
have been construed, but 'the late Bishop Challoner'. Useful
descriptions of the work of the Vicars-Apostolic can be found
elsewhere,[17] but two further points are perhaps worth making
here. One is that the Vicars-Apostolic do not seem to have met
on any regular basis; the anxiety and uncertainty of their exist-
ence was enough to prevent this. The other is that the ideal
credentials for becoming a Vicar-Apostolic in the eighteenth
century, if Bishop Petre is the example to go by, seem to have
been to have come from an ancient and noble family, to
have been educated at Douai, and to have private means.

The English priests of the eighteenth century were more fortunate than their predecessors of the seventeenth century, when
several priests had suffered the ultimate penalty for their Catholic allegiance, the last one being Oliver Plunkett. It is of interest
that no priest was executed in England during the eighteenth
century. Cynics may say that herein lies the reason for the
comparative somnolence of eighteenth century English Catholics; if the blood of the martyrs had been abundantly shed in
the sixteenth and seventeenth centuries then all that could be
hoped for in the eighteenth was a maintenance programme.
Certainly the priests could not show themselves openly and
adopted the dress of laymen. Since the jurisdiction of the Catholic Church in England was under four Vicars-Apostolic in four
Districts, we take four examples more or less at random of one
priest from each district.

William Anstead[18] (1737–91) was born in London and trained
for the priesthood at the Venerable English College in Rome.
He left for the English mission in 1762 and was attached to the
Sardinian Embassy in Lincoln's Inn Fields, London. It is of
interest that he is mentioned in William Mawhood's diary as
often saying Mass for the family at Finchley, the house at which
Bishop Challoner sought refuge during the Gordon Riots. He

seems to have served later at Woolhampton in Berkshire where he died in July 1791, the same year as John Wesley. Charles Fitzwilliams[19] (1700–50), later known as Williams, was a priest in the Midland District under Bishop Stonor. He left the Venerable English College in 1730, a year after ordination, and worked briefly at the French Embassy in London. His ministry was spent mostly in Wolverhampton where he was priest to about three hundred people, with an income of £30–£40 per annum, out of which he paid £12 for board, while striving to maintain a horse and find wine and wax for his church from the residue. In 1742 he retired to Harvington Hall in Worcestershire where he remained until his death. Another product of the English College in Rome was Edward Williams[20] (1707–76) who worked in the Western District from 1732 in the house of the Paston family at Horton, Gloucestershire. After two years he moved to Monmouthshire but by 1772 he was in Plymouth, having been by his own admission there for over twenty years and having opened up the mission in that place. His work was helped initially by two merchants but unfortunately they died young which caused the loss of the Catholic assembly room. The mission seems to have been based at Bearscombe, some twelve miles east of Plymouth, and it was here that he died and was buried in the local parish churchyard. John Hankin[21] (1706–82) was a native of Newcastle-upon-Tyne and was trained for the priesthood at Douai in France during the time when Challoner was a professor there. He left for the English mission in 1733, worked at Croxdale, Durham, and at the time of the Rebellion of 1745 was at Sunderland. While he was priest there a large number of people, mainly sailors, broke into the Mass-house where they found the people at prayers and a couple about to be married. After Hankin and the people had fled, the altar and crucifix and seats, with the priest's robes and the books, and all the other furniture, were burnt in the street outside. Hankin's library and personal papers were also committed to the flames. After the loss of the Sunderland chapel, Hankin moved to Witton Shields until 1772 when he retired to Douai. He died at St Omer in 1782.

These four priests are not remarkable in any way and their

detailed biographies have not been written. They serve merely to typify the kind of training they underwent (always overseas), the precarious nature of the mission (the loss of the place in Plymouth, the burning in Sunderland) and the dependence of the priests upon the gentry chapels and the chapels of the embassies, particularly during the periodic 'No Popery' paranoia of eighteenth century England. An illustration of the paranoia can be given from Burton's biography of Challoner. It concerns a particularly unpleasant person called William Payne.[22] Payne seems to have begun to take a close interest in Catholics around 1764 and succeeded in causing enormous perturbation among the London faithful until he was discredited in 1771. The 'Protestant Carpenter', as he was known, had problems with the Catholics of London not because of their behaviour but because they were present in the capital at all, since they were a sect which had no rights of public worship, except perhaps in the embassy chapels. By discovering their meeting places and being there as one of the putative faithful Payne had been able to ferret out the names of some of the London priests and even their home addresses. Barnard, in his life of Challoner,[23] tells us that Payne had applied to the bishop for instruction in the Catholic faith. Payne opened up a campaign against the Catholics, armed with the comprehensive knowledge he had gained in London. His greatest success came in 1767 with the arrest of John Baptist Maloney. This netted Payne £100 for his information leading to the priest's conviction. Shortly after this success, Payne tried an indictment against Bishop Challoner, four priests and a schoolmaster. By this indictment Payne probably hoped to obtain £600, although the schoolmaster was not a priest and therefore would yield no money. Challoner with his four priests and schoolmaster got off only because Payne so far over-reached himself as to forge some legal documents. He then agreed to drop the charges against the Catholics if they did not bring charges against him. For the clergy concerned it was an extremely close thing; Payne's receiving the £100 reward should have meant their perpetual imprisonment under the law of William III of 1700. Later on Payne was stopped by some legal acrobatics from Lord Justice Mansfield, who suggested that it was not sufficient to prove that a person acted as a priest, but the fact of his ordination must be proved. Most of the working priests in England had been ordained overseas, often in the seminaries of Douai, Lisbon and Rome, and clearly proof of ordination would have been almost impossible for Payne to unearth. Mansfield implied in his summing up against Payne during the Maloney case that only sordid gain was at issue and not the rights of the Protestant state. A final attempt to indict Bishop James Talbot, the co-adjutor of the London District, failed in 1771 when Payne's witnesses failed to make their case against Talbot; this was the last attempt by Payne to get Catholic priests convicted. The Payne history has been alluded to because it indicates the insecurity in which some of the priests were forced to live, especially in the London District. That only one priest was tried and found guilty should not leave us with the impression that all was secure.

When we try to decide how large the Catholic community was in the eighteenth century we come up against enormous problems. Magee[24] argued that numbers went down fairly quickly from the time of Charles I to the time of George III. At the end of his book, he suggests that as many as 10 per cent of all English people were probably Catholics during the reigns of Charles I and Charles II.[25] The rapid decline in Catholic numbers then began, first with the alarms of the Popish Plot, then with the flight of James II and then with the rising of 1715. The impression is thus given of a disastrous decline from about 1680 (10 per cent Catholic) to 1715 (5 per cent Catholic) until 1767 (1 per cent Catholic). This 'decline from the late seventeenth century' model has been challenged by Bossy in his work on the English Catholic community.[26] He begins by accepting a base figure of about 80,000 Catholics in 1770 (the publicized figure for 1767 was 69,376 and this probably needs a small adjustment upwards). Bossy draws what he hopes might be a more satisfactory conclusion from the available figures, which he feels is supported by other external evidence, that the English Catholic community was reasonably stable in size from before the middle of the seventeenth century to after the middle of the eighteenth century. He will not accept the suggestions of Berington in 1781, Burton in 1909, nor Magee in 1939, to the effect that the eighteenth century is the dark age of the Church's growth in England.[27] His graph shows a rise from about 40,000 in 1600 to about 60,000 at 1640, at 1640 it flattens out and then begins to move upwards at about 1720, continuing upwards for the rest of the century and beyond.

If the numbers held during the dark periods, it nevertheless seems that the temptation to apostasy proved too much for some of the aristocracy and gentry. It was essential that the Catholic aristocracy and gentry on their country estates should maintain both a chapel and a priest during the penal times. To choose just one of many examples, the Eyston family of East Hendred had held their lands since the time of Henry VI and had remained faithful during penal times. The chapel was held privately by the family and has been used continuously for Catholic worship from the thirteenth century until now, probably being the only one in continuous use although other chapels have claimed this.[28] In the eighteenth century, the Eystons were exemplary in their loyalty to the Catholic Church, and despite having their lands sequestered over and over again, they managed to keep hold of their estate. The problems that might be created for the people of the area by such a family apostatizing from the faith can be imagined. Berington[29] tells us that by 1781 there were only seven peers, 22 baronets and 150 gentlemen Catholics. This can be compared with the figures Magee gives for the 1715–20 registration period of Catholics when he lists twelve peers, 36 baronets, three knights, 227 esquires and 536 gentlemen.[30] Magee sees that Berington and he are talking of a different group of 'gentlemen', but the main point holds, namely that within some 70 years or so of the eighteenth century, there had been a large number of Catholics lost from the upper classes, through apostasy, through the consequences of the 1715 rising or through losses in family fortunes. If several influential families seem to have departed from the Catholic fold, such as the Gages, Shelleys, Ropers, Gascoignes and Swinburnes, causing several missions to close down, this does not of itself mean a wholesale apostasy. On the contrary, one draws the conclusion that the middle classes were beginning to take new responsibility for the Catholic mission after the apostasy of the aristocracy and gentry. In London, for example, the presence of Langdale, a distiller in Holborn, and of the Mawhoods, woollen merchants in West Smithfield, must have been predictive of the future strength of the Catholics not only in London but in the country as a whole.[31] There is some evidence in the life of Challoner that his interests and leanings are more towards the emergent merchant class of the district metropolis than towards the aristocrats and gentry. When the Gordon Riots broke out in 1780, he was not rescued and given refuge by a member of the gentry but by the Mawhoods in their small country house at Finchley.[32] Such small details predict the future strength of the Catholic Church in England. While old families such as the Petres of Essex still supported as many as six out of nine of the mission stations in Essex, there are signs that the new Catholic manufacturers and industrialists were beginning to bear some of the costs.

The London Catholics of the eighteenth century had one very great advantage over their fellow believers in the provinces. In London were gathered the embassies of the Catholic powers, where exercise of the Catholic faith was allowed by international law. Six such embassies were present in eighteenth century London: the Imperial, French, Portuguese, Spanish, Sardinian and Venetian. For the purposes of English Catholics the most useful one was the Sardinian embassy chapel as this was situated in Lincoln's Inn Fields, quite near to Holborn where a lot of Catholics had their homes. (Holborn, the area around St Giles, and Moorfields were the main Catholic areas.) The other embassy chapels were usefully distributed in Hanover Square, Greek Street, Golden Square, Ormond Street, and Suffolk Street (the present area codes will help to produce a picture[33]). Apart from these there were two small meeting places, in Butler's Alley off Grub Street, and in Moorfields. Catholics in London were used to meeting anywhere reasonably convenient if they were not near an embassy chapel. One of the famous descriptions of Richard Challoner is of when he preached to Catholics at the Little Ship in Little Turnstile, Lincoln's Inn Fields. The picture offered to posterity is one of each person sitting with a pot of beer in front of him, to serve as an excuse in the case of interruption, while the floor of the room where Challoner preached was partly movable so that people in two rooms could hear him preach at the same time.[34] John Milner, a future Vicar-Apostolic of the Midland District, often heard Challoner preach from a cock-pit, and Burton suggests that this spot may have been the famous Cock-Pit Alley, Drury Lane. Caution had to be exercised when services were held in non-authorized buildings, which in practice meant any building that was not an embassy chapel. An account of a Mass on a day around 1771 is recorded in Burton from the recollections of a Mrs Sidney who was received into the Church and received her first communion from Challoner on that day.[35] The service took place in the garret of a public house in the city. Before being admitted, members of the congregation had to offer a pass word, the key was turned after every admission and bolts were drawn across after all had been admitted. After Mass, the ornaments were locked away and the room left as ordinary in appearance as it had been before. It is difficult to decide whether Mrs Sidney's account can be the norm for the Mass in London. The account, on internal evidence, is dated to about 1771, around the time when Payne's activity in prosecuting Catholic priests was at its height. Since her offering is one of the few revelations we have into the worship life of Catholics in London, it would be a pity if it were not typical. Thus the romantic view of Mass behind bolted doors for fear of the Protestants may have come down to us as the eighteenth century norm.

Petty persecution seems to have been the major problem in the eighteenth century and there are plenty of examples to quote. In February 1735 a Mass was broken up by the peace officer in the garret of a public house in Shoreditch, the priest escaping via the back door and others being let go. In the evening a group collected together in the same place again, determined to have their Mass.[36] Burton offers another incident from Isleworth in 1758 where a chapel had existed for over 30 years in the house of Lord Shrewsbury. At an Anglican vestry meeting in November a resolution was tabled against the Catholic chaplain demanding his withdrawal within a month, with a threat to put the laws against Popery into execution.[37] This latter is one example of the penal laws being threatened, a threat which was hardly ever put into practice, but a threat under which the Catholic faithful always lived. As Richard Challoner grew older he seems to have used the Sardinian Embassy more and more as his 'cathedral' and a famous picture of him made three years after his death shows him in full pontificals, with mitre and crozier against the background of altar and sanctuary.[38] When the chapel was burnt down in 1759 Challoner used his good offices to ensure that it was rebuilt on the same spot since it occupied a crucial place for the English Catholics in that part of London. Most priests on the English mission had no opportunity to lead worship in such large centres. For them it was a case of making do with halls and attics in the towns or using the chapels of Catholic country houses. Challoner reckoned that in his District outside London proper there were between four thousand and five thousand Catholics. For the great majority of these, the centre of Catholic life and worship was the local Catholic estate. Where such an estate existed there was usually also a chapel and a resident priest. That the relationship between the priest and the patron could be a difficult one, almost that of employee and employer, is clear from the history, though one doubts whether every patron on arrival for Mass had quite the gall to say to his priest, 'Mr Smith, you may begin'. Joseph Berington has a famous passage often quoted from his *State and Behaviour of English Catholics* of 1780, which describes the way in which country house congregations could disappear if the patrons conformed to the Church of England or the Catholic line were ended by death:

> In one district alone, with which I am acquainted, eight out of thirteen are come to nothing: nor have any new ones risen to make up, in any proportion, their loss. When a family of distinction fails, as there seldom continues any conveniency either for prayers or instruction, the neighbouring Catholics soon fall away: and when a priest is still maintained, the example of the Lord is wanting to encourage the lower class particularly to the practice of their religion. I recollect the names of at least ten noble families that within these 60 years

have either conformed or are extinct; besides many Com-
moners of distinction and fortune.[39]

It is reckoned that in the whole of Challoner's London District something like 30 Mass-centres were to be found in chapels
on Catholic estates. That Mass-centres were even being sold by
Catholics elsewhere in the country is shown in two extracts
from Wesley's writings. In the first he describes a large chapel
at Osmotherley, at which he preached at ten o'clock at night,
which had once belonged to the Franciscans.[40] In the second
there is a reference to the use that the Methodists were making
of an old chapel of the Blessed Virgin Mary in Jersey, where she
was said to have once appeared.[41] Wesley showed little knowledge of the exact whereabouts of Catholic chapels in England
and there is only one mention in the letters. This is to the chapel
at Bath. In his letter to the printer of the *Public Advertiser* in
January 1780 he mentions the building of the Bath chapel as an
example of how the Catholics have interpreted the Relief Act
of 1778.[42] The Act was not meant as an act of toleration, but
Catholics have understood it as toleration, hence the chapels at
Bath and elsewhere, the new converts made day by day, and the
raising of seminaries. The latter reference may be to Challoner's
establishment at Sedgley, which was established in 1763 near
Wolverhampton. Wesley refers to it again in the *Journal*:

> Calling at Wolverhampton, I was informed that, some time
> since, a large old house was taken, three or four miles from
> the town, which receives all children that come, sometimes
> above four hundred at once. They are taught, *gratis*, reading,
> writing, and Popery . . . [43]

Park Hall, Sedgley, was not a seminary in the usual sense of
that word and the highest number of students, in 1810, was only
212. Among its early students were John Milner, later the Vicar-
Apostolic of the Midlands District, and several others who later
became priests and bishops.

When Richard Challoner died in 1781 he was buried in the
family vault of the Barretts at Milton in Berkshire and the
Church of England burial service was read over him by the

rector. His predecessors in the vicariate, Bishops Giffard and Petre, had been similarly buried, in their cases in the same vault in St Pancras' churchyard in London. The funeral rites had to be performed by Anglican incumbents. During the eighteenth century the Catholics had only one graveyard of their own, at St James in Winchester, and it was here in 1731 that Grace Challoner, the Bishop's mother, was buried. If there were difficulties with Catholic funerals, Catholic marriages created even more problems. The government produced a very sensible piece of legislation in 1753 which banned clandestine marriages but which created problems for Catholics. Before 1753 Catholics were legally married according to their own rites, after 1753 such a marriage had to be performed according to the rites of the Church of England and before a minister of that church. This left Catholics with the dilemma either of being married in the old way and therefore of being married illegally, or of being married in the Church of England while not sharing in the Anglican act of worship. Catholics were forced into deciding whether consent was offered first to the Anglican priest and then by extension to the Catholic priest at a later ceremony, or whether the true internal consent was withheld from the Anglican clergyman and only received by means of the Catholic priest at the second ceremony.

A fully Catholic education was impossible in early eighteenth century England, indeed it was made illegal in England and on the Continent by the famous Act of William III's government in 1700 (see Appendix A for this legislation). Education was obtained only for those who could afford it or who were intelligent enough to obtain scholarships in the English Catholic schools overseas. Richard Challoner was educated at Douai from 1705, having been recommended by the saintly John Gother and financed by one of the funds left in his will in 1688 by Bishop Leyburn, the Vicar-Apostolic of the London District. Challoner saw England only once during his 25 years at Douai, and in many instances of priestly formation abroad there must have been wide areas of study to which the English language and culture were largely alien. A school/seminary such as Douai had secular scholars as well as those training for the priesthood.

The figures at Douai in 1716 are instructive: theology 8, philosophy 16, rhetoric 9, poetry 9, syntax 12, grammar 14, rudiments 23, making 91 in all, of which only the theology and philosophy classes were training for the priesthood.[44] The majority of the others would of course find their way back to England and Catholic secular life. As early as 1699 there had been priestly complaints to the Vicars-Apostolic about the English College in Rome, the issues being the character of the students, their spiritual formation and the very small numbers being sent to the English mission. The average number of students from 1700 to 1739 was 24, the actual number in 1739 being only sixteen. In 1718 only one was sent to the English mission and in 1719 only one new student arrived.[45] This was the house that had been responsible for the protomartyr Ralph Sherwin and his martyr successors, the place where a Te Deum had been sung in the chapel when the news of martyrdom reached Rome.

That the dominant ethos of Douai, as of the Venerable English College in Rome, of Lisbon, Seville, Madrid and Valladolid, was Jacobite should probably not surprise us and it was only with the failure of the rising of 1745 that loyalty to the Hanoverian regime was cemented. The rise of schools on the Continent became less urgent once English schools became available. A school had existed in secret at Twyford about three miles from Winchester since the reign of James II, and it was here that Alexander Pope spent his earliest schooldays, but the 1745 rising and the subsequent panic brought the school to an end. In 1749 a replacement was founded at Standon Lordship in Hertfordshire. It was here that the refugees from Douai came in the wake of the French Revolution and it was from the nucleus of this that the later St Edmunds's College grew as the diocesan college for the London vicariate. Although its origins are more obscure than Standon Lordship, Sedgley Park School followed in the Midland District near Wolverhampton in 1763.

When Challoner wrote his report for Propaganda in 1773 he mentioned the zeal of the London clergy. Conversions in London were clearly common although outside the capital the situation was harder for Catholic proselytizers. One of the main factors in conversion must have been the liturgical worship available at the embassy chapels. It is clear from the eighteenth century accounts that we have that this open celebration of the Catholic Mass must have had a positive impact on those who observed it; perhaps even Payne might have enjoyed it. The other factor in conversion would have been by the marriage of Catholics with non-Catholics. Monox Harvey, having spent his earlier years as the head of a Catholic boarding school, mentioned in his diary in the 1750s that he has had some 90 converts in seven years, most of these being due to marriage. He was in perhaps the most favourable position to be an evangelist as he spent the last years of his life in London with no fixed commission. On the whole, the Catholic Church in England in the eighteenth century was neither a collection of individuals like 'the pebbles and *detritus* of the great deluge' nor a people living in the dark ages. The fidelity of its pastors, the availability of devotional and polemical literature of a high standard, meant that something greater than a maintenance programme was being sustained. When John Wesley met 'Papists' during his ministry and read some of their literature, he gives the impression that he is in contact with a once-great communion which has lost its way since the time of the early Church, but which is still significant and potentially seductive in eighteenth century England.

2

John Wesley – Meeting Papists

Accounts of the life of John Wesley are many and taken as a whole are accurate statements of his activities and thought.[1] Of relevance here are those aspects of his life that either helped or hindered his appreciation of the Catholics that he met during his lifetime. He was born in 1703, the second son of the rector of Epworth in Lincolnshire and one of seventeen children, eight of whom survived. Interestingly, both his parents, Samuel and Susanna, were brought up in the pattern of English dissent though both later became members of the Church of England. The spirituality of the home included small groups of earnest seekers who met in the rectory as well as the reading of spiritual writers who on Susanna's part included *The Christian's Pattern* or *Imitation of Christ* by Thomas à Kempis as well as the Catholic Lorenzo Scupoli's *Spiritual Combat*. After school at Charterhouse John Wesley went to Christ Church College in Oxford and after ordination he became a fellow of Lincoln College. From the Oxford period came the 'Holy Club', a meeting of earnest Christian gentlemen concerned for their spiritual formation and for the outworking of that in works of mercy. After Oxford and a period in Lincolnshire as curate to Samuel, John offered his services to the new colony of Georgia in the hope of converting the Indians. His lack of success in Georgia led to his return and the spiritual crisis that ended with the important experience at Aldersgate Street in 1738.

During his time in America he had come across the Moravians who were the followers of Count Zinzendorf. Zinzendorf and his people taught that an immediate experience of conversion by the grace of God was available to every person and a sense of assurance that they were right with God. Despite his past endeavours Wesley did not feel that he had yet received this experience of grace. The account of the experience that he went through on 24 May 1738 when at a religious society in Aldersgate Street in London is now engraved on a plaque outside the London Museum:

> In the evening I went very unwillingly to a society in Aldersgate Street, where one was reading Luther's preface to the Epistle to the Romans. About a quarter before nine, while he was describing the change which God works in the heart through faith in Christ, I felt my heart strangely warmed. I felt I did trust in Christ, Christ alone for salvation; and an assurance was given me that He had taken away *my* sins, even *mine*, and saved *me* from the law of sin and death.

This experience has been argued over for generations. Was it a conversion experience like Augustine's in the fourth century or was it an experience of assurance which excluded all doubt from Wesley's mind and heart? Whatever it was, it gave him the impetus to offer the gospel of Christ to all people and led to the birth of a new group within Christianity, the people called Methodists. His subsequent desire to preach Christ to the people led to the irregularities of field preaching (1739), lay preaching (probably 1740), registration of buildings as preaching houses (the first Model Deed was in 1763) and then the ordination of lay helpers for the work in America (1784). Wesley's aim was the building up of Christian societies with close links to the parish churches of the nation.

At the time of his death some 72,000 people in Great Britain were members of his societies. While Wesley died a sincere member of the Church of England, within a few years his movement had seceded from that Church. His reverence for the customs and liturgy of the Church of his parents is just one reason why the Roman Catholics that he met were regarded by him as such a strange and alien presence in the British Isles.

Wesley's opportunities for meeting members of the Catholic Church in England seem to have been severely limited. One suspects that the main reason for this was the low profile that

Papists felt they had to keep in what were still penal times, and their caution in the face of anything that, like eighteenth century Methodism, bore the impression of enthusiasm. As a result, Wesley had little face-to-face dialogue with Catholics and the impression of Catholic–Methodist dialogue in the eighteenth century is of the antagonists shouting their respective wares across a street full of the noise and bustle of carts, horses and people. Because they are on opposite sides of the street, they are barely heard by each other, and what is heard is only a snatch of the whole. Perhaps it would be fair to say that they are so convinced that they know what the other believes and know it to be wrong, that it is hardly worth listening.

One of the earliest contacts with a Catholic was in December 1735 when Wesley was on board the 'Simmonds' on the way to America. He made contact with a Mrs Patterson who may well have been a Catholic for he attempted to dissuade her by reading her a tract against Popery, after reading some William Law and having other serious conversation. The lady was 'seriously convinced'.[2] Another from the same period was probably a Mrs Fallowfield, who had been a convert to the Church of Rome but wanted to return to the Church of England. She was 'deeply convinced' by Wesley's preaching, particularly by what he said against the Church of Rome. At the same time he remarks in his *Journal*, and not for the last time, on the infatuation in England, and especially in London, for the Church of Rome and the alarming increases in Popery. Wesley wonders though why people are so concerned with Popery when Infidelity is increasing even more alarmingly. He makes three interesting points:

1) because as bad a religion as Popery is, no religion at all is still worse; a baptized Infidel being twofold more a child of hell than the [fiercest] Papist in Christendom;

2) because as dangerous a state as a Papist is in, with regard to eternity, a Deist is in a far more dangerous state, if he be not (without repentance) an assured heir of damnation;

3) because as difficult as it is to recover a Papist, 'tis far more difficult to recover an Infidel.

In his work at Savannah in Georgia Wesley was pleased to note the absence of Papists in the area, the only exception being a few Italians with whom he was unable to communicate.[3] Wesley considered that Deists were notoriously difficult to convert from their infidelity although he had some success with a Mr Mazine.[4] Mazine had once been a zealous Papist but had cast off Popery and Christianity altogether. His residual belief in God reads like a form of Deism which for Wesley was a form of infidelity. The outcome is unknown but an ambiguous reference in the Diary for 20 October shows that he may have administered the Holy Communion to Mazine and there are two further diary references to visits. The possible offering of the communion to a former Papist is of interest.

Although Wesley's contacts with Catholics in England were few, they seem to have been noisy. In April 1740 he was preaching in Bristol on the liberty we have to enter the Holy of Holies by the blood of Jesus, when he was interrupted by one John Beon or Darsy. The congregation, writes Wesley, had an opportunity to return good for evil and show love to the one who had interrupted the service. Darsy, it seems, was well known as a Romish priest in the area and had called out:

> Thou art a hypocrite, a devil, an enemy to the Church. This is false doctrine. It is not the doctrine of the Church. It is damnable doctrine. It is the doctrine of devils.[5]

The only priest this could refer to is John Darcy, a Capuchin friar, who served first the Portuguese and then the Bavarian embassy chapels in London. There is a record of his officiating at a wedding in 1739. Nothing else is known of him.

One of the more interesting encounters with a Catholic in England was described by Wesley in 1743. He met 'a cursing, swearing, drunken Papist' who wanted to bring him into a state of salvation.[6] No doubt Wesley felt that salvation might be best offered by him to the Papist, but perhaps he would have been too drunk to make a response. Wesley was urged to read *The Grounds of the Old Religion*, an anonymous book by Bishop Richard Challoner, first published in 1742. Challoner offers two main grounds for the old religion. The first is its foundation on

Peter, its perpetual visibility, and its infallibility. No new sects have a share in the scriptural promises to the true Church. The second ground is the Catholic rule of faith and its role as a judge in controversies. Here are put the arguments against the Protestant use of Scripture alone and the fallacy of private judgement. Further arguments are accumulated, including the evidences from antiquity, the Fathers, apostolic Tradition, perpetual succession in doctrine, the Creed, and the marks of the Church. The book also had an appendix exposing Anglican Orders, and arguments against the Reformers based on their unholy lives.[7] Wesley is extremely critical of the arguments. The Scriptures are heaped up by Challoner to show that only the Catholic Church is the one true Church. Wesley regarded this as the attempt of Challoner's Church, only a part of the Church Catholic, to call itself the whole. Challoner went on to make the important point that Scripture is not the whole rule of faith but needs the reinforcement of Tradition. If Scripture were the whole of faith it could lead to Christianity being at the mercy of the private judgement of individuals who interpreted the Scriptures in their own ways. Wesley then discourses on private judgement as being absolutely essential to decide between the rival claims of Churches.

An early encounter with Irish Catholics occurred in May 1749 when Wesley deliberately preached outside the rector Mr Glass's house in Ahascragh since the Catholics could not come into the parish church; nevertheless, he says, their attention was 'fixed and earnest'.[8] A few days before he had preached on Isaiah 55:1 and he wrote of a Papist who had declared frankly to him: 'I would fain be with you, but I dare not; for now I have all my sins forgiven for four shillings a year; and this could not be in *your* church.'[9] Other less-than-positive encounters with Catholics also occurred in Ireland. On many occasions Wesley had the opportunity of preaching to both Protestants and Catholics, as at Mardyke in Limerick in June 1765.[10] Here he was surprised at the 'indecent' behaviour of the Catholics who were talking and laughing as if at a play. They took it well when he reproved them and seem to have listened after that. Probably here Wesley was encountering a religious and cultural difference. At the Latin Mass, the congregation would have been spectators, and so participation in a service might well have been new to them and sermons would have been rare. In the next month, while he was preaching in the open air at Athlone, there were attempts to interrupt the Protestants and Catholics who listened to Wesley.[11] In the end a Catholic miller got up and began to preach against Wesley. He was countered by having dirt thrown in his face. This led to a fight from which the miller got off with only a bloody nose. In December 1765 Wesley had a conversation with a convert who had once been a Catholic priest.[12] Why were so many people converted to Catholicism and so few to Protestantism? Wesley replies:

> What wonder is it, that we have so many converts to Popery, and so few to Protestantism; when the former are sure to want nothing, and the latter almost sure to starve?

The response is intriguing. Is Wesley referring to the fullness of sacramental life offered to the Catholic when he says they want nothing? Why is it that Protestant converts have to starve? Does he mean that no groups or bands are available for most converts, and so, as with the converts of Whitefield, they usually fade away 'like a rope of sand'. Or does he mean that Catholics help their converts financially in a way that Protestants do not?

The majority of Wesley's contacts with Catholics would obviously have been in Ireland. In his work *The Doctrine of Original Sin*, written in 1757, he drew a horrific picture of the degradation of the bulk of the Catholics in Ireland.[13] They live in small cabins, with earthen walls, covered with straw or sods of earth. In one room are gathered the cow and the pig, as well as the husband, the wife, and the children. They know how to plant and boil potatoes, how to milk a cow, how to put clothes on and off. Other than that, they know nothing, except a little religion. They know the names of God, Christ, and the Virgin Mary. They know a bit of St Patrick, the Pope, and the priest, they know how to tell their rosary beads, they know the Ave Maria and the Pater Noster. They know how to do penance, to hear Mass, to confess and pay so much for the pardon of their sins:

But as to the nature of religion, the life of God in the soul, they know no more (I will not say, than the Priest, but) than the beasts of the field.

These remarks are not substantiated on the whole in the *Journal*, where Wesley has some very positive experiences with Irish Catholics. In April 1750 he describes, for example, a meeting with a young married woman who had been a zealous Catholic.[14] She had converted several Protestants in her area of Dublin to the Catholic faith. The local Methodists in turn converted her to the great truths of the Gospel. Her relations, in particular her husband, immediately renounced her. She was, writes Wesley, moved by none of this; she desired only to experience the new faith which once she persecuted. Another woman, a Papist, was cast out of the Church for hearing Wesley preach and Wesley tells of her later experience:

> While we were at prayer she cried bitterly after God, refusing to be comforted; nor did she cease till He revealed His Son in her heart; which she could not but declare to all that were in the house.[15]

At Mount Mellick in April 1758 he records that while his congregation were mostly Protestant, many Papists also stood on the skirts of the congregation.[16] They were liable, he says, to heavy penance for it. He states elsewhere that many of the people would be 'zealous Christians', were it not for their wretched priests 'who will not enter into the kingdom of God themselves, and diligently hinder those that would'.[17] His *Journal* records many examples of Papists hearing his words: at Tullamore 'many Papists' on 1 May 1758;[18] at Alaskra on 9 June some four-fifths were Papists;[19] 'an attendance of Papists' at Athlone on 11 June;[20] while at Ennis on 29 June some nine-tenths were Papists.[21] His remarks at Alaskra indicate his feelings about them:

> Would to God the Government would insure to all the Papists in the land, so much liberty of conscience, that none might hinder them from hearing the true word of God! Then, as they hear, so let them judge.[22]

Not all contacts were quite so positive and he notes at Minulla on 3 June 1758 that the Irish Papists were as they had been a hundred years before. They had the same bitterness and thirst for blood; they would as freely cut the throat of any Protestant in 1758 as they had in the last century.[23] In general, however, the Papists seem to have heard Wesley gladly, sometimes being part of a large congregation of which they were the majority, though sometimes preferring the fringe of the congregation out of fear of their priests.

One of the best stories of a Papist convert is that of Kath. Shea, told in the *Journal* for 13 June 1758. She heard the Methodist preaching in Athlone when she was just ten years old. Her parents moved into the country and she became a zealous Papist, as her parents were. At the age of thirteen she picked up a Mass Book to read the prayers and found that she was unable to see a word. She remained blind, just able to distinguish light from dark, until she lighted on a New Testament; at once she was able to see clearly. She decided, however, not to read the Protestant Testament but her own Mass Book. Immediately, the print appeared all dark and black. She could see the New Testament clearly but never the Mass Book. After trying three times, she threw away the Mass Book. On the family's return to Athlone, she heard the Methodist preaching regularly, although she was beaten by her parents and made to leave home. In the end, though the local priest disputed with her, even her father came to believe that she was in the right.[24] This story has been related in detail because it is one of the very few examples of a Catholic convert described by Wesley in his *Journal*. The particular indications of Providence would have appealed to the Puritanism that was part of his background.

Father O'Leary was an Irish Capuchin who entered into a lengthy correspondence with Wesley over the matter of the First Catholic Relief Act in 1778. On 12 January 1780 Wesley wrote a letter to the *Public Advertiser* in which he seemed to support the stand of the Protestant Association of Lord George Gordon against Catholic relief. O'Leary wrote several articles in the *Freeman's Journal* contesting Wesley's position on the allegiance of Catholics to the State. O'Leary made a lot of mistakes, especially when he put his six letters into one with Wesley's letter prefixed to them. Wesley's comments on O'Leary describe him as a 'wild, rambling . . . writer' who has 'only drollery and low wit to oppose to argument'. The controversy was keen on both sides, on O'Leary's there was the concern to vouch for the integrity of Catholics and their lack of antagonism to the State, on Wesley's there was the desire to counter the arguments for Catholic toleration which many had thought had come about in 1778. (This controversy is considered in full in Chapter 6.) The only contact between the two men came some seven years later:

> A gentleman invited me to breakfast, with my old antagonist, Father O'Leary. I was not at all displeased at being disappointed. He is not the stiff, queer man that I expected; but of an easy, genteel carriage, and seems not to be wanting either in sense or learning.[25]

It would be good to have recorded such reconciliations throughout the history of the Church. Imagine how different that history might have been if similar breakfasts could have been held of Augustine with Pelagius, of Bernard with Abelard, perhaps even of Manning with Newman.

While preaching at Doncaster towards the end of his life, on 5 July 1790, Wesley told the story of a Roman Catholic woman who broke her china crucifix and went to her priest exclaiming, 'O, sir, what must I do? I have broken my china crucifix, and now have nothing to trust to but the great God of heaven.' Wesley's Reformation rhetoric cannot resist this opportunity: 'What a mercy!' exclaimed the venerable preacher (raising his hands in his accustomed energetic manner), 'What a mercy this poor woman had at length nothing to trust to but the great God of heaven!' The *Wesleyan Methodist Magazine* of 1828, recording the growth of Methodism in Doncaster, relates that this illustration 'fastened a nail in a sure place' for a Roman Catholic named Jeweson, who renounced his papistical notions. The next Sunday he joined the Methodists and remained faithful to them till his death.[26]

Charles Wesley's sons were famous musicians in the London

society of their day. The *Journal* of January 1781 records an enjoyable hour at his nephews' concert in London, but he confesses to a preference for plain music and plain company.[27] John Wesley of course had a greater interest in their spiritual development than in their musical progress. In 1784, Samuel Wesley, the youngest nephew, joined the Church of Rome. Samuel had been persuaded to take this step by a young French friend and was now, to the delight of the Roman Catholics in London, to be open about it. John, his uncle, wrote to him on 19 August 1784 in a spirit of love.[28] His main point is that 'opinions', Protestant or Roman, are of no account. What really matters is the inward change of the earthly mind for the mind of Jesus Christ. Without this change of heart and mind, both Catholics and Protestants will perish everlastingly. Samuel can be damned or saved in the Church of Rome or the Church of England:

> If you are not born of God, *you* are of *no Church*. Whether Bellarmine or Luther be right, you are certainly wrong, if you are not born of the Spirit, if you are not renewed in the spirit of your mind in the likeness of Him that created you.

Once the love of God is shed abroad in Sammy's heart, if he then has nothing better to do, his uncle promises to discuss with him such matters as transubstantiation and purgatory. A few years later Samuel withdrew from the Church of Rome, with something like contempt in his heart for her doctrines. Sadly, he seems to have moved to having no religion. In his 1790 letter to Samuel, John feels himself to be on the edge of eternity, and feels that these could be his last words. He fears that his nephew wants the greatest thing of all – the religion of the heart:

> ... the religion which Kempis, Pascal, Fénelon enjoyed; that life of God in the soul of man, the walking with God and having fellowship with the Father and the Son.
>
> And I lament that fatal step, your relinquishing those places of worship where alone this religion is inculcated, I care not a rush for your being called a Papist or Protestant. But I am grieved at your being an heathen.[29]

Telford in his life of Charles Wesley[30] suggests that Samuel died in the faith of his father and uncle, with 'O Lord Jesus' on his lips and 'I am coming' as his last words.

As an outstanding example of a Catholic that he knows, Wesley offers the example of Mr Hook, a zealous Papist, who believes so much in the worship of God that he is not antagonistic to other traditions than his own:

> When I asked him, 'Sir, what do you do for public worship here, where you have no Romish service?' he answered, 'Sir, I am so fully convinced it is the duty of every man to worship God in public, that I go to Church every Sunday. If I cannot have such worship as I would, I will have such worship as I can.'[31]

Here we have a word, if not quite in the spirit of *de Ecumenismo*, at least closely parallel to the eirenicism of John Wesley's *Letter to a Roman Catholic*. We have to thank God for every gem of hope discovered in a polemical period when ecumenical contacts were few.

3

Accusations of Popery

It amazes us in this century that the early Methodist movement could have been suspected of being hand-in-glove with Popery. Yet such was the fear of the encroachment of Popery in any form that it was suspected of infiltrating everywhere, a situation rather similar to the 'reds under the bed' terrors of a few years back. Any new religious movement was bound to be suspect, especially if there was a return to some of the early Christian practices which had been retained by Rome, such as frequent confession, regular communion and a search for Christian holiness. At the end of his edition of the *Journal*,[1] Curnock, the editor, adds an extract from *A True Narrative of the State of Georgia* published by the principal land-holders of the colony. In it they accuse Wesley of Jesuitical arts during his Georgia pastorate. He has excluded dissenters from his church, desiring them to be rebaptized before communicating. Persons suspected of Roman Catholicism, far from being damned, 'were received and caressed by him as First-rate saints'. There follows a list of his 'usages': the re-establishment of confession, penance and mortifications; mixing water and wine in the sacrament; saying only 'the Body of Christ', 'the Blood of Christ' at the administration; the appointment of deaconesses. Finally, there is the linking of Wesley's Popery with a form of slavery, since his aim has been to break the spirits of his congregation by subjecting them to fastings and penances. This was of course the John Wesley of 1737, but the accusations of Popery seem to have been consistently made for the major part of his ministry in England.

In February 1744 there was a real fear of invasion by the

forces of the Young Pretender and a corresponding anxiety lest the Catholics in the capital should join his forces if he came there. As a result, the Papists of London were required to leave by the second of March. The Proclamation was published on the Monday requiring their total exit by Friday, and Wesley records in his *Journal* his intention to remain in London for a further week, against his original plan.[2] Clearly, the issue here was the possibility that his leaving at the same time as the Catholics might mean that the two groups would be firmly banded together in people's minds. On 20 March 1744 the *Journal* has a record of a summons to the Surrey justices. It is possible that Wesley may have been accused anonymously of being in league with the Pretender. At the request of a justice he took the oaths to George II and signed a declaration against Popery.[3] In his second letter to Bishop Lavington, Wesley records another incident where Methodists and Catholics were deliberately bracketed together:

> I remember well, when a well-dressed man, taking his stand not far from Moorfields, had gathered a large company, and was vehemently asserting, that 'those rogues, the Methodists, were all Papists'; till a gentleman coming by, fixed his eye on him, and cried, 'Stop that man! I know him personally; he is a Romish priest.'[4]

Archdeacon Blackburne, as late as 1768, was happy to quote words from a gentleman in Paris to the effect that the Papists rejoiced at the success of the Methodists and the groups were undoubtedly in constant correspondence with each other.[5] There are no records to back up such allegations but it is interesting that they could be offered sincerely as a distinct possibility.

In May 1768 we find him answering an accusation that he had recommended the use of the crucifix to a man under sentence of death.[6] He traces this to an Anabaptist preacher, Dr Stennett, who visited the cell and, discovering a picture of Christ on his cross, and knowing that Wesley used to visit the man, assumed that Wesley had brought it. Even within the Methodist Society there could be doubts about the true intentions of the move-ment. One poor woman was distracted by the thought that she and all her fellow Methodists were really Papists. She had caught this infection of doubt from a woman later diagnosed by George Whitefield as a lunatic. This lunatic woman claimed that Wesley had taught her to pray to the saints and to the Virgin Mary, but that this knowledge was as yet available only to the initiated. It reads like a sort of Methodist Gnosticism, a secret path into the Catholic Church. Wesley saw it as a subtle Catholic plot to have him numbered as a member of that Church.[7] A year earlier, in 1741, a rumour was circulating in London that Wesley had been forced to pay £20 'for selling Geneva', presumably a reference to discounting the Reformation in favour of Popery. Wesley also kept two Popish priests in his house, the rumour went on. A dissenting teacher suggested that Wesley was in the pay of Spain to collect poor people into an army of some 20,000 who would join the Spanish army when it landed. All three of these accusations came from the same place in the *Journal*, an indication of the fecundity of people's imaginations.[8]

But there were areas of practice within the Methodist groups that could be taken as Catholic, for example the practice of confession within the band meetings. Wesley always insisted that there was no analogy to Popish confession:

> An objection much more boldly and frequently urged, is, that 'all these bands are mere Popery . . .' Do not they yet know, that the only Popish confession is, the confession made by a single person to a Priest? – and this itself is in nowise condemned by our Church; nay, she recommends it in some cases. Whereas, that we practice is, the confession of several persons conjointly, not to a Priest, but to each other.[9]

This explanation of the practice of confession in the band meetings conveys the essence of the practice, yet it was still misunderstood. Lavington suggests that when the 'filthy jakes' have been uncovered, the sinners are brought before Wesley one by one for private confession. Wesley denies this and admits only to confession of the full bands once a quarter; he is no cryptopapist. Charles Peronnet had made the accusation that a man could be a user of the rosary and/or adore a cross and still be a Methodist. Wesley denies that there are any such in England or

Ireland. Many members in Ireland were once Papists but not one has remained so.[10]

There are other ways of attracting the accusation of Romanism. One is that of acting like a pope. In the *London Magazine* in 1760 there appeared an article describing Wesley as the first Protestant Pope. Another piece by John Langhorne in 1762 suggested that the Methodist preachers had become a thousand popes, with their doctrine of plenary inspiration.[11] In the *Large Minutes*,[12] Wesley attempts to answer the accusation of being 'Pope John'. Wesley refuses the title since the Pope affirms that every Christian must do as he bids and believe all he says, on pain of damnation. Wesley affirms that his preachers chose to serve him as sons in the Gospel and that the people who chose to accept Methodist discipline chose freely. The burden of caring for preachers and people is far greater in any case than the burden of preaching. Talk of papal authority merely undermines people's confidence and leads to evil surmises against John Wesley.

Other affinities with Rome were harder to discount, such as the one that suggested that Wesley failed to convert others from Popery.[13] Wesley's response is that he has, by the blessing of God, converted several from Popery who are alive and prepared to testify to it. He offers for example the briefest of references to Michael Poor, 'lately a Roman', from a letter he had received. Poor apparently has just read his recantation of Romanism in the parish church at Rathcormack in Ireland.[14] Wesley admits, however, that over the past 30 years, he has put on 'a more catholic spirit'. He means by this of course, not the doctrines of the Catholics, but a more tender regard for those whose religious opinions and modes of worship differed from his. When Lavington accuses him of praying for the faithful departed, Wesley cites the Book of Common Prayer Burial Service and the Lord's Prayer as evidence for this kind of prayer. He claims not to be corrupting the scriptural practice, as the Papists do when they pray for those who have died in their sins.[15] He is praying for those in heaven, not those in purgatory. The question might be asked, 'Why then do they need our prayer?' but Wesley does not engage with this.

Many who belonged to the revival begun by Wesley and Whitefield felt that it was not lawful for those who were true to scriptural teaching to remain within the Church of England. The main grounds for the possible separation were: a human liturgy, not subject to the norms of Scripture; laws of the Church which contained 'the very dregs of Popery'; ministers who neither taught the gospel nor lived by it; doctrines taught which were subversive of the gospel. On the second of these Wesley offers no solution and seems to go along with the criticism offered by his fellow evangelicals:

> As to the laws of the Church, if they include the Canons and Decretals, both of which are received as such in our Courts, they think 'the latter are the very dregs of Popery, and that many of the former, the Canons of 1603, are as grossly wicked as absurd'. And, over and above the objections which they have to several particular ones, they think '(1) that the spirit which they breathe is throughout truly Popish and antichristian; (2) that nothing can be more diabolical than the *ipso-facto* excommunication so often denounced therein; (3) that the whole method of executing these Canons, the process used in our Spiritual Courts is too bad to be tolerated not in a Christian but in a Mahometan or Pagan nation.

In this letter to Samuel Walker, Wesley reveals that he cannot answer these arguments to his own satisfaction, yet he feels that it is still lawful to continue within the Church. Here he feels something of the dilemma of the Puritans before him. The Church of England, with Protestant doctrine and semi-Protestant liturgy, with a still Roman Catholic polity, was indeed 'but halfly reformed'.[16]

Wesley perceived that few people in England really understood the basic doctrines of the Church of Rome, otherwise they would never accuse him of preaching Popish doctrines. These doctrines were those added to the Creed of the Church by the Council of Trent and amounted to some ten extra articles.[17] But these are not the doctrines of the Methodist. Could there be here a confusion between the Methodist and Arminian emphasis on the possibility that all people could be saved? This was controverted by the Calvinists who believed in limited salvation. Since the Calvinists of the evangelical revival were probably in a majority over the Methodists who were Arminian, this could have led people to believe that Methodists and Catholics preached the same doctrines.[18] Perhaps it was true that Papists and Methodists taught alike, with the exception of the doctrine of merit.[19] But did not the two groups believe exactly the same when they preached perfection? Sir Richard Hill thought so when he reviewed the doctrines of Wesley. Wesley's ideas of perfection were Popish, wrote Hill, the ideas had crept into the Church of Rome from the fifth century onwards, Luther had said as much. Wesley dismissed Hill's suggestions as invalid and second-hand. Even Hill's quotations from the Fathers were from Bishop Cowper and indirect. Wesley suggests that, far from there being evidence of perfection being a Popish doctrine, the true biblical doctrine has been condemned in Rome by the bull *Unigenitus* (the condemnation of Jansenism in 1713 by Clement XI). *Unigenitus* was the constitution written against the errors of the Jansenist Pasquier Quesnel in which some 101 errors are cited from the *Moral Reflections on the New Testament* of 1692 in which Quesnel took a strongly Augustinian line. This Jansenist theological stance seemed to regard the grace of God as irresistible. On looking through the constitution it is hard to find a reference which condemns what Wesley called 'the uninterrupted act of faith and love and giving thanks'. The nearest reference is in the condemnation of number XLIII where we read:

> The first effect of baptismal Grace, is, that we die unto sin, so that the spirit, the heart, and the senses, may have no more life for sin, than a dead man has for the things of the world. (Rom. 6:2, 1693 edition)

This article is clearly about the grace of baptism and not about perfection. There seems to be no other reference in *Unigenitus* that comes close to the condemnation of the true biblical doctrine of perfection. One has to assume that Wesley's knowledge was picked up from other Christians in England who knew little about papal writings or perhaps did not care to translate the

Latin carefully. The uninterrupted act of faith and love and giving thanks, was condemned as heretical, he says, though he offers no evidence for his statement. He asks whether the doctrine of perfection has been maintained in a public act of the Church of Rome. Perhaps the response, 'at every act of canonization', might be sufficient answer to his question today. Nevertheless, he insists that perfection is not a Popish doctrine, though no doubt he means by this his own doctrine of perfection.

It is difficult for us at this distance from the events of the Reformation in England, and its aftermath, to recover the sense of horror and fear aroused by the word 'Jesuit'. We have not lived through the period of treasonable priestly activity and the horrendous persecution which followed it in the Elizabethan age.[20] Nor have we known the fear of Jesuit-inspired conspiracies in the Armada venture of 1588, nor the Popish Plot of 1605, nor the fears of Popish ascendancy from Charles I to James II. The hostility of Catholic states to the Jesuits in the eighteenth century that led eventually to their suppression is also barely understood today. While Wesley rejected the epithet 'Jesuitical' for his movement, the words 'Jesuit' and 'Jesuitical' were often thrown at the Methodists. Here is an early example, from Bristol in 1739:

> Indeed, the report now current in Bristol was, that I was a Papist, if not a Jesuit. Some added, that I was born and bred at Rome; which many cordially believed.[21]

During the Cork Riots of 1749, Wesley appears to have been accused of purveying a subtle form of Jesuitism, the charge that may well have initiated the mob violence led by Nicholas Butler.[22] The people of Hayes, Middlesex, in 1749, just before the riots at Cork, seem to have circulated a story that Mr Wesley was certainly a Jesuit.[23] In spite of these fears of Popery, the people of Hayes nevertheless seem to have listened most attentively. Several anti-Methodist publications described the followers of Wesley as disguised Jesuits, *The Jesuit Detected* being the title used by at least two of them.[24] On several occasions, Wesley is accused of promoting arbitrary Popish power, the usual criticism against the Jesuits.[25] In his second letter to Bishop

Lavington, Wesley brings no reply to the argument that Methodists 'have a strain of Jesuitical sophistry, artifice, and craft, evasion, reserve, equivocation, and prevarication',[26] because Lavington offers no real evidence. Again, and perhaps more seriously, Lavington asserts that the Jesuits have infiltrated the ranks of the enthusiasts of the English sectarians. Wesley dismissed this by reminding Lavington that at no time has he been involved with these 'enthusiastic sectaries', not during his time in Germany, nor after his return from Georgia, nor at Lincoln College, nor before that at Christ Church or Charterhouse.[27] A 'serious clergyman' to whom Wesley responded in May 1748 had offered the example of the Dominican friar, Faithful Commin, who was examined by Queen Elizabeth and Matthew Parker in 1567. Commin had infiltrated Puritan ranks as had Thomas Heath, a Jesuit, who had spiced his sermons with extreme Puritanism before being discovered and imprisoned in 1568. Could the clergyman, by analogy, have taken John Wesley for a Dominican or Charles for a Jesuit?[28] That the charge of being a Jesuit could seriously be brought against Wesley in the eighteenth century shows how vehemently Wesley had to defend himself against it.

Anti-Catholic paranoia showed itself in many different forms. In a sermon of 1744 called *Scriptural Christianity*, preached before the University at St Mary the Virgin in Oxford, Wesley asks whom God will send to bring scriptural Christianity to England. If England will not listen to the 'enthusiasts', the Methodists gathered around Wesley, then they might fall to the armies of the 'Romish aliens'. This is a reference to the fears aroused of a French invasion in 1744 and the reinstatement of the Stuarts. Will England, he asks rhetorically, be thus reformed into her first love, i.e. scriptural Christianity?[29] One of the real fears amongst the English Protestants was that the Catholic Jacobite succession might be resurrected in England through the efforts of Charles Edward Stuart. Was this Methodist movement really a Jacobite cell in disguise? As early as autumn 1743 a rumour was circulating in St Ives, Cornwall, that Wesley had brought the Young Pretender with him to Cornwall, under the name of John Downes.[30] Some adherents at Rosemargay, in the same county, asserted in April 1744 that Wesley had been seen, just a few days ago, with the Pretender in France, and this inevitably shook the confidence of some in their understanding of Wesley's gospel.[31] Wesley drafted a loyal address to George II in 1744 on behalf of the Methodist societies, but his brother Charles dissuaded him from sending it on the grounds that the Methodists would be branded as sectarians.[32] Nevertheless, in 1745 Wesley did send a loyal letter to the Mayor of Newcastle just after Prince Charles Stuart had entered Edinburgh on September 17th.[33] At Tolcarn, a few months before the Jacobite Rebellion, another rumour reached Wesley: that he had spent a long time in France and Spain, and had been sent to Cornwall by the Pretender, in order that the societies of the Methodists should join the Rebellion.[34] Wesley believed that even the Jacobite gentlemen (of the drinking, revelling, cursing, swearing type) were making accusations that the Methodists were bringing the Pretender back to England.[35] By November 1745 Wesley, in Cheshire, was supposed by his denigrators to have been with the Pretender near Edinburgh. After a few lines Wesley judges that his accuser, Dr C., will have more regard for the truth in future.[36] The joy he felt after the victory of the English at Culloden was perhaps the strongest evidence against his regard for the Pretender,[37] while his brother Charles wrote some seven hymns especially for the day of Public Thanksgiving for the victory.[38] As late as 1785, Wesley had to write a disclaimer: his brother Charles was no Jacobite; his brother was a Tory, but not more a Jacobite than a Turk, neither was John Wesley himself.[39]

The most serious accusation of Popery was a doctrinal one. In 1752 one of his former followers, John Bennet, began to assert that Mr Wesley preached nothing but Popery, denying justification by faith, and making nothing of Christ.[40] In a sermon at Bolton, Bennet had disclaimed any further connection with Wesley and had spread out his arms in his bitterness, crying 'Popery! Popery! Popery!' That Bennet could make such a preposterous charge probably shows that there was a personal issue as well as a doctrinal one lying behind the accusation. It is well known that Wesley had formed a strong attachment to Grace

Murray, the matron of the orphan house in Newcastle upon Tyne. He lost her to John Bennet due to his own indecisiveness and no doubt Bennet was no lover of his wife's former suitor. Wesley, however, had always claimed that the doctrine of Justification was the very doctrine that excluded Popery:

> At this time, more especially, will we speak, that 'by grace are ye saved through faith'. Because, never was the maintaining of this doctrine more seasonable than it is at this day. Nothing but this can effectually prevent the increase of the Romish delusion among us. It is endless to attack, one by one, all the errors of that Church. But salvation by faith strikes at the root, and all fall at once where this is established. It was this doctrine, which our Church justly calls *the strong rock and foundation of the Christian religion*, that first drove Popery out of these Kingdoms; and it is this alone can keep it out.[41]

We leave the historical question as to whether Popery was excluded from England by the doctrine of Justification by faith or by Acts of Parliament and King, but we note Wesley's almost Lutheran insistence on the fundamental importance of the doctrine of Justification. Over twelve years before Bennet's accusations Wesley had categorically stated that the difference between Popery and Protestantism was the question of works and justification. Popery was 'justification by works' or 'by faith and works'. Wesley reacts against this with the thirteenth of the Thirty-nine Articles, though quoting it as follows:

> No good works can be done before justification; none which have not in them the nature of sin.

Before 1738, he claims, he was a Papist and knew it not. Even the erroneous teaching of transubstantiation is a trifle compared with the error of teaching justification by anything other than faith alone:

> O ye fools, when will ye understand that the preaching of justification by faith alone; the allowing of no meritous cause of justification, but the death and righteousness of Christ; and

no conditional or instrumental cause but faith; is overturning Popery from the foundations.[42]

At late as 1768, Wesley had to protect his Protestantism against a connection between Methodists and Papists suggested by Archdeacon Blackburne in an article on the anti-Catholic penal laws. Blackburne hoped that some doubt concerning the connection might be offered by Wesley, as it had been by George Whitefield. Wesley replied that he had written to remove such suspicions on several occasions, as early as August 1738, and in a long letter to a *Popish Priest* in August 1739. The gist of the letter of 1739 was, 'No Romanist, as such, can expect to be saved, according to the terms of the Christian covenant'.[43] Elsewhere, he claims, he has made the same case: in the *Journals*, in *An Earnest Appeal to Men of Reason and Religion*, in *A Word to a Protestant*, in *A Roman Catechism* and in *The Advantage of the Members of the Church of England over Those of the Church of Rome*. We might add to his list a few other pieces: *A Short Method of Converting all the Roman Catholics in the Kingdom of Ireland, Popery Calmly Considered, A Letter to the Printer of 'The Public Advertiser' occasioned by the late Act passed in favour of Popery, A Disavowal of Persecuting Papists*, and several relevant letters. Most of these were written after 1768, but the *Journal* at the end of 1768 says it all:

> What amazing ignorance then, not to say impudence, does it imply, for any one at this time of day to tax me with having any connections with Popery![44]

4

The Cork Riots and the *Letter to a Roman Catholic*

... open, barefaced, noonday, Cork persecution, breaking
open the houses of His Majesty's Protestant subjects, destroying their goods, spoiling or tearing the very clothes from their
backs; striking, bruising, wounding, murdering them in the
streets; dragging them through the mire, without any regard
to either age or sex; not sparing even those of tender years;
no, nor women, though great with child; but, with more than
Pagan or Mahometan barbarity, destroying infants that were
yet unborn.[1]

Thus John Wesley, with some rhetorical skill, describes the Cork
Riots which began in May 1749 and ended a year later. Although
the description is as vivid as the passages in *Barnaby Rudge*
concerning the Gordon Riots, the scenes can be paralleled elsewhere in the *Journal*, of popular disturbances in opposition to
the Methodist movement.[2] The incitement to violence against a
peaceful movement that sought the holiness of its members
usually came by 'the great Vulgar stirring up the small'.[3] In
other words, clergymen, members of the gentry, or local farmers
were behind the minor vulgar who constituted the mob. In the
case of the Cork Riots, the ringleader was a Protestant, one
Nicholas Butler, although it is fair to say that Daniel Crone, the
Mayor of Cork, was sympathetic and at times kept such a low
profile as to have been practically invisible,[4] thereby encouraging
the rioters. In 1749 Wesley paid his third visit to Ireland, arriving
at Dunleary in mid-April.[5] On 3 May Nicholas Butler, in
parson's gown and bands, with ballads in one hand and a Bible
in the other, assembled a large mob outside the house of Thomas

Jones, a merchant of Cork.[6] A Methodist woman was so terrified at the language of this singer of ballads that the sheriff allowed her to sojourn in jail for a couple of days. Jones sought the help of Crone, the Mayor, who said he had not given Butler permission, nor would he hinder him. A larger mob that evening threw dirt and caused injury to several of the Methodist people as they came out of the preaching house. The next evening, in spite of Crone's word of honour to stop the mob, there was a larger gathering and this time swords, clubs and hangers (short swords hung from the belt) were used and many Methodists were badly wounded. Only after two days of rioting did Crone appear with his esquires, sheriffs and aldermen; the response of the authorities was to board up the preaching house and let the people out to the devices of the mob. The riots continued with increased intensity all through May and it was clear that nobody was going to oppose Butler. The reasons for this mob violence are not obvious from Wesley's account in the *Journal*, but there is the possibility that the theory that the Methodist movement might be 'all Jesuitism at bottom'[7] could have been behind it. Businesses were ruined and whole houses torn apart by the rioters. Apart from being called abusive names like 'heretic bitches', women suffered sword cuts and in at least two cases were caused to miscarry.[8]

It is against this background of violence that Wesley wrote *A Short Address to the Inhabitants of Ireland* on 6 July 1749.[9] It is a short piece of some nineteen paragraphs and is said to have been 'occasioned by some late occurrences', on which Wesley enlarges:

> But the generality of men treat them (the Methodists) in a different manner, – with utter contempt, if not detestation; and relate abundance of things in order to prove that they are not fit to live upon the earth.

The Methodists were vulgarly known as 'Swaddlers', a reference given to one of them who preached in Dublin on Luke 2:7. Wesley, in his *Journal*, suggests that the nickname, given by a priest, only highlighted the ignorance of Scripture among the Papists of Ireland. In the *Address* he asks who these Methodists are, what they teach, and what effect they have. The outcome is a typical account of 'Methodism according to Wesley', found elsewhere in such works as *A Plain Account of the People Called Methodists*.[10] These people are living witnesses to the substance of true religion and the change wrought in them shows all of this to be of God. As a result, any man of religion, any man of reason, any lover of mankind, any lover of his country, should rejoice at this movement of holiness in the nation. That the *Address* was aimed at the Protestants of Ireland and not at the Catholics is shown by the reference to the manufacture of linen in paragraph eighteen. Protestants were at the head of all the manufacturing in Ireland in this period, so it is clearly addressed to them.

Some sixteen days after he began the *Address*, Wesley wrote his *Letter to a Roman Catholic*.[11] This has become an ecumenical classic and deserves to be quoted in full.* It was clearly written in the wake of the first outbreak of the Cork Riots, although there is only an oblique reference to them when Wesley writes of the malice between Protestants and Catholics 'which have frequently broke out in such inhuman barbarities as are scarce named among the heathens'. There is no hint of the identity of the recipient of Wesley's letter. Albert Outler prefers to think of a friendly Irish Roman Catholic, while Michael Hurley sees it as an open letter to all Catholics in the wake of the Cork Riots. The problem with Hurley's theory is that it implies Catholic participation in anti-Methodist riots at a time when Catholics had no legal rights in Ireland and therefore could have reaped no benefits from participation in the riots. However, since Wesley does mention Catholic mobs elsewhere, perhaps Catholics were at least a part of the Cork mobs. Ultra-Protestants might well co-operate with Catholics to rid themselves of the Methodist threat. Unlike the *Address*, the *Letter* contains a description, not of Methodism, but of true Protestantism. The term 'Methodism' is avoided in the *Letter*, possibly because Wesley wanted to ally his movement with all good Protestants against the ultra-Protestantism of Nicholas Butler.

Wesley attempts to remove something of the root of bitterness

* See Appendix B, p. 211.

by appealing to the principle of love, while allowing both sides to retain their own opinions (1–4). He then offers the belief of the true Protestant in a credal passage containing the Trinity, the Church, forgiveness and the Last Things. While much is of interest here (5–10), two matters have importance for Protestant–Catholic dialogue. One is Wesley's acceptance of the perpetual virginity of Mary (7), a doctrine he must have obtained from his Caroline forebears in the Church of England.[12] The other might have inferred more to Catholics than Wesley meant. Wesley believes that members of the Church have fellowship with the Holy Trinity, with the holy angels, and with all the living members of Christ on earth, as well as all who are departed in his faith and fear (9). This may well be 'the communion of saints' as the Creed states it, but a Catholic reading it in Ireland would certainly infer the invocation of the saints as Wesley's belief. This would have been far from Wesley's mind and intention. He realizes that Catholics will of course want to believe more (11), but asks whether his statement of faith is not all that is needed for salvation? Wesley goes on to talk about what we have come to call 'orthopraxy' (12–15), suggesting that one who does not practise can hardly be called Christian in any sense. Paragraph 15 is almost a Catholic examination of conscience, which might be found in Ignatius Loyola's *Spiritual Exercises* or Lorenzo Scupoli's *Spiritual Combat*. After this, Wesley describes all debate about anything other than the central core of faith as 'jangling about opinions'. Perhaps, in Reformation language, he might have called these matters, *adiaphora* or 'things indifferent' (16). 'I hope to see you in heaven. And if I practise the religion above described, you dare not say I shall go to hell.' And here is the core of the argument: 'Then, if we cannot as yet think alike in all things, at least we may love alike.' The final section suggests that we no longer hurt another, no longer speak harshly of each other, think no unkind thoughts, and help each other to the kingdom. Wesley finishes magnificently with a string of Pauline quotations, six in all. The *Letter* was reprinted only three times in Wesley's lifetime: in 1750 in Dublin, in 1755 in London and in the collected *Works* of 1773, and, sadly, we have no record of the reaction to it from the Catholic side.

In April 1750, writing of the whole of February, Wesley recorded in his *Journal*, 'King Nicholas reigned' (meaning Nicholas Butler) and there are further accounts of Methodists still suffering from mob violence.[13] At the Lent Assizes of 1750, it was made clear that riots would no longer be tolerated and so Methodists in Cork at last had the law to back them. Yet in May 1750 when Wesley was back in Cork, the mayor once again tried to stop him. The preaching house was surrounded and ripped apart. Wesley, as Jesus before him, walked through the midst of the mob unafraid.[14] They were able only to burn him in effigy. After Wesley had written a strong letter to the mayor, suggesting that it would be good even to be treated like a Jew, a Turk, or a Pagan,[15] the turn around came when an army colonel told the mob, with the mayor at its head, that he would have no riots in that place. It is sad to relate that within a fortnight of this Wesley, on his way to Waterford, learned at the ferry outside the town that Butler had been gathering mobs against the Methodists for the past week. There is a note concerning Butler in Crookshank's *Methodism in Ireland*, quoted in Wesley's *Journal* by Curnock.

> Soon after, Butler, having quarrelled with some of his companions, lost his right arm in the affray, and, thus disabled, fled to Dublin, where, according to one account, he dragged out the remainder of his life in well-deserved misery, and was actually saved from starving by the charity of the Dublin Methodists; and, according to another, he rendered himself amenable to justice and was transported for life.[16]

5

Toleration and the Gordon Riots

Wesley's reaction to Catholics in England was consistent with the reaction of most of the enlightened members of the Church of England in the eighteenth century. He knew few English Catholics personally, the exception being of course his nephew Samuel, Charles Wesley's son, who may have returned to the Methodist fold on his deathbed. John Wesley was a man of his own era and probably was more a product of the Enlightenment than he would have liked to believe. That he was in favour of toleration in some sense cannot be doubted. Unfortunately, he also was a product of the age of Locke and as such believed in only a limited form of toleration for Catholics.

A very brief outline of the history of toleration in England may be helpful at this point. Toleration does not of course become an issue until people begin to believe different things. Thus it might be defined as the granting of liberty to those who differ in religion. Toleration was hardly thought of as a possibility in the Reformation period although John Foxe does stand out as one who felt differently from most:

> It is tyrannical to constrain by faggots, consciences love to be taught. The most effective master of teaching is love.[1]

Unfortunately, the author of the *Acts and Monuments* wrote only about Protestants who died for their faith. James I was inclined to the toleration of Catholics, as indeed were all his Stuart successors until 1688, only a few Catholics being executed during his reign. Sadly the matter of the Gunpowder Plot of 1605 jaundiced English opinion against the toleration of Catholics and this became another *cause célèbre* for anti-Catholic feeling, to rank with the papal bull *Regnans in Excelsis* of 1570 and the Catholic Spanish Armada of 1588.

Under Cromwell's Protectorate liberty of conscience became a fundamental feature of the constitution and even Catholics achieved a level of toleration unknown to them before. Two significant moments for Catholics occurred during this period. One was the Act for the relief of religious and peaceable people of 1650 when most penal legislation against Catholics was repealed as from the time of Elizabeth I.[2] While on the one hand recusancy fines were no longer invoked, on the other hand the legislation of 1580 against the Mass and against Catholic education remained in force, and indeed was not removed from the statute books until 1791. The other important moment was a vote in parliament in 1657 when about a third of the Commons opposed the imposition of an anti-transubstantiation oath on Catholics in the wake of the outbreak of war against Catholic Spain. It was noted that the Commons were prepared to practice toleration with some groups but not with others.

The arrival of Charles II was heralded by the Declaration of Breda in 1660 when the king promised liberty to tender consciences, though few good effects came to the Catholics. In 1687 the future monarchs William and Mary had indicated their intention to maintain the penal laws against Catholics but to grant them full liberty of conscience to worship in their own way. The Toleration Act of 1689 which followed their accession failed to fulfil the hopes of their 1687 declaration.

The letters of John Locke have often been referred to as a major breakthrough in the theory of toleration. His best known work on the subject is the first *Letter Concerning Toleration*,[3] published in 1689 though his views were almost certainly conceived as early as 1667. Locke wrote four letters concerning toleration, the first containing by far his most important arguments, thus there is no need to consider here the contents of the other three. It is almost certainly the first letter which influenced Wesley's views on toleration as Locke's points occur frequently in Wesley's writings. Locke begins with criticism of his own government for partiality in religion. On the other hand, the chief characteristic of the true Church in every age is toleration. How can men continue to torture and burn other men under the pretext of religion when religion is clearly about loving our enemies? God never gave to men in authority the power to compel others into religion. True religion always consists in the inward persuasion of the mind and so compulsion for the sake of religion is bound to be illogical. Toleration does not imply that the Church has not the right of excommunication of offenders, nor does it imply that one Church, however right it may appear to be, has the right to destroy another Church. 'I cannot be saved by a religion I distrust', writes Locke, 'and so there is no safety in following the religion of the monarch unless I am thoroughly persuaded that it is true.'[4] The magistrate must tolerate all congregations because they are all, including the religion of the state, concerned with the salvation of souls. Does this apply even to an idolatrous religion? Locke suggests that the power that might be given to a magistrate to suppress an idolatrous church might at another time and place be used to ruin an orthodox one. The only criterion for forbidding particular beliefs is if the opinion were inimical to the rights of other citizens. Thus the Catholic believes that what others call bread is the body of Christ, but he is welcome to that opinion since it does not hurt his neighbour in any way. Locke describes such belief as 'speculative opinions', and the word 'opinion' was used by Wesley in much the same sense in the next century.[5]

It is when Locke comes to what he calls 'some peculiar prerogative covered over with a specious show of deceitful works' that he sees danger to the civil rights of the community. No sect teaches openly that people are not to keep their promises, that princes may be dethroned by those that differ from them in religion, that authority over all things belongs only to them. (Locke at this point is clearly referring to Catholics but does not make actual reference to them.) But some sects say these things in other words. 'Faith is not to be kept with heretics'[6] means that some do not need to keep their word. 'Kings excommunicated forfeit their crowns, and kingdoms' implies the deposing power claimed by some (the Catholic hierarchy) down the centuries. 'That dominion is founded in grace', means that they lay claim to the possession of all things. These people have no right to be tolerated by the magistrate, says Locke, as they are far from wanting to tolerate others in matters of religion; indeed the doctrines indicate that they are ready to seize the government and the estates of their fellow-subjects. Worse still, they are subjects of a foreign prince. For all these reasons, he denies the possibility of toleration for Catholics in England without actually mentioning them. Locke had given his high philosophical sanction to the traditional prejudice and ignorance against Catholics in England and created another block against the toleration of Catholics and their emancipation.

Wesley clearly shared much of Locke's thinking on the subject of toleration. The period before the Hanoverian monarchy had been one when fears on the one hand of arbitrary government, as during the Interregnum, and on the other of a return to Popery, as during the reign of James II, had been constant in the minds of those who controlled the Church and State. Wesley grew up and began his ministry in a much less anxious period of Whig ascendancy when annual acts of indemnity were offered to Dissenters and the penal laws against Catholics were administered only half-heartedly. Wesley's views on Dissent do not concern us overtly here but it might be noted that he regarded it as having strong political tones and therefore as potentially inimical to sound government as he perceived the Catholic faith to be.

The best example in the Wesley corpus of his early understanding of toleration is the sermon on the *Catholic Spirit*, to which reference will be made later.[7] The sermon dates from 1749 and was presumably written at about the same time as the *Letter to a Roman Catholic*. While it looks like a piece of Lockeian theology, with the expressed sentiments of a latitudinarian, Wesley is extremely anxious to guard against this view. His understanding of the catholic spirit is far from 'speculative latitudinarianism' and is closer to that Anglican tradition which attempted to distinguish between things essential to the faith (and these Wesley lists in his sermon as he does in his letter of 1749) and things not essential to the faith, the things indifferent or *adiaphora* discussed first by Melanchthon in Germany and then in England by Hooker. Wesley's considered view of the matter was that 'things indifferent' in the faith were those 'opinions' held by so many different groups within the Christian Church. He quoted a letter to him from James Erskine, written around 1744/5, in the *Journal* for 1745 where this extract is to be found:

> Is it not the duty of both ministers and private Christians, in their several stations, to show that our particular opinions are not so important but that one in whom the grand characteristic is found may hold different, nay, contrary opinions.[8]

The 'grand characteristic' was of course love to God and neighbour. It was in this sense that Wesley could believe that de Renty and Lopez, though Catholic in their 'opinions', could possess the heart of Christian faith. 'Opinions' were to be distinguished from essential doctrines:

> Whatever is 'compatible with love to Christ, and a work of grace', I term an *opinion* . . . [9]

In his *Thoughts on Liberty* of 1772 Wesley offers a definition of 'religious liberty' which he must have felt to be an important statement as he repeated it in 1776 in his *Some Observations on Liberty*:

> Religious liberty is a liberty to choose our own religion, to worship God according to our own conscience, according to the best light we have. Every man living, as man, has a right to this, as he is a rational creature. The Creator gave him this right when he endowed him with understanding. And every man must judge for himself, because every man must give an account of himself to God. Consequently this is an indefeasible right; it is inseparable from humanity. And God did never give authority to any man, or number of men, to deprive any child of man thereof, under any colour or pretence whatever.[10]

Wesley goes on to remind his readers of the horrors brought on by the lack of liberty in England's past compared with the liberties of the reign of George III. A later reference to the subject, written in 1787 well after the horrors of the Gordon Riots,

comes in his sermon *On God's Vineyard*.[11] Wesley is describing
earlier opposition to the Methodist movement and a conversation between a great man and George II in which the King
was begged to stop the run-about preachers of Methodism. 'His
Majesty, looking sternly upon him, answered without ceremony,
like a king, "I tell you, while I sit on the throne, no man
shall be persecuted for conscience' sake." ' Some persecution
continued in spite of George II's words; but after an incident in
Kent in 1760 Methodists appealed to His Majesty's Court of
King's Bench, and won their case; ever since they have been free
to worship God according to their conscience. Wesley then
suggests that it is strange that every mode of worship and every
opinion were tolerated in the past, however superstitious, but
true, vital scriptural religion was not tolerated. That it is now
tolerated is a reason for praising God. At the end of the sermon
Wesley asks his hearers: 'Are you truly thankful for the amazing
liberty of conscience which is vouchsafed to you and your brethren?' A note in the new edition of Wesley's sermons adds: 'The
Methodists profited from the growing spirit of religious toleration even more than the Nonconformists or the Roman Catholics.'[12]
  In 1788 we find Wesley remarking on the breadth of the
Methodist movement and its lack of emphasis on personal
religious 'opinions':

> Look all round you, you cannot be admitted into the Church,
> or Society of the Presbyterians, Anabaptists, Quakers, or any
> others, unless you hold the same opinions with them, and
> adhere to the same mode of worship.
>   The Methodists alone do not insist on your holding this or
> that opinion; but they think and let think. Neither do they
> impose any particular mode of worship; but you may continue
> to worship in your former manner, be it what it may. Now, I
> do not know any other religious society, either ancient or
> modern, wherein such liberty of conscience is now allowed,
> or has been allowed, since the age of the Apostles. Here is our
> glorying; and a glorying peculiar to us. What society shares it
> with us?[13]

Unfortunately there is no record of an English Catholic trying to join the Methodist movement except by being a convert from the Catholic faith. Allowing that his/her priest might not hear of it and prevent it, one wonders whether the potential convert would have been allowed still to hold all the Catholic 'opinions' within the Methodist society. Toleration could presumably only go so far. Wesley's final comment on the toleration of opinions comes in one of his last sermons, *On the Wedding Garment*, written in 1790:

> When things of an *indifferent nature* are represented as necessary for salvation it is a folly of the same kind, though not of the same magnitude [as persecution, see paragraph above]. Indeed it is not a little sin to represent trifles as necessary for salvation, such as going on pilgrimages or anything that is not expressly joined in the Holy Scripture.[14]

We return to the position of the Catholics in England. The Toleration Act of 1689 tells it all in its official title, 'An Act for exempting their Majesties' Protestant Subjects, dissenting from the Church of England, from the Penalties of certain Laws'. Here there was no hint of hope for the Catholic subjects of William and Mary, it was aimed only at Protestant Dissenters ('neither this Act nor any clause, article or thing herein contained shall extend or be construed to extend to give any ease, benefit or advantage to any Papist or Popish recusant whatsoever . . .'). The Act gave a list of penal laws still directed against Catholics but which now applied no longer to the Dissenters. The laws included those against Catholics from the reigns of Elizabeth and James I along with those most recently passed in the reign of Charles II: the Test Act of 1673 ('An Act for Preventing Dangers which may happen from Popish Recusants') whereby government office holders had to declare their rejection of belief in transubstantiation, receive the sacrament at an Anglican communion and take the oaths of supremacy and allegiance; a second Test Act of 1678 entitled 'An Act for the more effectual Preserving of the King's Person and Government by disabling Papists from sitting in either House of Parliament' which included a specific rejection of the invocation or adoration of the saints or the Blessed Virgin Mary and the sacrifice of the Mass as superstitious and idolatrous. Further legislation forced Catholics with property to pay the Land Tax at a double rate. The tax was high during the reigns of William, Mary and Anne and every attempt was made to make the tax effective, Catholics being known experts in the evasion of it.

By 1700 ('An Act for the Further Preventing the growth of Popery') – the notorious one of 11 and 12 William III – Catholics no longer had the right of succession to the throne and a Protestant marrying a Catholic would lose the right of succession. They were excluded from the militia and from the Bar. They were excluded from being able to purchase or inherit land; Protestants who were next of kin could now exclude Catholic heirs from their inheritance by applying to the courts. Catholics who ventured out of their districts or who travelled into London without proper licence could be convicted of recusancy. The Test Act oaths were invoked on those convicted and the penalties were £5 for a first refusal of the oaths, £10 for the second and binding over for good behaviour for the third. That Catholics could not own arms or horses over the value of £5 gives some idea of the restrictions that these penal laws caused them to suffer. Informers were encouraged to give details of the presence of Catholic mission priests or of parents sending their children to Catholic schools on the continent. The payment for informers was raised in 1700 from £50 to £100 for every proven case, which made the role of informer a very lucrative one. Arrested priests were to be subjected to lifelong solitary confinement in remote jails.

The movement towards the Relief Act of 1778 can be told briefly. Abercrombie[15] suggests that the tide of persecution against Catholics was turning by 1760s. Although the penal laws were still ranged against them, Charles Butler in *Memoirs of the Catholic Relief Bill* (London 1829) wrote:

> The wisdom and mildness of government, and the good sense and humane spirit of their countrymen, had come to the aid of the Catholics, and generally prevented the execution of the severer parts of the penal codes . . . [16]

The movement towards Catholic relief came about through the need to recruit Catholic soldiers for service in America and was taken up by Sir John Dalrymple. Dalrymple, a Protestant Scotsman and fourth baronet of Cranstoun, had already investigated the possibility of raising Catholic regiments in Ireland and was asked to look unofficially at the possibility of doing the same in England and Scotland. Dalrymple's contact in England with Challoner only raised the bishop's timidity and many difficulties, so he turned to William Sheldon, a lawyer and former student of St Omer's. Sheldon was anxious to move to a relief bill without the interference of the priests of his Church. A loyal address from the English Catholics to the king would be followed by legislation to relieve Catholics of major disabilities. Edmund Burke drafted the loyal address which was agreed by some 206 leading Catholic laymen and published in the *London Gazette* on 2 May 1778. On 14 May Sir George Savile introduced a bill 'for relieving his Majesty's Roman Catholic subjects from certain penalties and disabilities imposed on them by the Act of the 11th & 12th of William III'. One of Savile's principal aims in proposing the repeal was to 'vindicate the honour, and assert the principles of the Protestant religion, to which all persecution was, or ought to be, wholly adverse'.[17] Would Locke or Wesley have said less?

Royal assent was given to the bill, after several amendments, on 3 June 1778. The bill had been, amazingly, only ten weeks in its gestation. The Act deliberately states the intention of relieving Catholic subjects of George III from 'certain penalties' of 11 and 12 William III. This meant that the apprehending of Catholic bishops, priests, and Jesuits for their Catholicism was no longer legal; that those who professed Catholicism could now freely keep schools in Britain; that inheritance could now pass to Catholic and not only to Protestant next of kin. The Oath of Allegiance which was appended to the Relief Act demanded of Catholics: loyalty to the Hanoverian succession; a denial of the principle 'no faith is to be kept with heretics'; a denial of the deposing power of the Pope of Rome, and a denial of his temporal or civil jurisdiction in England. All these assertions of loyalty and the denials of Catholic power in

England were to be made without any mental reservations and without the understanding that the pope could dispense from them.[18] Although the Relief Act left Catholics with the status of second-class citizens until 1829, it did at least mean an end to persecution and an increase in the building of chapels. Bishop Challoner required his people to pray for the King and the Royal family, and to take the Oath without scruple, even though he and the other clergy had been consulted about none of the matters concerned with the Relief Act.[19]

John Wesley made no immediate public response to the Savile Relief Act of 1778. It is not clear whether the work *Popery Calmly Considered* of 1779 should be regarded as some kind of response to the Act or whether it was something he felt he had to write in any case. In a letter written just one year later, on 12 January 1780,[20] he remarks a daily increase in the number of Papists. As indicated in Chapter 1, Professor Bossy has given figures which he believes show that Catholic numbers were increasing gradually in the eighteenth century, thus giving some objective confirmation of Wesley's subjective view. The other points made by Wesley in this letter make it important in the history of Wesley's relations with Catholics. It was written to the printer of *The Public Advertiser* and contains his thoughts on the Savile Relief Act of 1778. It was this letter which gained the thanks of Lord George Gordon's Protestant Association and a total response of 101 pages from Father Arthur O'Leary of Cork (for details see Chapter 6). The Catholic Relief Act of 1778 met with little opposition in England but when the repeal of the penal laws in Scotland was proposed, enormous opposition followed. In 1779 the Protestant Association was formed in Scotland and rioting led to the abandonment of the provisions for Scotland. Lord George Gordon, becoming president of the English Protestant Association in November 1779, began to collect signatures for a petition to Parliament for repeal of the 1778 Act. Gordon in Parliament suggested that parliamentary indulgences offered to Papists had alarmed the whole country and that he had 120,000 men to back him. Gordon called the Association to assemble at St George's Fields on 2 June 1780 to present a monster petition to Parliament. Over 60,000 made the march on Parliament accompanied by the petition with over 100,000 signatures on it.

The disgraceful scenes outside Parliament have often been described. 'No Popery' was the constant cry, while supporters of the Savile Bill of 1778 were pelted with mud and manhandled. George Savile had his coach demolished, the Archbishop of York was covered with mud, Lord Mansfield had his coach windows smashed and then later his house burned by the mob. Eventually the mob, which had come close to invading the Commons, was dispersed from the area by the Guards, with the promise from Gordon that the repeal of the Relief Act would follow in a few days.

That the mob should move away from Parliament to attack Catholic buildings might have been expected. Two of the embassy chapels were attacked: the Sardinian embassy in Lincoln's Inn Fields had its chapel burned down; the Bavarian embassy chapel was ransacked and its furniture made into a bonfire in the street. Two days later, the Catholic chapel in Moorfields, the nearest Catholic place of worship to Wesley's new chapel in City Road, was attacked and its contents were set on fire in the street outside. During the following days further Catholic property was attacked and burned, the most spectacular instance being Thomas Langdale's gin distillery in Holborn. Langdale, a noted Catholic, had at first tried to conciliate the mob with free gin, but in the end the mob set light to his house and the large gin vats. Men and women drank the flaming gin as it ran down the streets. Dickens, in *Barnaby Rudge*, offers the best description:

> The gutters of the street, and every crack and fissure in the stones, ran with scorching spirit, which being dammed up by busy hands, overflowed the road and pavement, and formed a great pool, into which the people dropped down dead by dozens.[21]

Wesley wrote on several occasions of his intense dislike of distilled liquors, but it is doubtful whether even he would have approved of the work of the mob in Holborn.[22]

The king insisted that the provisions of the Riot Act should be observed even without it being read, and this saved the capital

from further devastation. Over 10,000 troops patrolled the capital by 9 June, the blue cockades of the Association gradually
became less obvious, and eventually Gordon was arrested and
put into the Tower of London. The verdict of history on Gordon
is best left to Dickens who puts these words into the mouth of
Gordon's servant Grueby:

> 'Between Bloody Marys, and blue cockades, and glorious
> Queen Besses and No Poperys, and Protestant Association,
> and making of speeches . . . my Lord's half off his head.'[23]

The riots were the most serious ones in eighteenth century
England; Stevenson gives the figures of 210 killed, 75 dying
subsequently in hospital, 450 arrested of which only 62 were
sentenced to death and 25 eventually hanged.[24] Compensation
paid to individuals was over £70,000, an enormous sum for
those days. The rioters seem to have singled out the wealthier
Catholics and the wealthy supporters of the 1778 Act for their
worst assaults, showing that their antagonism was not just
against Popery but against the rich. In the end the Protestant
Association sought to dissociate their giving of the petition to
Parliament from the subsequent riots in London of which they
were not the instigators. Gordon was eventually found 'not
guilty' of inciting the people to violence, and was acquitted. His
biography indicates that he became a Jew and died in Newgate
in 1793, having been imprisoned for two libels.[25]

Wesley's support for the Protestant Association in 1780 does
not mean that he was in some way the instigator of the Gordon
Riots, even if later Catholic writers seem to have pointed to him
as the chief theoretician. Recent writers on the topic of the
Gordon Riots are generally of the opinion that there is nothing
in the sources to show that either Wesley or his Methodist
people were sympathetic to the rioters.[26] Wesley wrote on 5
November 1780:

> I preached at the new chapel on Luke ix 55: 'Ye know not
> what manner of spirit ye are of'; and showed, that, supposing
> the Papists to be heretics, schismatics, wicked men, enemies
> to us, and to our Church and nation; yet we ought not to

persecute, to kill, hurt or grieve them, but barely to prevent their doing hurt.[27]

When the riots broke out in June 1780 Wesley was away from London in the north east. During the riot his brother Charles wrote a satirical poem in four cantos, ridiculing both the mob and the magistrates.[28] After Gordon's imprisonment Wesley paid him a visit, Gordon having indicated a desire for this on two occasions. He spent an hour at the Tower of London with him and they discussed 'Popery and religion' particularly 'experimental religion'. Gordon, wrote Wesley, was well acquainted with the Bible and had plenty of books. Wesley was surprised that he was uncomplaining and offered the pious hope that imprisonment would be a blessing for him.[29] When Gordon's indictment was known Wesley thought it was an insult to truth and common sense.[30] The short tract *A Disavowal of Persecuting Papists* came out in 1782 in the *Arminian Magazine*. Wesley accepts the right of all to worship according to their conscience, including members of the Church of Rome. Although some Catholics (à Kempis, de Sales, de Renty) have loved God and neighbour, such behaviour is rare in Catholics who still believe in papal indulgences, priestly absolution and not keeping faith with heretics. He gives two recent examples of Papists freely owning that they would like Protestant blood. Nevertheless, he refuses to persecute them and prefers toleration. He closes with a paragraph that must have been written with the Gordon Riots in mind:

> But still I say, Persecution is out of the question. And I look on all vague declarations upon it, which have been lately poured out, as either mere flourishes of persons who think they talk prettily, or artful Endeavours to puzzle the cause, and to throw dust into the eyes of honest Englishmen.[31]

The leader of the Methodist movement was still the disciple of John Locke.

6

Keeping Faith with Heretics

Since the Gordon Riots were anti-Catholic riots, they must have had their origin in Protestant thinking and writing. In Catholic thought for many years, as indicated in the previous chapter, the major cause of the riots was held to be the letter written in 1780 by John Wesley to the printer of the *Public Advertiser*. In this letter he had applauded 'An Appeal from the Protestant Association to the People of Great Britain' as being a plea for the preservation of the British Constitution against the encroachments of Catholicism. In his *Journal* for 18 January 1780 Wesley had written:

> Receiving more and more accounts of the increase of Popery, I believed it my duty to write a letter concerning it, which was afterwards inserted in the public papers. Many were grievously offended; but I cannot help it: I must follow my own conscience.[1]

The letter to the *Public Advertiser* set out the three main reasons why Roman Catholics could give no guarantee of civic behaviour or allegiance to the state. The main one was the maxim, said to have been declared at Constance in 1415, that 'no faith is to be kept with heretics'. The others were: that priestly absolution meant that Catholics could receive pardon even for the sins of perjury and high treason against the state; and that the Pope had pardons and dispensations that could pardon rebellion, treason and any other sins.

The major issue quickly became the question of whether the Council of Constance had in fact passed a decree that faith should not be kept with heretics, according to which decree

John Hus had been burned at the stake for heresy. It may help
to relate the major points of the episode in order to understand
the issues.[2] John Hus (c. 1369–1415), the proto-Reformer of
Prague, had taken John Wycliffe as his mentor and taught much
that was Wycliffite; his tract *Adversus Indulgentias* for example
being pure Wycliffe.[3] In 1403 the University of Prague condemned 45 propositions of Wycliffe, and in 1408 and 1412
Wycliffite doctrines were proscribed by Pope Gregory XII. In
his teaching, Hus denied the worth of priestly absolution by
clerics and bishops in mortal sin and, like Wycliffe, proposed
Scripture as the ultimate test of belief. As a result, he was
excommunicated in 1412 by his own Archbishop, and in the
following year he was condemned by the Pope, this time by
John XXIII (called this at the time, though later recognized as
an anti-pope). During this period, Hus received support from
King Wenceslas, and from the nobles and people, and there were
fears in the Empire of a Bohemian schism. By 1414 the Emperor
Sigismund was able to force John XXIII to call a Council to
end the papal schism and also to settle the matter of Hus and the
Bohemians. Hus's excommunication was lifted and Sigismund
offered Hus a safe conduct to and from Constance where it was
hoped that Hus would be able to clear himself of the charge of
heresy. Historians differ at this point as to whether Sigismund
could offer a safe conduct both to and from the Council,
especially if the Council should find Hus guilty of heresy. The
written safe conduct seems to have been ambiguously phrased
so that it was not clear whether it covered Hus at Constance
and on the return journey. Clearly, Hus believed in the oral
assurance given by Sigismund and went to Constance in good
faith. He made two major mistakes, one in leaving Prague without the written safe conduct which he received only after reaching Constance, and a second in entering Constance without
waiting for the retinue of Sigismund. The charges against Hus
were serious: he had declared that Wycliffe was orthodox; he
had advocated communion in both kinds for all in the Mass;
he had stated that no cleric in mortal sin could validly celebrate
a sacrament. That all the three charges were false seems to be
correct; Hus was probably guilty of heresy only in his under-

standing of the papal supremacy.[4] When Hus asked for leave to speak with the Pope and cardinals, he made his third mistake. He left the safety of his lodging and companions, and was arrested and kept incarcerated on an island until Palm Sunday. Sigismund had surrendered his right to free Hus in January 1415 and by April had renounced all safe conducts granted to anyone in Constance. Here perhaps is the chief cause of Hus's condemnation and death: Sigismund's retraction on the grounds that a safe conduct could not be insisted upon after heresy had been proved. Hus was given no opportunity to make a defence before the Council. As a suspected heretic, he was given lists of articles to condemn, mostly abstracted from Wycliffe. Hus wanted scriptural proof of what was being offered as orthodox but sought this in vain. Although he maintained his orthodoxy even on transubstantiation, as a suspected heretic and no longer an independent theologian, he was not free to make his case. He was subjected to a trial, was condemned, degraded from his priestly orders, and burned at the stake on 6 July 1415. To complete the catalogue of the Emperor's acts of duplicity in the affair, it was Sigismund's suggestion that Hus should be burned by the secular powers.

There is no doubt that while it was not only his theology that brought about his condemnation, Hus had never attempted to avoid the collision course between his theology and the magisterial theology of the early fifteenth century. He had violently opposed the clerics who unworthily celebrated the sacraments of the Roman Church. His espousal of the doctrines of Wycliffe was no way to make friends with the hierarchy of the Church. Some of his presentation of these themes looked a little bit like exhibitionism, for example when he used quotations from Wycliffe while defending orthodox positions. Hus was clearly close to Catholic orthodoxy but his perception of it was clouded by his use of Wycliffe's ideas.

After this brief excursus into the history of Hus, we return to the controversy stirred up by Wesley's letter of 21 January 1780. Before 1780 it is difficult to find any reference in Wesley's works to the condemnation of Hus at Constance. In *A Word to a Protestant* of 1745 he discusses three major errors of Popery which strike at the heart of the Christian faith.[5] The third of these errors is the doctrine of persecution, and here he discusses his views which are reproduced in the letters of 1780, though there is no direct reference to the Council of Constance. Of the doctrine of persecution he writes:

> This has been for many ages a favourite doctrine of the Church of Rome. And the Papists in general still maintain that all heretics (that is, all who differ from them) ought to be compelled to receive what they call the true faith; to be forced into the Church, or out of the world.[6]

In his treatise, *The Doctrine of Original Sin* of 1757,[7] Wesley misses the chance to illustrate his list of Romish persecutions with the example of Hus and Constance but instead refers to the Dukes of Savoy against the Waldensians, to the horrors of the massacre of St Bartholomew in France, and to the Inquisition and 'a thousand other methods of Roman cruelty'. He suggests that since the Reformation perhaps 45 million have been the victims of Roman Catholic persecution. With all these grossly exaggerated figures to hand, perhaps Hus and Constance could be forgotten. There may, however, be an implied reference to the condemnation of Hus in Wesley's examination of the Roman Catechism in 1756. In his response to Question 40 concerning the Virgin Mary, he reminds his readers that at the Council of Constance the Blessed Virgin was invoked rather than the Holy Spirit.[8] No doubt in Wesley's mind, though it is not stated, the 'light from heaven' granted through Mary was deficient compared with the enlightenment of the Holy Ghost. Why else would the Fathers of Constance have ordered the burning of Hus?

The controversy of 1780 was played out mainly between Wesley and Father Arthur O'Leary, an Irish Capuchin. Since the order of events is very confusing and was further confounded by the differing titles of O'Leary's works, we look at the controversy in chronological order. In his *Public Advertiser* letter of 21 January[9] Wesley set out in a mere three pages his usual three major reasons why Catholics should not be tolerated. He went on, the encouragement offered by the Relief Act of 1778, while not the same as toleration, has been interpreted by the Catholics as the equivalent of toleration. As a result, their seminaries and chapels are increasing, their numbers are increasing too, and their intolerant persecuting principles are spreading. Around the same time there was printed an anonymous pamphlet entitled *A Defence of the Protestant Association*. This work deplored the growth of Popery in Britain, claimed that Catholics were potentially disloyal to the government, and that the Protestant Association had been wrongly calumniated for its attitude to Roman Catholics. In the *Defence* Protestants were reminded once more of the fires of Smithfield and of the Catholic persecutions. Surely it was now the duty of all Protestants to stop the spread of Catholic superstition? The *Defence* is important because O'Leary believed that it was written by Wesley. That Wesley received the thanks of the Protestant Association on 17 February for his 'excellent letter' and the almost unanimous approval of readers of the *Gospel Magazine*, might have confirmed O'Leary in his suspicion that Wesley had written not only the *Advertiser* letter but the *Defence* as well. O'Leary wrote some 'Remarks' on Wesley's letters in the *Freeman's Journal*.[10] Wesley, writes O'Leary, has foisted a false creed on the Catholics. 'Violation of faith with heretics' was never authorized at Constance and O'Leary has searched the libraries to find references to it. He quotes from the words of the Pope elected at Constance, Martin V, who wrote in a bull: 'That it is not lawful for a man to perjure himself on any account, even for the faith.' This presumably settled the matter for O'Leary as it put Constance in the right for burning Hus and Sigismund in the wrong for his revocation of the safe conduct. Mr Wesley was guilty of ransacking and misconstruing the events of an old Council held 400 years ago, for his own ends.

John Wesley's response to the 'Remarks' was not published in the *Freeman's Journal* until 23 March but must be taken next. He is scathing of the lightness of tone in the 'Remarks' and feels that O'Leary has failed to prove the case for Constance, only nibbling at an explanation. Where O'Leary denies that a decree was ever made at Constance that permitted the Church to violate faith with heretics, Wesley points to Father L'Abbé's *Concilia Maxima* of 1672 where a decree of Constance is stated:

> That heretics ought to be put to death, *non obstantibus salvis conductibus Imperatoris, Regum etc.*, notwithstanding the public faith engaged to them in the most solemn manner.[11]

For Wesley, this proves the case against Constance. Could Father O'Leary answer the other two charges?

In the interim, Father O'Leary had written five further letters to the *Freeman's Journal*, on March 12, 14, 16, 18 and 21. He claimed that Hus had abused his safe conduct and had tried to escape. But the most interesting passage is a quotation from the Council of Constance that Wesley will use in his 23 March letter to the *Freeman's Journal*. O'Leary's quotation reads:

> That every safe conduct granted by emperors, kings, or other princes, to heretics, or persons accused of heresy, ought not to be of any prejudice to the Catholic faith, or to ecclesiastical jurisdiction; nor to hinder that such persons may and ought to be examined, judged, and punished according as justice shall require, if those heretics refuse to revoke their errors: and the person who shall have promised them security, shall not, in this case, be obliged to keep his promise, by whatever tie he may be engaged, because he has done all that is in his power to do.[12]

Safe conducts, remarks O'Leary, cannot suspend the execution of the laws of the Church and State. The clergy of Constance decided the case against Hus on points of doctrine and left Hus to be burned by the State. O'Leary's quotation does not go so far as Wesley's in suggesting the death penalty, but it is clear that they are referring to the same passage from Constance. He does answer Wesley's other two questions in the later parts of his work. Roman Catholics would, he writes, rather forfeit all civic privileges than take oaths against their consciences; perjury is not a part of their creed.[13] If the Pope, as Wesley implies, can dispense any vow, how could civil society exist even for one year in a Catholic country? If indeed a priest's ability to absolve a penitent actually encourages sin of any kind, let alone perjury and treason, then so does the Gospel declaration that God forgives sins! O'Leary has strong arguments against the 'Appeal' from the Protestant Association even though Wesley had pronounced it benevolent. The calumnies it listed against the Catholic faith were really extraordinary: the costs for absolution from murder, incest and for sleeping with a woman in the sanctuary; that toleration of Popery would be prejudicial to souls and bring destruction on the fleets and armies of Britain. All these calumnies are countered by O'Leary with a paragraph that could have come from Wesley's *Letter to a Roman Catholic* or from the sermon on the *Catholic Spirit*:

> May the ministers of religion of every denomination, whether they pray at the head of their congregation in embroidered vestments, or black gowns, short coats, grey locks, powdered wigs, or black curls, instead of inflaming the rabble, and inspiring their hearers with hatred and animosity for their fellow creatures, recommend love, peace and harmony![14]

Wesley's response in the *Freeman's Journal* of 31 March 1780[15] is based on the second group of O'Leary's remarks, printed on 12 March in the same journal. After making his usual three points about the reasons why Catholics cannot be expected to behave peaceably, he criticizes O'Leary's skipping and rambling manner which though entertaining, does not amount to an argument. Hus, argued O'Leary, struck at the root of temporal power and civil authority by asserting that princes, magistrates etc in the state of mortal sin are thereby deprived of all power and jurisdiction. Wesley cannot find this in his sources, nor the attempted escape of Hus noted by O'Leary. He rejoices that O'Leary also finds in the material concerning Constance the declaration that no safe conduct issued by a prince to a heretic need prevent the heretic from being punished. Wesley then rehearses the history of the arrest of Hus, the articles brought against him, and his condemnation. He notices four things: i) that Hus was guilty of no crime; ii) that he was not guilty of sedition; iii) that his only fault was opposition to papal usurpations; iv) that Sigismund was a perfidious murderer and that the Council of Constance, by extolling Sigismund, was guilty of innocent blood in laying down that the solemn promise made to a heretic could be broken. If public faith with heretics may be broken once, the instance might be multiplied a thousandfold. Arguments that Sigismund could not in law grant a safe conduct to a heretic mean nothing; a safe conduct was offered and then retracted, and a Council agreed to it. Until the doctrine is repealed, it remains that 'the public faith, even that of kings and emperors, ought not to be kept with heretics'.

O'Leary's six articles were printed together in *Miscellaneous Tracts* as 'Remarks on the Rev Mr Wesley's Letter in Defence of the Protestant Associations in England; to which are prefixed Mr Wesley's Letters'. The 1781 version of *Miscellaneous Tracts* is subtitled, 'In which are introduced, the Rev Mr Wesley's Letter, and the Defence of the Protestant Association'. Hempton[16] sees each successive issue as a partial retraction by O'Leary of the implication that Wesley wrote to defend the Protestant Association. Because Wesley perceived that O'Leary wrongly saw him as the writer of the *Defence*, and had printed only his first letter of 21 January and not the two he had written to the *Freeman's Journal* in March, he decided to reprint all three letters with a brief explanation to the reader on 29 December 1780. The date may be significant. In the *Journal* he records a visit on 19 December to Lord George Gordon in prison. On 29 December he heard about the indictment against Gordon.[17] Perhaps he felt the need to set the record straight concerning his involvement in the matter.

This was not the end, however. O'Leary made a 'Rejoinder' to Wesley's 'Reply'.[18] The thirtieth proposition in Hus's condemned articles at Constance was seditious: no king, no pope, no bishop can function in a state of mortal sin. It was as seditious as Wesley's defence of the Protestant Association; see the embers of London for proof! Why did Hus never complain to Sigismund about his breach of promise? He must have realized that the Emperor would have had to obey the law of the Church concerning heretics. Jerome of Prague came to Constance a year later under safe conduct and under this clause, *salvo jure concilii* (saving the Council's right to judge). Jerome came to Constance like Hus, believing himself to be in the right, and clung obstinately to that belief, so he was burned at the stake. 'Many go to the market for wool, that come home shorn.'[19]

As early as next year, Wesley was once again writing about Hus and Constance in the third volume of his *Ecclesiastical History*.[20] The work was an abbreviation of Lawrence's translation of the work by Mosheim, the Chancellor of Göttingen. Here again we have Hus's exclamations against the court of Rome, his recommendation of Wycliffe, the breach of the safe conduct by Sigismund, his essential doctrinal orthodoxy. As to why Hus was burned, Wesley offers the traditional explanations: that the clergy was made odious in the eyes of the people by Hus; that there was theological jealousy; that the Germans expelled from Prague in 1408 wanted revenge. The theological jealousy is sharpened under the influence of Mosheim's work. The battle is between the Realism of the Hussites and the Nominalism of Gerson and d'Ailly. The latter group hounded Hus to his death.

In the penultimate year of his life Wesley wrote at Madeley the sermon *On the Wedding Garment*.[21] Here again the Catholic Church is accused of the spirit of persecution. It was avowed at the Council of Constance and has been practised for many ages:

> But have the heads of that community as openly and explicitly renounced that capital doctrine of devils as they avowed it in the Council of Constance, and practised it for many ages? Till they have done this they will be chargeable with the blood of Jerome of Prague, basely murdered, and of many thousands, both in the sight of God and man.

It is interesting that this debate about the keeping of faith with heretics was still around after the death of Wesley. Charles Butler, a member of the Cisalpine Club formed in 1792, offered in 1807 the following affirmation of the Roman Catholic position.

> That there is no principle in the tenets of the Catholic faith by which Catholics are justified in not keeping faith with heretics, or other persons differing from them in religious

opinions, in any transaction either of a public or private nature.[22]

Thus Wesley's allegation was still being answered in the period before Catholic Emancipation.

7

John Wesley and Richard Challoner

If John Wesley and Richard Challoner had met, one suspects that Wesley would have been surprised at the gentle and conciliatory nature of the leading Papist of London, while Challoner would have been surprised at Wesley's essentially Christian and rational orthodoxy. Sadly, they never met, although they were often in the capital at the same time, perhaps only a few streets apart. Challoner (1691–1781) was the elder by twelve years.

By the time that Wesley took over the Foundery for his London society in 1739, Challoner had already been in London as a priest for some nine years. In 1741 he was consecrated coadjutor to Bishop Petre with the attribution of the see of Debra *in partibus infidelium* and in 1758 succeeded Petre as Vicar-Apostolic of the London District. It seems that he lodged most of his life with Mrs Hanne: in Devonshire Street, Red Lion Street, Lamb's Conduit Street and then Gloucester Street.[1] During the Gordon Riots his lodgings were threatened by the mob who looked forward to chasing the Papist bishop through the streets in mock homage, but Challoner escaped to Finchley where he was looked after by the Mawhoods.

As a Catholic priest and bishop Challoner had to lead a celibate life, and here there is a contrast with Wesley who married Molly Vazeille in 1751. It has been suggested that Wesley's vocation was in fact to the single life, as might seem to be consistent with being the leader of a religious order within the Church of England. It could be argued that his disastrous marriage was undertaken outside the will of God for him, for he was in fact called to the celibate life. Wesley's thoughts on the single life are therefore of interest to us. Three times he urges

Zachariah Yewdall to be free rather than to seek a wife[2] and commends his *Thoughts on a Single Life* and *A Word to Whom it may Concern*. In 1751 he urged his younger preachers to remain single for the sake of the work if at all possible, although he himself a few days before had made the decision to marry.[3] His *Thoughts on a Single Life* were written in November 1764 and were consistent with a previous tract from 1743 called *Thoughts on Marriage and a Single Life*.[4] His first thought is that he will not allow that the single life is essential to ministry as do the members of the Church of Rome. He finds that the married state is commended in Scripture and must not be branded as 'licensed fornication' as some Roman Mystics have written. Wesley's main reason for his advocacy of the single life is that the single person can devote his full time to the work and glory of God, without the distractions of wife and children. Abstinence from marriage can be received as a vocation at our justification but the inclination to the vocation is later lost by our own fault, he believes. The arguments offered for the single life are of course the ones offered within the Catholic Church: liberty from the things of the world such as homes and families; the temptation to love any other person more than God; the leisure to do more in the way of prayer and service. The ways to avoid the devices of Satan which move us to marriage are: the company of our own sex who are like-minded; the avoidance of conversation and any intimacy with those of the opposite sex; allowing every hour to be turned to good account. Blessed, says Wesley, are those who have made themselves eunuchs for the sake of the kingdom, 'who abstain from things lawful in themselves, in order to be more devoted to God'. It is interesting that Challoner in his *Meditations for Every Day in the Year* has little on celibacy, presumably because he writes more for the Catholic laity than for the clergy and Religious. He does not mention the devotion to full time work for God which celibacy offers but rather lauds chastity as a great evidence of the truth of Christianity:

> Chastity is the lily of virtues; the bright ornament of the soul; the profession and practice of which, by so many thousands,

is one of the greatest evidences of the truth and the excellency
of the Christian religion; of the wonderful grace it communi-
cates to its followers, and of the purity and sanctity of the
Author of it.[5]

Here the emphasis is less on the value of celibacy and more on
the divine work shown in chaste members of the Catholic faith.

Both Challoner and Wesley advocated the use of the fasts
prescribed in the Church year. For Challoner these were the
Fridays of each week and the appropriate vigils before certain
festivals. The record of fasting in the Wesley corpus is even more
impressive.[6] Wesley even criticizes the Romans for repealing the
Wednesday fast from the early Church; this he kept with
the Friday as well.[7] The *Journal* and *Letters* refer to fasts for the
King and nation at times when Popery raised its head in England
– such as in 1745 with the fear of the Young Pretender's
invasion,[8] and even fasts for slaves.[9] Wesley enjoined prayer and
fasting upon his people at critical times in the life of his Methodist societies.

Both Challoner and Wesley reacted to the events of the earthquakes, in London in 1750, and in Lisbon in 1755. Burton
offers Challoner's thoughts from his *Instructions and Advice to
Catholicks upon occasion of the late Earthquakes*. The earthquakes had hit London early in 1750 and it was rumoured that
an earthquake on 8 April would destroy the city. Challoner
takes the view that the earthquake was a judgement for the sins
of London since it was not felt elsewhere. Scripture and the
Fathers show that earthquakes indicate the wrath of God:

> And what else, indeed, can any one expect, who seriously
> reflects on the multitude and enormity of the blasphemies,
> perjuries and other crying sins that are so common amongst
> all sorts of people . . . besides that general lewdness, injustice,
> profane swearing and other vices which everywhere reign,
> together with an utter contempt of all religion, and profanation
> of all that is sacred.[10]

Catholics should turn to God in prayer and penitence, Collects against earthquakes were to be used in all services and the *Miserere* was to be sung after Compline or Benediction.

John Wesley has a sermon on earthquakes often attributed to him though it is almost certainly by Charles.[11] His *Serious Thoughts Occasioned by the Late Earthquake at Lisbon* was printed in 1755.[12] In it he says that such disasters should fall upon Lisbon is hardly surprising, for there is a God who judges the world and he has begun in a place of iniquity where riches have been piled up by merchants and where the Inquisition, that bloody 'House of Mercy', has insulted heaven and earth. Recent events in England have indicated God's displeasure; the earth has been shaken and cattle disease has spread. These are not 'natural causes' but are signs of God, who is hoping to bring us back to himself by these means. This God is not an epicurean who sits at ease in heaven but one who has created heaven and earth. Human beings need to make this terrible God their friend, then even if the earth should be moved, the Lord of hosts will be an everlasting refuge. Wesley ends the piece with an evangelical appeal to people to change their ways and turn to God, who will create for us happiness in life, death and eternity. Here the Methodist and the Catholic are at one, even if the Catholic did not have the same opinion concerning Lisbon's housing of the Inquisition.

It is fair to say that by the end of their lives both Wesley and Challoner had performed immense services for their followers. The parallels are illuminating. Both had been responsible for reissuing classic Christian writings in a form that could be easily appropriated by their people. In 1735 Wesley had produced a new translation of Thomas à Kempis' *Imitation of Christ*, which he called *The Christian's Pattern*.[13] It is probable that Richard Challoner's edition of à Kempis, called *The Following of Christ*, which he produced in 1737, was a deliberate attempt to draw Catholics away from Wesley's translation of the work. Two years later Challoner produced the *Confessions* of St Augustine. Other works that the now Vicar-Apostolic edited included a *Life of St Teresa of Avila* (1757) with extracts from her works, and *Philothea*, better known as *An Introduction to the Devout Life* by St Francis de Sales (1762). In 1746 Challoner edited

John Gother's spiritual works, a link here with his past since it was Gother who had received him into the Church.

Wesley's main work as an editor of Christian classics is found in his *Christian Library* of 50 volumes, mostly abridgements of larger works. To give a full list would be tedious but apart from the Protestant and Puritan classics here are to be found the Apostolic Fathers, Macarius of Egypt, Blaise Pascal, Brother Lawrence, Archbishop Fénelon, Miguel de Molinos, Juan d'Avila and Gregory Lopez.[14]

Challoner was perhaps more concerned than Wesley with making appropriate books of prayers and worship material available for his people. Challoner was responsible for what became the best-known book of prayers, devotions and meditations in the English Catholic Church for over a century. It was called *The Garden of the Soul* and came out in 1740. So influential was it that 'Garden of the Soul Catholics' was a description used of the English Catholics before the more Roman forms of devotion became popular both before and after the restoration of the hierarchy in 1850. Crichton described this Catholicism of the Challoner period as 'strong in faith, somewhat reticent, solidly instructed and devout with a deep interior piety'.[15] *The Garden of the Soul* was an extremely useful manual of prayers for lay Catholics at a time when all but Sunday Mass was impossible, and by its use each lay person became his or her own minister. It contains an exposition of Christian doctrine, what every Christian must believe and do to gain life everlasting; Gospel lessons to be pondered at leisure; feast and fasts for the year (at the time there were 36 holy days of obligation for the Catholic); a Morning Exercise with acts of faith; ten meditations based on Francis de Sales' 'Introduction'; instructions and devotions for hearing Mass; other devotions proper for Sundays and Holy Days; Vespers and Benediction; the seven Penitential Psalms; Evening Devotions for families; necessary virtues to be practised each day; preservatives and remedies against sin; instructions and devotions for confession, communion, confirmation, and for the sick; prayers and litanies for the living and departed. This book, often over 300 pages, served the Catholics as the Book of Common Prayer did the

Anglicans, probably proving even more useful than the BCP because of the practicality of its contents. It is still as moving to read in our time as it no doubt was in the eighteenth century and breathes the devotion of its author and compiler. Challoner's *Meditations for Every Day of the Year* of 1754 also went through many editions in his lifetime and after. As a work it would have been of great interest to Wesley with its use of biblical material, a use Wesley thought was not important in the Catholic tradition. It is interesting that the *Meditations* are very insistent in their emphasis on sin, death and hell, thus making them less than replete with that 'optimism of grace' which Wesley seems to have preferred in his spirituality.

Wesleyan parallels to Challoner here are not abundant. In 1733 he published *A Collection of Forms of Prayer for Every Day in the Week* for the use of his Oxford pupils.[16] It is a short piece when set alongside the *Garden of the Soul*. The same comment applies to his *A Collection of Prayers for Families*, probably of 1745, a pamphlet of some 24 pages with prayers for each day to help a family in their daily devotions.[17] Green believes it be an extract from an unknown author rather than Wesley's own work. In 1772 Wesley published *Prayers for Children* with brief prayers for the morning and evening of each day of the week.[18] The paucity of Wesleyan material here is probably accounted for by Wesley's reverence for the Book of Common Prayer, a book which he felt already contained all the set prayer forms his Methodists could ever want. The large body of Methodist hymnody also helped to provide his people with 'a little body of experimental and practical divinity', thus offering a major source for private devotion.

The vast amount of polemical writing in Challoner has often been noticed, mostly writings which attempted to explain the Catholic position and oppose the theology of the English Protestants. The titles indicate their contents: *The Unerring Authority of the Catholic Church* (1732); *A Short History of the First Beginnings and Progress of the Protestant Religion* – drawn from Protestant writers (1733); *The Touchstone of the New Religion* – 60 assertions of the Protestants on 'Scripture alone' (1734); *The Young Gentleman Instructed in the Grounds of the Christian*

Religion – against Atheists, Deists, Freethinkers and Arians (1735); *The Grounds of the Old Religion* (1742); *A Papist Misrepresented and Represented* – Gother's work with selected portions (1752); *A Caveat Against the Methodists* (1760).[19] Wesley responded to two of these, *The Grounds of the Old Religion* and *A Caveat Against the Methodists*, and even then all too briefly (see Chapter 8). As a controversial writer he was a reluctant starter and although he made several ventures into controversy against the Moravians and Calvinists (e.g. 'A Short View of the Difference between the Moravian Brethren, lately in England, and the Rev Mr John and Charles Wesley' of 1741 or 1745 and 'A Dialogue between an Antinomian and his Friend', also of 1745), the controversy with Catholics does not seem to have been taken up too often. We have noted above that the controversy was important at the time of the Jacobite Rebellion. To this 1745 period belong *A Word in Season* and *A Word to a Protestant*. [20] In the 1750's there were three polemical pieces: *A Short Method of Converting all the Roman Catholics in the Kingdom of Ireland* (1752), *The Advantage of the Members of the Church of England over Those of the Church of Rome* (1753) and *A Roman Catechism, with a Reply thereto* (1756).[21] There seems then to have been a lull before the Catholic Relief Act of 1778 after which we have *Popery Calmly Considered* (1779) and the letters to the printer of the *Public Advertiser* (1780).[22] Nothing controversial appears after 1780. Over against the controversial material have to be set the *Letter to a Roman Catholic* of 1749 and the sermon on *Catholic Spirit* of 1755.[23] It has to be said, however, that in controversy against Catholics the polemical Wesley wins over the eirenical Wesley in terms of the volume of work that he produced.

Wesley in his *Christian Library* devoted about four and a half books of the 50 to extracts from John Foxe's *Acts and Moments of the Christian Martyrs* and to a supplement of Foxe's which were published in 1751. Some ten years before, Challoner had pulled together the accounts of the English Catholic martyrs, of which there had been no previous account in English, in his *Memoirs of the Mission Priests* which appeared in two volumes in 1741 and 1742. Challoner's work included over four hundred martyrs, not only priests but laity as well, who had died for the faith between 1577 and 1684. Lingard, the Catholic historian, described the volumes as superseding 'Foxe's lying stories'.

Both Wesley and Challoner were forced to reply to the works of Dr Conyers Middleton. Middleton had been in Rome in 1724–5 and in 1729 had written a *Letter from Rome showing an exact conformity between Popery and Paganism: or, the Religion of the present Romans derived from their heathen ancestors.* Middleton's writings showed a tendency to scepticism and before his death it was noted that he had suspended belief in revelation. Challoner in 1737 answered Middleton in *The Catholick Christian instructed in the Sacraments, Sacrifice, Ceremonies and Observances of the Church.* His preface to the work swept away Middleton's arguments and the remainder of the book became a standard work for Catholics for over a century. Challoner had suggested that the royal coat of arms over the communion tables of the Church of England and the royal head on coins were a subtle form of royal idolatry. As a result Middleton had attempted to commit Challoner under the penal laws for disloyalty to the sovereign.[24]

Wesley's controversy with Middleton was over his *A Free Inquiry into the Miraculous Powers, which are supposed to have existed in the Christian Church...* of 1748. Wesley's response took him some twenty days to formulate and he attempted to show that miracles were indeed performed by Christ and his Apostles and in the primitive Church, and that Christ, the Apostles and the Early Fathers were neither fools nor knaves.[25] The letter is one of the longest Wesley wrote. This is his conclusion, following his insistence on the element of the miraculous:

> I reverence these ancient Christians (with all their failings) the more, because I see so few Christians now; because I read so little in the writings of later times and hear so little of genuine Christianity; and because most of the modern Christians (so called), not content with being wholly ignorant of it, are deeply prejudiced against it, calling it 'enthusiasm' and I know not what.[26]

Under Challoner the London priests met weekly to encourage

each other to keep the apostolic spirit alive amongst them.
Challoner drew up some seventeen rules for their guidance and
perhaps here there are some parallels with Wesley's *Rules of a
Helper*. The emphasis in Challoner's rules is on the continuing
sacramental life of the Catholics and so eight of the rules concern
the sacraments and catechisms. Brief excerpts from the rules are
however of interest:

1. Our first care shall be to endeavour to labour for our
   own sanctification ...
2. We will neglect no opportunity of labouring for the conversion and sanctification of our neighbours ...
4. When we shall be desired to go to the poor that are sick,
   we will never decline it ...
7. We will endeavour to turn our common conversation, as
   much as may be, to edification.
13. We will exact nothing for our Functions from the rich;
    and take nothing from the poor ... [27]

It is certain that Wesley would have agreed that these were
consistent with his ideals for the Methodist preachers, and each
of the above can be paralleled in his writings.

The disciplined life of John Wesley is of course well docu-
mented as is his refusal to waste time in being 'triflingly
employed' from his waking at 4 a.m. for prayer until his retirement at bedtime. Challoner's life was similar, if less frenetic.
Butler's account tells of his rising at 6 a.m. for meditation, his
recital of the Daily Offices, his daily Mass, his short but frequent
visits to his people and his time in the confessional.[28] When not
employed in the pastoral round he set himself to write for the
edification of his people and the Catholics owed to this disciplined endeavour such classics as *The Meditations* and *The
Garden of the Soul*.

That the English Catholics were not anti-biblical is shown by
Challoner's work on the Douai version of the Bible. By the
eighteenth century the Douai version was 150 years old and not
only difficult to understand but difficult to procure. The Bible
was a crucial ingredient in Challoner's works, providing the
woof and warp of his arguments for the Catholic faith. He

decided to attempt a recension of the Douai Bible, relying on his translation from the Vulgate for the Old Testament and common English usages for the New (including the careful use of the Authorized Version, while purposefully retaining differences between his version and the AV). His New Testament appeared in 1748 and the Old Testament in 1750. He continued work on the New Testament and the third edition differed from the first in over 2,000 places. Wesley also produced a more reliable translation of the New Testament in 1790, his last important publication.[29] It is reckoned to contain 12,000 alterations from the text of the Authorized Version, many of them very detailed and indicating the pains that Wesley took over the work. The parallel here between Wesley and Challoner shows the falsity of contrasting a biblical teacher (Wesley), with a non-biblical teacher (Challoner). Sadly, even towards the end of his life, Wesley was still accusing the Catholic leaders of removing access to the Bible from their people.[30]

Both men regarded charity as being an important part of their ministry.[31] Wesley left the money from the sale of his many books to the poor. In the snowy winter of 1785 we find him in the streets of London begging for the poor men who had been employed in completing the new chapel on City Road. Both men spent time and money in relief of the prisoners in the London jails. Challoner similarly left bequests to the poor in his will, including the money that would be obtained from his unsold works.

> He himself lived in that poor and humble style, in which we have all beheld him, barely allowing himself the indispensable necessaries of life, whilst through his hands flowed an inexhaustible stream of bounty to the necessitous of different descriptions.[32]

In a letter of 1757, harassed as he was by the duties of the episcopate, he wrote that he longed to be 'absolutely released from all kinds of superiority and left in a lower station to preach to the poor'.[33] As he was stricken with a stroke in his last illness he indicated his pocket where money for the poor was to be found and uttered his last word, 'Charity'.[34]

That both men were concerned for a true spirituality both in themselves and in their people has been amply demonstrated. We shall end with quotes from both Challoner and Wesley:

> He is a fire that ever burns; this fire is the very centre of our souls; how is it that we feel so little of its flames? It is because we will not stand by it. It is because we will not keep our souls at home, attentive to that great guest who resides within us, but let them continually wander abroad upon vain created amusements.[35]

> One design ye are to pursue to the end of time – the enjoyment of God in time and in eternity. Desire other things so far as they tend to this: love the creature, as it leads to the Creator. But in every step you take, be this the glorious point that terminates your view. Let every affection, and thought, and word, and action, be subordinate to this. Whatever ye desire or fear, whatever ye seek or shun, whatever ye think, speak, or do, be it in order to your happiness in God, – the sole end, as well as source, of your being.[36]

Both of these pieces could have been written by either Challoner or Wesley.

8

A Caveat Against the Methodists

In 1760 Richard Challoner took up the cudgels against the Methodist movement, which he perceived to be a threat to the Catholic Church in England, claiming as it did to be based on the teaching of the earliest Apostles. Apostolicity existed in England, said Challoner, but it was to be found only where the uninterrupted succession of teachers had existed from the beginning, namely in the Catholic Church. Challoner set out his ideas in a work of some 48 pages called *A Caveat Against the Methodists*. Some editions have the date 1756 but it is clear from the date of Wesley's reply and from Burton's biography that the date of the *Caveat* was 1760. Burton in his life of Challoner gives no context for the piece, neither does Wesley in his *Journal* for 1761.[1] This is a great pity as the impression gained from reading what Challoner and Wesley had to say is of two great Christian leaders who would have agreed on a great deal had they had any contact with each other. Challoner's work was published anonymously, like all Catholic works in penal times, and was subtitled, 'Showing how unsafe it is for any Christian to join himself to their Society or to adhere to their teachers'. The tract went to six editions[2] and was last printed in 1817. The tract usually has with it another small tract called *The Devotion of Catholics to the Blessed Virgin Truly Represented, written in the Year 1764*, though this was almost certainly by Robert Manning and not by Challoner.

Challoner set out his *Caveat* in six major headings:

    I   The Methodists are not the People of God: they are not

true Gospel Christians: nor is their new raised Society
the true Church of Christ, or any Part of it.

II   The Methodist Teachers are not the true Ministers of
Christ: nor are they called or sent by him.

III   The Methodist Teachers have not the Marks by which
the Scriptures would have us to know the true Ministers
of Christ; nor do their Fruits any ways resemble those of
the first Teachers of Christianity.

IV   The Methodist Rule of Faith is not the Rule of true
Christian Faith.

V   The Methodists' pretended Assurance of their own Justification, and their eternal Salvation, is no true Christian
Faith; but a mere Illusion and groundless Presumption.

VI   The true Scripture Doctrine concerning Justification.

John Wesley's answer to the *Caveat* was published in the
London Chronicle of 16 February 1761 and is reproduced in
the *Journal*.[3] It is said to be an answer to the tract but is in fact
only the beginning of an answer to the first two points, namely
that Methodists are not the People of God and that Methodist
Teachers are not the true Ministers of Christ. Wesley does not
unfortunately here enter into the discussion of the other topics:
namely the Fruits of the true Ministers of Christ, the Methodist
Rule of Faith, the Methodist understanding of Assurance, and
the scriptural doctrine of Justification. These can of course be
found elsewhere in his works. Before looking at Challoner's
first two caveats, he makes a general point. A blanket caveat
against all Methodists is really directed against all Protestants;
the names of Whitefield and Wesley are used but the Church of
England and Protestants of all denominations are meant. Wesley
pleads his 'scarecrow name' as an inadequate person to make a
retort and suggests that one with more skill and time might be
persuaded to make a better response.

In the first section Challoner sets out the proposition that the
Methodists are not the People of God, not the true Gospel
Christians, nor is their Society the true Church of Christ.[4] He
offers proofs from the Old Testament and New Testament of a
society founded by Christ, universal, one, holy, and orthodox.

In this society there has never failed a succession of pastors and teachers, directed by the Holy Spirit, but this Catholic society has nothing to do with this newly-raised sect. The weight of Challoner's argument from Scripture is really impressive and must have daunted Wesley when he saw it. Over 50 verses from the Old Testament are listed and over twenty from the New. This must have looked formidable to one who, like Wesley, adhered to the letter of Scripture. It is of interest that he does not use Scripture as a part of his argument against Challoner.

Wesley begins by agreeing with Challoner concerning the marks of the Church, its perpetuity, its universality, its unity, its holiness, its orthodoxy. He agrees that there has always been a perpetual succession of pastors and teachers, divinely appointed and assisted. But he alludes to a task that they perform under God which Challoner does not even mention; they convert sinners to God. This perhaps was the difference between Challoner's 'true ministers in apostolic succession' and Wesley's 'helpers', the itinerant lay preachers in connection with him; the former were in right apostolic succession but converted nobody,[5] the latter might not be true ministers, but they converted sinners to God.

Wesley denigrates Rome for doctrines and practices which are additions to and unscriptural corruptions of the original faith and suggest that the 'marks' of the Church are not found there. The Church of Rome is not at unity with itself as there are parts of the Catholic Church not found in it; Wesley here seems to be suggesting the alienation of such groups as the Eastern Orthodox, Coptic and Russian Orthodox from Roman Catholicism. It is not holy as he sees its members in London and Dublin. There is no security against error as history shows with Pope against Pope, and Council against Council. Again, he makes the suggestion that God does not reveal that Catholic pastors have been sent by him. They convert others to their own opinion but do not convert sinners to God; the drunkard remains a drunkard, the flocks wallow in sin together. Roman Catholics in general are not the People of God.

In the second section,[6] Challoner suggests that Methodist Teachers are not true ministers of Christ, neither called nor sent by him. If the Methodists are not the People of God, then the ministers cannot be true ministers. In particular, there is no succession from the Apostles. A divine commission must come in one of two ways, either directly from God as the commissions given to Moses and the Apostles, or from men who have had authority handed down to them by the Apostles. A direct commission from God would have been attended with miracles; the Methodist teachers have not had these miraculous visitations; the commission from men would have come via apostolic succession, this has not been given. The doctrine of Justification which Whitefield and Wesley preached is not the one that the heirs of the Apostles have taught. Presumably Challoner is here describing the doctrine of Justification of the Council of Trent, a topic that he will take up again later in section VI.

Wesley argues that Challoner has not proved that Methodists are not the People of God and that therefore the idea that their ministries are not true ministries comes to nothing. He argues that if Roman ministers come down from the Apostles, then so do Protestant ministers, in particular the English. He uses the work of le Courayer to make his point from the Roman side. Pierre François le Courayer was a French Augustinian canon from St Geneviève near Paris who was well known in London during Wesley's time for his positive appreciation of the catholicity of the Church of England. He had written in 1721 a 'Dissertation on the Validity of the English Ordinations and of the Succession of Bishops in the Church of England'. Courayer escaped from France after his works were condemned and lived in England for the next 40 years, dying in 1776 and being buried in the cloisters of Westminster Abbey.[7] It is fair to say that le Courayer was one of the few Catholic theologians who held that the Anglicans had maintained the apostolic succession. Wesley points out that the anathemas thrown by the Council of Trent against the Protestants are equally anathemas thrown against St Paul. Not for the first time, he denies that the uninterrupted succession is provable in any sense. At this point he takes up the doctrine of 'intention'. It is a Roman doctrine that the 'intention' of the administrator of any sacrament is necessary for its validity, whether it be baptism, the sacrament of the altar, or ordination. Suppose that the intention to do what the Church does was ever lacking as the basis of the sacrament; this would imply that the ministry of the person would be wholly worthless. Thus Wesley believes that he disposes of the uninterrupted succession, if intention were lacking at even one point in that succession. He then finishes with a final argument, that a priest can hardly teach others the way to heaven if he is not himself on the way. If the blind lead the blind, both shall fall into the pit. Clearly Wesley does not understand the doctrine that the efficacy of the sacraments does not depend on the state of grace of those who purvey them. Here, sadly, his comments cease, with only two sections of Challoner's work criticized. It could be that he had only the first two sections to hand, but it would have been of interest to hear his direct comments on the other parts.

Wesley would no doubt have countered Challoner's third heading that the Methodist Teachers had not the marks of the true ministers of Christ nor the fruits of the first teachers, with the affirmation that the fruits of the Spirit were manifest in his preachers. The effect of the Gospel preaching was manifest in changed lives. His preachers brought souls from the power of Satan to God:

> What is the end of all ecclesiastical order? Is it not to bring souls from the power of Satan to God; and to build them up in his fear and love? Order, then, is so far valuable, as it answers these ends; and if it answers them not, it is nothing worth.[8]

Probably he would have turned the argument further to the advantage of his preachers and asked whether the Catholic priests of the eighteenth century bore the marks of the Apostles of the first century.

One of the responses one would have liked to have had from Wesley concerns Challoner's fourth point, the identity of the Methodist Rule of Faith with true Christian Faith. Perhaps Wesley's comments on the nature of true faith in his *Letter to a Roman Catholic* of 1749 might be a sufficient answer. Clearly he believes that Catholics and Protestants are only divided on opinions and share the same basic faith. Challoner insists that although the Methodist rule is based on Scripture, it is interpreted by the private judgement of individuals and not by the body of Church authority down the centuries. Wesley would no doubt have insisted on the right of private judgement as being the basis of the Reformation from Popery. He argued this in his refutation of Challoner's *The Grounds of the Old Religion* in 1743.[9] In his sermon on the *Catholic Spirit*[10] he argues against the idea that the place of one's birth should fix the church to which we belong, as it would mean that the Reformation would have been impossible, and then writes:

> Not the least of which is that if this rule had took place, there could have been no Reformation from Popery, seeing it entirely destroys the right of private judgement on which that whole Reformation stands. (Sermon 39, I.10)

Thus to Challoner's question, 'Can one private Christian be wiser than the whole Church of Christ?' Wesley offers his Protestant answer of 'Yes'.

Challoner's fifth section concerns the presumption and illusory nature of the Methodist doctrine of the Assurance of Justification and Salvation. This doctrine of Assurance is not taught by the word of God or by the early Christians, writes Challoner, nor is anybody promised that he will persevere to the end. Fear should be the note and constant warnings should be offered less the Christian be presumptuous about his salvation. Romans 8:16, where the Spirit witnesses with our spirit that we are children of God, is about those who live in mortification and obedience and charity, not about Methodists. People may have a highly probable assurance that from the fruit of the Spirit, they are in a state of grace, but this is not an infallible certainty. To this failure to see a doctrine of Assurance in the New Testament at Romans 8:16, let Wesley reply:

> None who believes the Scriptures to be the Word of God can doubt the *importance* of such a truth as this: a truth revealed therein not once only, not obscurely, not incidentally, but frequently, and that in express terms; but solemnly and of set

purpose, as denoting one of the peculiar privileges of the children of God.[11]

The final, sixth, section of the *Caveat* discusses the true doctrine of Justification under twenty headings. Although Challoner states them argumentatively, assuming that Wesley would have disagreed, it is clear from Wesley's works that he would have taken Challoner's twenty headings as representing much of his own understanding of Justification. We indicate Challoner's twenty points, abbreviating them drastically, indicating their sources in Trent. We then set alongside them Wesley's own views.

1. The original sin of Adam put all men under the sentence of death and hell.[12] [Trent, *Decree on Justification*, Ch. 1]
   This was hardly controversial in any branch of Christian theology. Wesley writes: 'By the sin of the first Adam, who was not only the father but likewise the representative of us all, we all "fell short of the favour of God" (Rom. 3:23) we all became "children of wrath" (Eph. 2:3); or, as the Apostle expresses it, "Judgement came upon all men to condemnation" (Rom. 5:18).'[13]

2. Christ was sent by the Father to set us free from sin, Satan and hell.[14] [Trent, *ibid.*, Ch. 2]
   Here there are many quotations possible from Wesley's writings, and the sermons are full of them.[15]

3. The Son of God died for all (2 Cor. 5:14, 15) and this translation from the state of sin to the state of grace is called Justification which is obtained by Christ who regenerates us – we are brought into a new dispensation by baptism (Jn. 3:15).[16] [Trent, *ibid.*, Chs III, IV]
   As Wesley puts it in his *Treatise on Baptism*: 'By water then, as a means, the water of baptism, we are regenerated or born again . . .'[17]

4. Prevenient grace disposes us to turn to God in baptism with hope and fear.[18] [Trent, *ibid.*, Chs V, VI and Canon III]
   Wesley writes on prevenient grace as follows: 'No man living is entirely destitute of what is vulgarly called "natural

conscience". But this is not natural; it is more properly termed "preventing grace".'[19]

5. Paul does not mean that faith alone is enough for justification, just the first disposition of man; hope, love and repentance and the sacrament of reconciliation are required as well.[20] [Trent, *ibid*., Ch. VII]

A close Wesley parallel to this is: 'The first usual objection to this is, that to preach salvation or justification by faith only is to preach against holiness and good works . . . But we speak of a faith which is not so, but necessarily productive of all good works and all holiness.'[21] The sacrament of reconciliation in its Catholic form was of course alien to Wesley's thinking.

6. All hope, fear, faith, love etc. are free gifts of God, nor can works of one's own justify. Nothing that goes before justification can merit justification (e.g. even faith).[22] [Trent, *ibid*., Ch. VIII and Canon I]

'As on the one hand, though a man should have everything else, without faith, yet he cannot be justified; so on the other, though he be supposed to want everything else, yet if he hath faith he cannot but be justified.'[23]

7. Faith in Scripture is not the Methodists' presumptuous confidence, or absolute assurance; such faith was not heard of in 1500 years of Christianity (it is no part of the faith first delivered to the saints, Jude 3); rather it is a close adhesion of the soul to divine truth.[24] [Trent, *ibid*., Ch. IX]

Wesley's reasoning on assurance goes as follows: 'He that now loves God – that delights and rejoices in him with an humble joy, an holy delight, and an obedient love – is a child of God; But I thus love, delight, and rejoice in God; Therefore I am a child of God . . . Of the former proposition he has as full an assurance as he has that the Scriptures are of God. And of his thus loving God he has an inward proof, which is nothing short of self-evidence.'[25] Romanists have held it too, says Wesley, and turns to St Augustine and St Bernard. Augustine in his *Confessions* gave an account of the full assurance of faith, what Wesley calls 'the naked experience of his heart'.[26] Bernard of Clairvaux is introduced into the argument against 'John Smith' (a pseudonym for a serious opponent who wrote some six letters to John Wesley between 1745 and 1748) and Wesley creates an artificial argument between Bernard and his neighbour on 'The Spirit of God bears witness with my spirit that I am a child of God'. This witness, argues Bernard, is inward, perceptible testimony, by which we cry, Abba, Father![27]

8. The justice of Christ is not just imputed and man remains unjust; we are made holy by the love of God shed into our hearts (Rom. 5:5), living temples of the living God (1 Cor. 3:16).[28] [Trent, *ibid.*, Canons IX, XI]
   This was of course a major difference between Wesley and Luther, and Wesley wrote in 1741 or 1745 (Outler believes that either date is possible): 'So that faith in general is the most direct and effectual means of promoting all righteousness and true holiness; of establishing the holy and spiritual law in the hearts of them that believe.'[29] Wesley is closer to Challoner than to Luther.

9. We grow in justice and sanctity and are still more justified and sanctified. Paul v. James; Paul means works prior to justification, James speaks of him that is becoming more just (Jas. 2:24).[30] [Trent, *ibid.*, Ch. X]
   Here Challoner and Wesley part company: Wesley says: 'What is "justification"? . . . it is evident from what has been already observed that it is not the being made actually just and righteous. This is *sanctification* . . . The one implies what God *does for us* through his Son; the other what he *works in us* by his Spirit.'[31] In the Conference Minutes for 1744 Wesley is close to Challoner when he writes of James and Paul: 'Because they do not speak of the same works; St Paul speaking of works that precede faith; St James of works that spring from it!'[32]

10. David and Peter were justified and both fell into mortal sin, by adultery and denial – Christians need to remember the possible fall (1 Cor. 10:12) – only God's special revelation (unusual) can make a man absolutely certain of election or perseverance.[33] [Trent, *ibid.*, Chs XII, XIII, and Canon XVI]
    Wesley agrees the possibility of continuing sin in believers, and attacks the doctrines of the Moravians: 'It has been observed before, that the opposite doctrine, "that there is no

sin in believers", is quite *new* in the Church of Christ; that it was never heard of for seventeen hundred years, never till it was discovered by Count Zinzendorf.'[34] On perseverance, Wesley had some hard things to say against the Calvinists and here agrees with Trent and Challoner: Once saved, always saved, 'leads the way by easy steps, first to presumption, and then to black despair'.[35] Colin Williams is helpful here when he suggests that Wesley freed the doctrine of Assurance from long neglect. Assurance had been associated with the certainty of final salvation (perseverance). When Wesley discarded the doctrine of double predestination, he enabled the doctrine of Assurance to be what it ought to have been, a statement of our *present* state with God, not our *future* state .[36]

11. The justified Christian must keep all the divine commandments (1 John 5:3).[37] [Trent, *ibid*., Ch. XI]
There is no controversy about this: 'This is perfect freedom; thus to keep his law and to walk in all his commandments blameless.'[38]

12. Belief is not enough to remain in God's favour – if we sin deadly sin then we forfeit eternal life (e.g. Gal. 5:19–21).[39] [Trent, *ibid*., Canons XIX and XX].
'But in the meantime let it be carefully observed (for eternity depends upon it) that neither the faith of a Roman Catholic nor that of a Protestant, if it contains no more than this, no more than the embracing such and such truths, will avail any more before God than the faith of a Mahometan or a heathen, yea of a deist or materialist . . . Can it save any man from sin or hell?'[40] There is in Wesley no distinction between deadly and venial sin; all sin can lead to death.

13. Heresy and schism exclude the soul from the kingdom of God (the Methodists are a sect) unless invincible ignorance excuses them (not so, because Scripture shows they are in schism).[41]
Wesley objects to the use of 'heresy' in the history of the Church as one that has no basis in Scripture, where the word means 'opinion' rather than something for which the deviant Christian is burned at the stake.[42]

14. The just pass through this life with sin still (1 John 1:8) through venial sins which they overcome.[43] [Trent, *ibid*.,

Canon XXIII]

Wesley's attitude to this is best seen in a passage where he discusses the Moravian concept that sin remains *in the flesh*, but not *in the heart* of the believer. The absurdity of this being clear he suggests that sin *remains* but does not *reign* in the one who is born of God.[44] Again we note that there is no distinction in Wesley between mortal and venial sin.

15. Absolution is available to deadly sinners who confess with right dispositions (as John 20: 21–23).[45] [Trent, *ibid.*, Chs XIV, XV, Canon XXIX]

    Wesley comments on John 20:23, 'whosoever sins ye remit', that this means 'without sacerdotal absolution'. Therefore that the text indicates, i) the power of *declaring* pardon, as in the Book of Common Prayer, or ii) the inflicting and remitting of ecclesiastical censures.[46] Here the Catholic and the Protestant views concerning the priesthood conflict strongly.

16. Free will has no part in justification but concurs by working with God – good works are our works (done by grace with our concurrence) and God's works (of grace).[47] [Trent, *ibid.*, Canons IV and V]

    In a rather tortuous passage in *Predestination Calmly Considered*, Wesley makes a similar point: 'If man do at all "work together with God", in "working out his own salvation", then God does not do the whole work, without man's "working together with him". Most true, most sure: But cannot you see, how God nevertheless may have all the glory? Why, the very power to "work together with Him" was from God. Therefore to Him is all the glory.'[48]

17. The justified Christian labours in good works with God's grace (see Matt. 16:27, Rom. 2:6 etc.).[49] [Trent, *ibid.*, Canon XXIV]

    See 11 and 16 above for Wesley's agreement on this.

18. Eternal life is promised in the Scriptures not to faith alone but to good works done by faith (Matt. 25:31ff, Jas. 2:14, 17, 20) – we are condemned for our omission of good works, not lack of faith.[50] [Trent, *ibid.*, Ch. XVI]

    The true Christian, writes Wesley, ' "As he had opportunity", therefore, if he could no good of a higher kind, he fed the hungry, clothed the naked, helped the fatherless or stranger, visited and assisted them that were sick or in prison.'[51]

19. Grace and predestation do not take away the power of doing evil (free will can still choose the bad), (Matt. 24:37, 2 Cor. 4:1).[52] [Trent, *ibid*., Canon VI]

One of the best parallels to this in the Wesley corpus is in the sermon *On Predestination*, where it is argued that God's knowledge of my sins does not mean that he causes them. 'In like manner God knows that man sins; for he knows all things. Yet we do not sin because he knows it; but he knows it because we sin. And his knowledge *supposes* our sin, but does not in any wise *cause* it.'[53]

20. God does not predestinate people to sin or hell – Calvin and others imply that God created some of mankind just to damn them – he really is a false prophet, robber etc., and to be shunned by all Christian people.[54] [Trent, *ibid*., Canons XV, XVI, XVIII]

Wesley here agrees with Challoner against the Calvinists, but has to give answer to the question, why are not all saved? 'If you ask, "Why then are not all men saved?" the whole law and the testimony answer, First, Not because of any decree of God; not because it is his pleasure they should die; for, "As I live, saith the Lord God," "I have no pleasure in the death of him that dieth" (Ezek. 18:3, 32). Whatever be the cause of their perishing, it cannot be his will, if the oracles of God are true; for they declare, "He is not willing that any should perish, but that all should come to repentance" (2 Pet. 3:9); "He willeth that all men should be saved." '[55] Wesley suggests that Predestinarianism was hatched by Augustine, made into a system by Peter Lombard and Aquinas, taught by Loyola and the Jesuits, and only disclaimed at Trent against Luther and Calvin.[56]

It would be unfair to leave the impression that Wesley and Challoner were at one in their understanding of Justification. We have indicated the differences under the above headings as concerned with, i) the sacrament of reconciliation and priestly absolution in Catholicism which Wesley did not adhere to, ii) the doctrine of Assurance regarded by Challoner as presumption, while Wesley held it with careful qualification, iii) the distinction between justification and sanctification which is not in Challoner and iv) the contrast between venial and mortal sin which Wesley did not hold. Where Wesley seems to hold a more 'Catholic' view than previous Protestants is in his understanding of the significance of works, both before and after justification:

> (3) We have received it as a maxim, that 'a man is to do nothing in order to justification'. Nothing can be more false. Whoever desires to find favour with God, should 'cease from evil, and learn to do well'. Whoever repents, should 'do works meet for repentance'.[57]

Wesley guarded himself from the accusation of Catholicism here when he added these words at the Conference of 1771:

> ... though no one is a real Christian believer (and consequently cannot be saved) who doth not good works, where there is time and opportunity, yet our works have no part in meriting, or purchasing our salvation from first to last, either in whole or in part.[58]

If the attitude of Challoner to the nature of faith seems to be somewhat intellectual as we read it in his *Caveat*, this may be the most important contrast between him and John Wesley. After all, Wesley's experience of 24 May 1738 was more than a purely intellectual matter and Wesley saw himself after 1738 as one in a sort of apostolic succession of warmed hearts that would have included not only Paul, Augustine, and Luther, but Francis of Assisi and Philip Neri as well. It is sad that Wesley's admittance into this apostolic succession remained unknown to Challoner, although it happened in Aldersgate Street, about 400 yards from one of his worship centres in Moorgate. If they had met and understood each other properly, there might have emerged a consensus document on Justification from Catholics and Protestants between the bilateral talks at Regensburg in 1541 and the Anglican/Roman Catholic International Commission document *Salvation and the Church* in 1987.

9

Popish Doctrines

John Wesley set out his major objections to the doctrines of the
Church of Rome in two small tracts. One, called *A Roman
Catechism, faithfully drawn out of the allowed writings of the
Church of Rome: With a Reply thereto*,[1] is based on a seventeenth century abstract from the Catechism of the Council of
Trent. Wesley's source for the Reply was a duodecimo tract by
Mr John Williams, later Bishop of Chichester. Williams' tract
was written in 1686 and was entitled, *A Catechism Truly Representing the Doctrines and Practices of the Church of Rome with
an Answer thereunto*. It contains no indication of author but
the copy in the Bodleian Library has a note on the flyleaf in
ink, 'by Mr Williams'. The original author was anonymous, but
described himself 'a Protestant of the Church of England'. Like
most polemical works of its time, it does not reproduce the gist
of the catechism but concentrates solely on the controversial
issues between Catholics and Protestants. Wesley's use of it
extends to 89 controverted points and in his conclusion he
admits that he could have included other matters such as the
jurisdiction of the Church over princes, the canonization of
saints and the consecration of items for use in worship. This
lengthier conclusion would have meant a great deal more
research than he had so far undertaken since Wesley simply
drew all 89 points from Williams' original, except that here and
there he abbreviated a few passages. The only major difference
between Wesley and Williams is that, whereas Williams puts the
Catholic answers on the left hand page and the Protestant replies
on the right, Wesley prefers to put them in a continuous form.
Williams makes it clear that his appeal is to Scripture and

antiquity over against Councils, Missals, Breviaries, Rituals and Catechisms. It is summarized for him in the precept of Vincent of Lérins that the truth faith of the Church is that which has been held everywhere, always and by all (*Quod ubique, quod semper, quod ab omnibus creditum est; Commonitorium*, II.6, AD 434). It might seem a little unfair to accuse Wesley of the same attitude to Catholic doctrines as John Williams in 1686. However, because he did decide to lift Williams' catechism almost verbatim, we have used 'Wesley said', rather than 'Williams said', in this chapter. Williams' thoughts on Popish doctrines had become Wesley's by 1756, the date of Wesley's work. If there should be any doubt about this, the material in *Popery Calmly Considered* [2] of 1779 is extremely close to that in *A Roman Catechism* of 1756. Hence we are on the right path in putting 'Wesley said' even where Williams said it before him.

In the second tract, *Popery Calmly Considered*, Wesley offers an exposition and examination of the chief doctrines of the Church of Rome, followed by the natural tendency of a few of these doctrines. The tract is a good deal shorter than the examination of the catechism and both works are explorations of the same themes. Here and there in other parts of his writings Wesley deals with points of Catholic doctrine, but the main investigations are centred in these two tracts. In order to give the theme some coherence we shall look firstly at the Catholic view of the sacraments and then at other controversial points of theology.

Wesley begins his piece on the sacraments with the Catechism of Trent's questions and answers (Q 50).

Q. What is a sacrament?
A. A sacrament is a sensible thing which by the institutions of God hath a power, as well of causing, as of signifying, holiness and righteousness. (*Catech. Rom.* par 2, cap 1, n 11)

The sacraments are then listed and the appropriate anathema pronounced for those who deviate from the seven. These are: baptism, confirmation, eucharist, penance, extreme unction, orders and matrimony. Wesley makes the historical point that

Augustine thought in terms of only two in the fifth century, and not until Peter Lombard in the twelfth century was there an attempt to define the number. After questioning the validity of form and matter as parts of the sacrament, Wesley suggests that the doctrine that grace comes in sacraments *ex opere operato* (by the work itself) is defective and that adult people need the appropriate disposition of faith in order to benefit from the sacraments (Q 54). To the answer that the ministers must 'intend to do what the Church does' in order to make the sacrament 'work', Wesley objects that intention can never be absolutely certain and so all sacraments are potentially defective (Q 55).

After sacraments in general, Wesley looks at baptism. The Tridentine catechism insists that while ordained ministers are the normal administrators of baptism, in case of necessity any person, even a non-christian, may do it provided that they intend to do what the Church does. Wesley's response to this is somewhat High Church: baptism was given by Christ to the Apostles and their successors in ministry, not to women, Jews and infidels (Q 56). Presumably, then, for Wesley only ordained ministers may baptize. In the next question Wesley goes into the ceremonies of baptism in the Roman Church. He pours scorn on the multiplicity of ceremonies and describes eight different priestly actions performed on the infant. His worst scorn is reserved for the exorcism of the salt and he quotes the, to him ludicrous, prayer for the exorcism after his question:

> Can we think it for the majesty of it, to have salt exorcized in the name of the Father, Son and Holy Ghost; and to be put into the mouth of the child, for a propitiation unto eternal life? (Q 57)

When he passes to confirmation, Wesley uses the authority of Alexander of Hales (d. 1245) to affirm that at least one Catholic theologian has thought that Christ did not declare confirmation a sacrament. For Wesley, there is no understanding of initiation as a two-phase process and this reflects the practice of eighteenth century Anglicans to whom confirmation was an almost forgotten sacrament (Q 58). After comments on the chrism and the episcopal words (Q 59 and Q 60), Wesley wonders at the Catholic bishop breathing on the oil of chrism and at the blow given on the candidate's cheek and the binding of the anointed head with the head band (Q 61).

The true, real and substantial presence of Christ under the appearances of bread and wine are explained in terms of transubstantiation (Q 62 and Q 63). In an early letter to his mother in 1732 he explained that his understanding of it was similar to that of his father and mother:

> One consideration is enough to make me assent to his and your judgement concerning the Holy Sacrament; which is, that we cannot allow Christ's human nature to be present in it, without allowing either con- or trans-substantiation. But that His divinity is so united to us then, as He never is but to worthy receivers, I firmly believe, though the manner of that union is utterly a mystery to me.[3]

Wesley objects, of course, that no change can be inferred from the Saviour's words at the Last Supper and that this comes only from the authority of the Church. It is the usual way of Scripture to describe the mystical relation of one thing to another by using the same word; hence the elements can be called Christ's body and blood without needing the explanation of transubstantiation. The distinction between substance and accidents so beloved of the scholastic theologians is dismissed; if transubstantiation be granted and yet our senses perceive bread and wine, how can we believe that the perceived flesh of the risen Christ when he appeared to the disciples was true flesh and not mere appearance (Q 64)? The doctrine that the whole Christ is present under every particle of bread and wine in the Eucharist is totally unreasonable (Q 65). Wesley is at his most perturbed when the people are denied communion in both kinds and feels that 'just and weighty' causes such as the danger of spilling it, its scarcity, the need to disprove those who deny Christ to be contained wholly under both species, are not to be allowed to overrule the Saviour who said, 'Drink ye all of this' (Matt. 26:27) (Qs 66–67).

The propitiatory nature of the sacrifice of the Mass is next set out as available for the sins, punishments and satisfactions of the living and for the souls in purgatory (Qs 68–70). Wesley objects to the repetition of the sacrifice made 'once for all' and quotes Hebrews 9:22, 25 and Hebrews 7:27:

> He needeth not daily, as those High Priests, to offer up sacrifice etc.; for this he did once, when he offered up himself.

Solitary Masses of the priest alone are disapproved of; the Lord's Supper is a communion from which many partake (Q 71). While Wesley is happy to adore Christ in the Lord's Supper, he refuses adoration to the elements, since *latria* or worship is due to God alone. Christ is in heaven and not corporally present anywhere on earth; therefore the adoration of the consecrated species is idolatry (Q 72). Wesley completes his discussion of the Eucharist (Qs 73 and 74) with the ceremonies and garments used for the Mass. Here he is perhaps at his least sympathetic and most clearly a man of his period. In another age the mystical significance of the amice, the alb and the girdle, indications of the divinity of Christ covered under his humanity, the whiteness of faith and innocence, the cords of fasting and prayer, might have affected his aesthetic sense if not his religious perceptions. He seems to want to imply that they are not from apostolic tradition nor in any sense from the Holy Spirit (as Bellarmine had suggested that they were) but are superfluous and vain things that cannot raise the mind to the contemplation of the divine things concealed in them. The bowings, sprinklings and genuflections with their mystical significance must have seemed alien to Wesley's mind, raised as it was in an era when the Enlightenment had done its best to rob English Protestant worship of all rumours of the transcendent.

That Wesley recommended private confession to the band meetings is well known and often pointed to as one of the parallels between Catholicism and Methodism. It was by no means similar in his eyes and he was forced to point this out on several occasions, for example in his second letter to Bishop Lavington in 1752:

> Therefore, every unprejudiced person must see that there is no analogy between the Popish confession to a Priest, and our

confessing our faults one to another, and praying one for another, as St James directs.[4]

However, his strictures against Popish confession need to be seen in the light of the practice within his own movement. His criticisms concern the following: the need for confession to a priest; whether absolution can be judicial or whether it is merely declarative; the distinction between attrition and contrition; the question of satisfaction; and the vexed question of merit and indulgences. Confession, according to Trent, is the disclosure of all mortal sins to the priest, without which neither confession nor forgiveness can be obtained. Wesley objects that, while confession may be a great help to many, God has not made auricular confession, or particular confession to a priest, necessary for salvation (Q 76). Earlier he complained that the sacrament of penance is defective in matter as the matter in question, namely contrition, confession, and satisfaction, cannot be measured sensibly in the case of contrition (Q 75). As a true son of the Church of England, Wesley recalls the Book of Common Prayer where in the service of Morning Prayer it reminds the Anglican faithful that Almighty God:

> hath given power and commandments to his Ministers, to declare and pronounce to his people, being penitent, the Absolution and Remission of their sins . . .

Absolution and remission are 'declared' or 'pronounced' but in the writings of the Council of Trent absolution is not only declarative but judicial. Wesley quotes St Ambrose against Trent:

> Men show a ministry in the forgiveness of sins, but do not exercise a right of power. They pray, but it is God forgives. (*De Spir.*, 1.3, c. 19)

The reference is not quite correct. In the more recent edition of the Post-Nicene Fathers it says:

> But men make use of their ministry for the forgiveness of sins, they do not exercise the right of any power of their own. For they forgive sins not in their own power but in that of the Father and of the Son and of the Holy Spirit. They ask, the

Godhead gives, the service is of man, the gift is of the Power
on high. (*Of the Holy Spirit*, BK III, Ch. XVIII, 137)

The passage is the same but the omission of the second sentence
with 'they forgive sins' is crucial. Sadly, Wesley follows Williams
word for word and does not check his sources at this or other
points. A further quotation from Ambrose will make this clear:

> In like manner it seemed impossible that sins should be for-
> given through repentance, but Christ gave this power to his
> Apostles, which has been transmitted to the priestly office.
> That, then, has become possible which was impossible.
> (*Concerning Repentance*, Bk II, Ch. II, 12)

In this Father, then, the work of the priest looks to be judicial
rather than declarative. The sentence of the priest is the sentence
of the Judge. Wesley refers at least three times to the important
distinction between attrition and contrition (*Roman Catechism*
Q 14, Q 78; and *Popery Calmly Considered*, Section II, para.
1). Attrition comes merely from the fear of hell.[5] It is obviously
less perfect than contrition which is sorrow for past sin plus the
intention of not committing sin in the future. Trent teaches that
attrition plus confession is equivalent to contrition but that even
contrition is not enough unless confession to a priest follows,
with an appropriate act of penance (Q 14, quoting Council of
Trent session 14, chapter 4). Repentance, writes Wesley, is the
same as contrition, and repentance is the only qualification for
forgiveness:

> Repent and be converted, that your sins may be blotted out.
> (Acts 3:19)

Such texts make contrition sufficient, without priestly confession, and also make attrition insufficient even with priestly
confession. The idea of satisfaction being made to God for our
sins brings out Wesley's deepest scorn (Qs 79 and 80). It seems
to take away from the satisfaction made by Christ for our sins
upon the Cross:

> who made there (by his one oblation of himself once offered)
> a full, perfect, and sufficient sacrifice, oblation, and satisfaction,

for the sins of the whole world . . . (Book of Common Prayer,
Holy Communion, Prayer of Consecration)

Only the Son by his obedience and suffering can make satisfaction to God. Penance might be given by the Church to
notorious offenders as a means of discipline, but this penance is
offered to the Church and not to God. As to good works and
merit, Wesley refers again to Trent; good works done by justified
persons do truly deserve eternal life (Q 15, Council of Trent,
session 6, chapter 16). Wesley reminds the Catholics that we are
all unprofitable servants (Luke 17:10) and that when we have
done all, we have only done our duty. Later, in 1773, he has
more difficulty in making hard and fast distinctions, and he
quotes the 1770 *Minutes of Conference* to make his point:

> In the *Minutes* I say, 'We are rewarded *according to* our works,
> yea, *because of* our works (Gen. 22:16, 17). How differs this
> from *for the sake of* our works? And how differs this from
> *secundum merita operum*, or "as our works deserve"? Can you
> split this hair? I doubt I cannot.' I say so still.

Wesley's theological position may be put thus: a person is justified by Christ with no pleading of his/her own merits. As a
result of that justification he/she begins to live a life in grace
that enables him/her to reach that holiness without which no
one sees the Lord. Thus he/she might be said in some sense to
merit the life of heaven, although in another sense all is of
grace. That our merits are in any case inadequate is clear to the
Tridentine theologians who insist that there exists an overplus
of merit available through the application of the satisfaction of
Christ and the saints. These merits can be transferred by decree
of the Church and are then called indulgences (Council of Trent,
session 25). Wesley will have no truck with indulgences; will sin
be pardoned merely by standing in front of the doors of St
Peter's at Easter for papal plenary indulgence? Despite the scan-
dals of the Reformation, the Papacy has continued to offer them
ever since and Wesley lists a few of the recent ones. For example,
Clement X in 1671 granted a plenary indulgence upon the
canonization of five saints. Indulgences have been offered for

monetary gain (sometimes called alms), for simple pilgrimages to sites in Rome, for taking up arms against the Albigensians, and even for the recital of a prayer to the Blessed Virgin Mary and St Anne in the time of Alexander VI:

> Hail Mary, full of grace! The Lord be with thee, thy grace with me! Blessed be thou among women; and blessed be St Ann thy mother, from whom, O Virgin Mary, thou has proceeded without sin and spot; but of thee hath Jesus Christ been born, the Son of the living God. Amen.

Wesley cannot believe that works of supererogation, that is, works that are more than those that are necessary for salvation, could be predicated of any other person than Christ, as his own Church's 39 Articles stated:

> Voluntary Works besides, over and above God's commandments, which they call Works of Supererogation, cannot be taught without arrogance and impiety. (Article XIV)

Is there any need for this superabundance of satisfaction in the saints when there is infinite merit in Christ's sufferings? Merit is not transferable:

> For if there be no comparison betwixt the reward and the sufferings, then no one has merit to transfer to another; and if every one must give an account of himself to God, then no one can be saved by the merit of another. (*Popery Calmly Considered*, Section II, para. 4)

On the topic of the penitential system of the Church, then, Wesley shows himself to be a true son of the Reformation.

Extreme unction (Qs 81 to 84) is described in terms of its matter, olive oil, and its form (by this anointing God pardons the sinner) and the parts which are anointed. Wesley's argument against it is mainly on scriptural grounds: the rite was used for curing the sick but was not absolutely necessary to it as the sick were cured also by laying on of hands; it was merely a rite in apostolic times whereas the Church of Rome has made it a sacrament; in the time of the New Testament it was for bodily ills but is now properly for the soul and incidentally for the body; it was used at first for the recovery of the sick but is now applied to those at the point of death.[6] A point of interest in Wesley's criticism is the implicit understanding that healing as described in James 5:14–15 no longer takes place in the Church:

> And as long as this power continued in the Church, so long there was a reason for continuing this rite ... But when the power ceased, there was no reason for the continuance of this sign.

The 'forgotten talent' of healing was not rediscovered in the Church until the next century.

Ordination, according to Wesley, while of divine institution, is not to be admitted as a sacrament (Q 85):

> We account ordination to be of divine institution, and that by it a ministerial commission is conveyed; but how necessary soever this office is in the Church, and grace for the exercise of it, yet as that grace is not promised to it, we cannot admit it to be properly and truly a sacrament.

His strongest words are offered in opposition to the seven orders of the Catholic ministry: priest, deacon, sub-deacon, acolyte, exorcist, reader and door-keeper (Q 86). He rightly does not include the episcopate as the primary grade, for according to the Council of Trent, priesthood was the highest grade because of its power to offer the sacrifice of the Mass. Vatican II, of course, has since moved the bishop to centre stage, as the one who primarily shares in the priesthood of Christ. Wesley's knowledge of church history is here shown to be a little deficient as he should have known from his reading that at Rome under Cornelius (AD 251–3) there are all seven of the orders. He knows of no authority for any order under that of deacon, he writes. He illustrates his dislike of the whole idea of lower orders by concentrating on the idea of the office of the exorcist in the Church of Rome and the books of exorcism handed to the exorcist on his ordination:

> We know of no authority for this kind of procedure, for those forms of conjuration contained in these books; or for the use

of those rites therein prescribed, for exorcising persons, houses, cattle, milk, butter, fruits, etc., infested with the devil.

Behind this lies the fear that he shared with those of the eighteenth century of anything remotely resembling superstition. There is no space here for any discussion of Wesley's views on the ministry but some fascinating insights will be found elsewhere.[7]

Marriage can no more properly be called a sacrament than can using the sign of the cross, and even Bellarmine does not allow the use of the sign of the cross to be described as a sacrament (Q 87). That those in Holy Orders may not marry was a very early ruling within the Western Church although only the Second Lateran Council of 1139 made the marriage of clergy both unlawful and invalid. Wesley quotes Lateran II also to the effect that those in Holy Orders are to be the temple of God and are not to serve uncleanness. While canon 6 of Lateran II actually reads, 'it is unbecoming that they give themselves up to marriage and impurity' and is not quite as harsh as Wesley implies, the almost manichaean implication is not lost on Wesley:

> The Apostle, on the contrary, saith, 'Marriage is honourable in all' (Heb. 13:4); and gives a hard character of that doctrine which forbids it (1 Tim. 4:1–3). And how lawful it was, the direction of the Apostle about it (1 Tim. 3:2) doth show. (Q 89)

The *Explanatory Notes on the New Testament* include a reference to Titus 1:6, 'the husband of one wife'; 'surely the Holy Ghost, by repeating this so often, designed to leave the Romanists without excuse'.[8] That the prohibition of clerical marriage is to be regarded as mischievous receives support in Wesley's quotations from Polydore Virgil's *De Inventoribus* of 1499 and Cassander's *Consultatis de Articulis Fidei inter Catholicos et Protestantes Controversis* of 1565. Virgil's book considered the origin of all things lay and ecclesiastical, while Cassander's attempted to put a Catholic interpretation upon Protestant understandings, with reflections on Catholic practices. Both books that Wesley cites were put on the *Index Expurgatorius* by subsequent popes and appear to have attracted little following from the majority of Catholics. With this discussion of marriage Wesley's treatment of the sacraments ends.

Wesley begins his discussion of the Roman Catechism with the Church of Rome which is said to be 'that Society of Christians who professes it necessary to salvation to be subject to the Pope of Rome, as the alone visible head of the Church' (Q 1). Elsewhere he made it clear that Popery in his understanding was not merely justification by works but the supremacy of Rome and its bishop.[9] He appends the notorious sentence from the bull *Unam Sanctam* of Boniface VIII promulgated in 1302:

> We say, define, and pronounce, that it is absolutely necessary to salvation, for every man to be subject to the Pope of Rome.

Wesley's response is that Christ alone is the head of the Church (Col. 2:19) and that neither in Scripture nor antiquity is there any evidence for a visible head, nor evidence that salvation depends on subjection to him. In any case, when there were two popes or even three, as during the Great Schism of the fourteenth century, which pope did we need to acknowledge as our head? Question 2 concerns Peter's successors who as Vicars of Christ claim supreme power over the whole Church. Wesley does not here discuss the 'papal' texts such as Matthew 16:18ff, Luke 22:31ff, John 21:55ff etc., but states categorically that Christ did not give one Apostle pre-eminence over the rest. Such power they were told not to desire for themselves (Matt. 20:26). St Paul not only claimed equality with the Apostles (Gal. 1:15–17) but withstood Peter to his face (Gal. 2:11). He adds a quotation from Cyprian, one that he uses elsewhere:

> The other Apostles are the same Peter was, endowed with an equal fellowship of honour and power. (*On the Unity of the Church*, 4)

Rome's claims to be the mother and mistress of all Churches have to be set against similar claims for Jerusalem:

> We wish to inform you that the most venerable and God-

beloved Cyril is bishop of the Church in Jerusalem, the mother
of all the churches. (Letter of AD 382 from the Synod of
Constantinople to Damasus of Rome *et al* concerning the
Council of Constantinople, 381)

and the claim of Constantinople to be on a par with Rome:

That the Church of Constantinople should have equal privileges with that of Rome, because she is the imperial seat.
(Council of Chalcedon, canon 28)

Wesley omits, whether consciously or not, the rider that while
Constantinople should be elevated to the level of Rome in
ecclesiastical affairs, she should also 'take second place after her'.
He is on safer ground historically when he quotes Pius II who
as Cardinal Piccolomini wrote, 'before the time of the Nicene
Council, little regard was had to the Church of Rome'. All
persons, however, are obliged to receive and believe her doctrine
in order to be saved (Q 4). Since Rome has added to the Gospel,
writes Wesley, she comes under the anathema of Paul:

Though we, or an angel from heaven, preach any other gospel
unto you, than that which we have preached, let him be
accursed. (Gal. 1:8)

and indeed the anathema of Revelation:

If any man shall add unto these things, God shall add unto
him the plagues that are written in this book. (Rev. 22:18)

This is precisely what he accuses the Romanists of doing:

... All Romanists, as such, do add to those things which are
contained in the Book of Life. For in the Bull of Pius IV,
subjoined to those Canons and Decrees, I find all the additions
following:
1. Seven Sacraments; 2. Transubstantiation; 3. Communion
in one kind only; 4. Purgatory; 5. Praying to saints; 6.
Veneration of relics; 7. Worship of images; 8. Indulgences;
9. The priority and universality of the Roman Church; 10.
The supremacy of the Bishop of Rome. All these things

therefore do the Romanists add to those which are written in the Book of Life.[10]

Here, in the extract from the *Journal*, there is a more complete list than in Question 6 of the *A Roman Catechism* where he excludes veneration of relics, the priority of the Church of Rome and the supremacy of the Bishop of Rome. The point is that if transubstantiation, purgatory, etc., are not in Scripture, they cannot be doctrines of faith. The basic problem is that the Romanists have departed from the proper use of the Scriptures and replaced the priority of Scripture with the priority of Scripture with Tradition:

> ... she requires that the traditions be received with the like pious regard and veneration as the Scriptures; and whosoever knowingly condemns them, is declared by her to be accursed. (Council of Trent, session 4, *Doct de Can Script*) (Q 7)

Wesley regards this as teaching for doctrines the commandments of men and does not hesitate to quote from Jerome's *Commentary on Haggai*:

> The sword of God doth smite those other things, which they find and hold of their own accord, as by Apostolic tradition, without the authority and teaching of Scripture. (Chapter 1, verse II)

Unfortunately, this quotation is offered without due regard to its context. Jerome is making the point that God has called a drought on everything: land, hills, grain, wine, oil, on men and cattle. He describes this drought as God's sword upon the people. He speaks then of the gatherings of heretics. The 'other things' that the sword of God smites are not their unscriptural traditions but the heretics themselves who need to be confounded by the authority and testimony of the Scriptures which have come straight from the Tradition of the Apostles. In context, Jerome's words mean something very different from the meaning Wesley offers.

The Church of Rome does not agree with other Churches concerning the canonical books of Scripture (Q 10). She has added to the Old Testament, Esdras, Tobit, Judith, Wisdom, Ecclesiasticus, Baruch, I and II Maccabees and new parts of Esther and Daniel. In addition, the faithful of the Church of Rome are not permitted to read the Scripture in their native language (Q 11), the argument being that to read the Bible would do more harm than good. Wesley responds that people 'wrested the Scriptures to their own destruction' even in apostolic times but the Apostles merely cautioned them not to be 'led away by the error of the wicked' (Q 12). Far from the scriptural text being interpreted by the Church alone, namely the Church in communion with the see of Peter, at all times the Scripture must be preferred to the Church and not the Church to Scripture. Scripture in fact is its own interpreter, as Clement of Alexandria states:

> The way for understanding the Scriptures, is to demonstrate out of themselves, concerning themselves. (*Stromateis* or 'Miscellanies', Book VII, Chapter XVI)

However, earlier in the same work Clement has commented on the knowledge or *gnosis* to be acquired by a truly Christian gnostic, which reads very like a secret tradition:

> And the *gnosis* itself is that which has transcended by transmission to a few, having been imparted unwritten by the Apostles. (*Stromateis*, Book VI, Chapter VII)

In other words, Clement's position appears to be 'interpret Scripture by means of Scripture', but in the meantime the true initiates have a special knowledge which is unwritten and comes direct from the Apostles. The only difference between Trent and Clement is that Trent regarded the unwritten tradition of the Apostles as open and not secret, imparted to all by the agency of the Church.

As indicated above, Wesley's criticism of Tradition in the Catholic Church is that it is an attempt to add to the biblical revelation, something forbidden by the New Testament itself. The faith of Protestants, on the other hand:

> . . . embraces only those truths as necessary to salvation, which

are clearly revealed in the oracles of God. Whatever is plainly declared in the Old and New Testament is the object of their faith. They believe neither more nor less than what is manifestly contained in, and provable by, the Holy Scriptures.[11]

In this same sermon, Wesley is a little more eirenical to the Roman Catholics than he is elsewhere concerning their use of Tradition. They are 'volunteers in faith', that is, they choose to believe more than God has revealed as necessary for salvation. Yet although they have added to 'the faith once delivered to the saints', their new articles, added at the Council of Trent, do not contradict the ancient articles and so they still believe all that God has revealed to be necessary for salvation. Elsewhere he lists the ten[12] or twelve[13] pieces of Tradition added at Trent. These 'extras' were often listed by Protestant polemicists during the reign of James II and later. Altham, an Anglican writing against the Catholic John Gother in 1687 and 1688, has a list of the twelve new articles added to the twelve articles of the Nicene Creed:

13. Apostolical and Ecclesiastical Traditions.
14. Holy Scripture in the sense of the Church and the unanimous consent of the Fathers.
15. The seven sacraments instituted by Christ.
16. Trent on Original Sin and Justification.
17. Mass and propitiatory sacrifice and Transubstantiation.
18. Sacrament under one kind.
19. Purgatory.
20. Saints prayed to and relics.
21. Image-honour and veneration.
22. Indulgences.
23. Roman Catholic Church as Mother of all Churches and Bishop of Rome as successor of Peter and Vicar of Christ.
24. Definitions of Ecumenical Councils and Trent.[14]

Wesley thinks that these additions began only in the reaction to the Reformation which then received some shape in the decrees of Trent:

On the contrary, at the very beginning of the Reformation,

the Church of Rome began to oppose this principle, that all articles of faith must be provable from Scripture, (till then received throughout the whole Christian world) and to add, if not prefer, to Holy Scripture, Tradition, or the doctrine of Fathers and Councils, with the decrees of Popes.[15]

This process was finalized at Trent when the faithful were commanded to receive the Scriptures and the traditions of the Church 'with equal piety and reverence'. The remedy of Trent was sought because many doctrines, practices, and ceremonies of the Church not only could not be proved by Scripture but flatly contradicted it. When he relates his own understanding of Tradition in the Catholic Church (Q 8), Wesley differs somewhat from Trent:

> Such things belonging to faith and manners as were dictated by Christ, or the Holy Ghost in the Apostles, and have been preserved by a continual succession in the Catholic Church, from hand to hand, without writing.

Wesley's concept looks like 'secret traditions', after the mode of Clement of Alexandria, while Trent is more concerned to highlight the role of the Holy Spirit in the Church than the remembering of a whispered tradition from bishop to bishop. Wesley quotes Cyril of Jerusalem's *Catechetical Lectures* to justify his position of 'Scripture alone':

> It behoveth us not to deliver, no, not so much as the least thing of the holy mysteries of faith, without the Holy Scripture. That is the security of our faith, not which is from our own inventions, but from the demonstration of the Holy Scriptures. (*Catechetical Lectures*, V, 12)

In the same paragraph, however, Cyril writes concerning the Creed he is about to offer to his catechetical class:

> Take heed then, brethren, and hold fast the traditions which ye now receive, and write them on the table of your heart.

The statement of the Creed was clearly becoming part of the Tradition of the Church, indeed perhaps even a summary of the most important points collected out of Scripture, as Cyril writes elsewhere. Wesley has only one more important criticism of Tradition; if it is a collection of optional opinions, then it cannot be religion.[16] His view is clear in a letter to Gilbert Royce in 1750: 'If I were in the Church of Rome, I *would* conform to all her doctrines and practices as far as they were not contrary to plain Scripture.'[17]

Wesley's main problem with Catholic devotion to the Blessed Virgin Mary is that she is not merely held in reverence but worshipped. Such worship is gross, palpable idolatry, he says; we can only honour her as the mother of Holy Jesus and a person of eminent piety. Wesley distinguishes elsewhere (Q 46) between *latria* and *doulia*, the former meaning 'worship' and the latter 'reverence', but in the section on the Virgin Mary he fails to make the distinction between the two. In the Second Council of Nicaea, AD 787, the use of images to represent Jesus Christ, the Virgin Mary, the angels and the saints, is encouraged while an important distinction is made:

> The more frequently they are seen in representational art, the more are those who see them drawn to remember and long for those who serve as models, and to pay these images the tribute of salutation and respectful veneration. Certainly this is not the full adoration in accordance with our faith, which is properly paid only to the divine nature ... [18]

The distinction is between 'veneration' and 'adoration' (in the original Greek *proskunesis* and *latreia*, while confusingly in Latin *adoratio* and *latria*). One wonders whether the confusion in Wesley and others at this point is not caused by the ambiguous use of *adoratio* which looks like 'adoration' and is translated 'reverence'. Wesley clearly believes that worship is offered to Mary: 'What is the worship they give to the Virgin Mary?' (Q 38). He objects to the Catholic faithful applying to Mary as the mediatrix of the gifts bestowed by Jesus and quotes from a book printed in 1685:

> ... whatever gifts are bestowed upon us by Jesus, we receive them by the mediation of Mary ... such is the acceptableness

of the mother of Jesus to Jesus, that whosoever is under the verge of her protection, may confide in her intercession to Jesus. (*Contemplations of the Life and Glory of Holy Mary*, pp. 7–9, 14)

He remembers that even a Council, the notorious Council of Constance that burned John Hus, invoked the Virgin Mary to its aid, while previous Councils had always invoked the Holy Spirit (Q 40). We read little in the Scriptures of the acts of Mary on earth, nothing of her bodily assumption, nor of her being the mother of grace and mercy, the queen and gate of heaven, the advocatrix of sinners, nothing of her power to destroy all heresies or to be all things to all. Wesley brings Epiphanius to his aid who called it an act of impiety when a sect of women in his time offered cakes to the Virgin Mary. He wonders what Epiphanius would have said of the eighteenth century, when not cakes but litanies and prayers are offered to her, in more abundance than prayers to Christ himself.

He adds a similar thought in his *Explanatory Notes on the New Testament* in a comment on Luke 1:28:

> This salutation gives no room for any pretence of paying adoration to the virgin; as having no appearance of a prayer, or of worship offered to her.[19]

In the same *Notes* at Matthew 1:25 he suggests that from 'he knew her not' it should not be inferred that he knew her afterwards. The brothers of Jesus described in Matthew 12:46 are he says cousins, sons of Mary, the wife of Cleopas or Alphaeus, his mother's sister. A similar thought is found in his *Letter to a Roman Catholic* of 1749 where he makes the perpetual virginity of Mary part of the common creed of Catholics and Protestants. The horror that Wesley feels at the worship of Mary is seen in the assessment of some Catholic figures in his sermon on John Fletcher of Madeley. He compares Fletcher with Gregory Lopez and the Marquis de Renty, all three being examples of Christian perfection in Wesley's eyes. Fletcher, by implication, was better than the two Catholics because he did not worship the saints or the Virgin Mary. The religion of Christ, he said, had nothing to do with the worship of our Lady of Loreto.[20] The Virgin had no authority over Christ, as Wesley made clear in his comment on John 2:4:

> May we not learn hence, if his mother was rebuked for attempting to direct him in the days of his flesh, how absurd it is to address her as if she had a right to command him on the throne of his glory?[21]

His comment on Mark 3:34 is even more forthright:

> In this preference of his true disciples, even to the Virgin Mary, considered merely as his mother after the flesh, he not only shows his high and tender affection for them, but seems designedly to guard against those excessive and idolatrous honours which he foresaw would in after ages be paid to her.[22]

It is of interest that Bengel, his source for the *Notes*, does not have these comments, which almost certainly therefore have come directly from Wesley.

Wesley has similar objections to the cult of the saints, being concerned not primarily with worship of the saints but with their function as mediators and intercessors (Qs 34 to 37). 'There is one God, and one Mediator between God and man, the Man Jesus Christ; who gave himself a ransom for all' (1 Tim. 2:5–6). Christ Jesus is at the right hand of God and makes intercession for us (Rom. 8:34). Origen is invoked as an authority:

> All prayers, and supplications, and thanksgivings, are to be sent up to God the Lord of all, by that High Priest who is above all angels, being the living Word of God. (*Against Celsus*, V, 4)

> We ought to pray only to the God over all, and his only Son, the first-born of every creature, who, as our High Priest, offers his prayer to his God, and our God. (*Against Celsus*, VIII, 26)

Elsewhere, in his work *On Prayer* (15–16), Origen states that prayer should strictly speaking be made only to God the Father, not to Christ himself since he also prayed. Thus, prayer through the mediation of Christ is justifiable but in absolute terms not strictly correct. This follows from Origen's subordinationist christological position. Hence there is a danger involved in using Origen as an authority for the teaching of the undivided Church. When Wesley discusses the veneration of the relics of the saints (Qs 42–43), he has little to say. He offers as criticism of the practice the scriptural passage where Moses' body is buried without knowledge of its location (Deut. 34:6) with the implication that veneration of bodies and relics must be unlawful. God's brazen serpent (Num. 21:8) was cut down when it became idolatrous (2 Kings 18:4) and so the relics of the saints should be decently interred and forgotten. Wesley has a keen sense of the communion of saints which almost might make us think that we could ask their prayers:

> It is not improbable their fellowship with us is far more sensible than ours with them ... But we have in general only a faint and indistinct perception of their presence, unless in some particular instances, where it may answer some gracious ends of Divine Providence. Then it may please God to permit that they should be perceptible, either by some of our outward senses or by an internal sense for which human language has not any name.[23]

In a letter of 1771 he comes very close to it:

> Right precious in the sight of the Lord is the death of his saints! And I believe many of the blessings which we receive are in answer to their dying prayers.[24]

The Catholics might ask, 'If the saints are helpful so close to death, why not ask their aid when they could be even more useful in heaven?' Some of Wesley's strongest words are offered against the sin of idolatry. In the sermon On Schism he writes: 'Suppose, for instance, you are a member of the Church of Rome, and you could not remain therein without committing idolatry, without worshipping of idols, whether images or saints or angels; then it would be your bounden duty to leave that community, totally to separate from it.'[25] 'None of these idols were known in the Christian Church till some centuries after the time of the Apostles'.[26]

The concept of purgatory, the place to which those go who die in a state of grace yet are not sufficiently purged from sin to enter into heaven, is clearly contrary to Scripture (*Popery Calmly Considered*, Section II, 5). The same point is made against Ramsay's *Principles of Religion* where Ramsay had suggested that sufferings and expiatory pains were necessary to purify lapsed beings to make them fit for heaven. ' "Expiatory pains" ', writes Wesley, 'is pure, unmixed Popery', finding no warrant in the Bible.[27] The only fires are the fires of hell, not the fires of purgatory, he writes, against William Law.[28] Wesley describes purgatory as a place of torment (Q 21) and objects that 'there is no condemnation to them which are in Christ Jesus' (Rom. 8:1). There can be no condemnation if a person is justified (Rom. 8:33–34). If the Catholics are right, should not the penitent thief have been sent to purgatory and not to paradise? Wesley opts for Cyprian's statement that when life is completed we are divided for everlasting death or everlasting life (*To Demetrianus*, 16). Unfortunately Wesley seems to have a mistranslation. The version in the Ante-Nicene Fathers seems to be about believers lifting themselves above earthly things into a dependence on high and heavenly things. A better quotation comes later in the same letter:

> Believe him who will give to all that believe the reward of eternal life. Believe him who will call down on them that believe not, eternal punishment in the fires of Gehenna. (*To Demetrianus*, 23)

It ought to be noted here that in the Western Church the doctrine of purgatory is taught systematically by Ambrose and Augustine, though there are the beginnings of the belief in AD 203 in the *Passion of Saints Perpetua and Felicitas*. Cyprian, interestingly, does not follow the hint in the *Passion*, although he must have known of it, and prefers his own, 'When you have once departed thither, there is no longer any place for repentance, and no possibility of making satisfaction' (*To Demetrianus*, 25). That souls could be delivered from a situation outside heaven, seems to Wesley to be nonsense (Q 23). Prayers, alms, Masses, indulgences cannot bridge the gap, as Jesus indicated in the parable of Dives and Lazarus (Luke 16:26). 'After death,' says Epiphanius, 'is no help to be gotten by godliness or repentance.'[29] Epiphanius obviously changed his mind on this as he is one who reckoned the denial of the value of prayers for the dead to be a heresy (*Panarian*, 75, 8). Wesley contests the idea that purgatory has to be believed (Q 24). He does not believe that prayer for the dead in the early Church was to procure their release from purgatory.[30] Even the martyr Cardinal Fisher believed there was little evidence for it among the ancients, as did Polydore Virgil at about the same time. On the other hand, the article in the *Oxford Dictionary of the Christian Church* finds it in the Eastern Fathers Clement of Alexandria, Origen, Cyril of Jerusalem, Chrysostom and Epiphanius, and in the Western Fathers Ambrose, Augustine, Caesarius of Arles and Gregory the Great. Wesley ends his discussion of purgatory (Qs 25–28) with a look at the doctrine of limbo, for infants and for the Old Testament patriarchs. Scripture reads that Abraham is in heaven (Luke 16:23), as are Elijah and Moses (2 Kings 2:11 and Luke 9:30). He will have nothing of the assertion that Christ harried hell and released the patriarchs from limbo. He fails to discuss the case of infants in limbo. During 1738, after the Aldersgate experience, he was in Mayence where he read a paper on the door of the cathedral which he described as 'extraordinary'. It was a papal indulgence for the souls in purgatory and he quotes it in full in the *Journal*:

> A Full Release for the Poor Souls in Purgatory His Papal Holiness, Clement the XIIth, hath this year, 1738 on the 7th of August, most graciously privileged the cathedral church of St Christopher in Mayence; so that every priest, as well secular as regular, who will read Mass at an altar for the soul of a Christian departed, on any holiday, or on any day within the octave thereof, or on two extraordinary days, to be appointed by the Ordinary, of any week in the year, may each time deliver a soul out of the fire of Purgatory.[31]

At the end of this discussion of controverted doctrines, it may be of interest to quote some other words of John Wesley, from his *Journal* of 27 August 1739:

I have neither time nor inclination for controversy with any; but least of all with the Romans. And that, both because I cannot trust any of their quotations, without consulting every sentence they quote in the originals: And because the originals themselves can very hardly be trusted, in any of the points controverted between them and us. I am no stranger to their skill in mending those authors, who did not at first speak home to their purpose; as also in purging them from those passages which contradicted their emendations.[32]

Perhaps we do not need to discuss a passage such as this. Similar claims would have been made in the eighteenth century by a Roman Catholic writing against Anglicans or Methodists. In an ecumenical century we use the same editions of texts and our respective positions are beginning to be known to each other. That these positions are not yet fully understood provides the agenda for the ecumenical endeavours of the future. As we have come to enjoy our differences in our experience of other ways of worship we have begun to live in other traditions and to value them as ways into God while the theological dialogue continues.

10

Mr Wesley's Misrepresentations
Answered

In the recusant archives at Oscott College there are no traces of any contemporary Roman Catholic responses to John Wesley's attack on Popish doctrines. The first responses date from early in the nineteenth century. In 1811 Nicholas Gilbert, a priest in Whitby, produced *An Answer to the Reverend John Wesley's Misrepresentations of the Catholic Doctrines*.[1] This was a response to the republication in 1810 of Wesley's *A Word to a Protestant*. A slightly later production, in four parts, came from the Catholic priest in Stourbridge, J. A. Mason, entitled *Strictures on Wesley's Pretended Roman Catechism, pointing out its numerous misrepresentations, false glosses and gross falsehoods, addressed to the Methodists of Stourbridge and its Vicinity*, dated 1828.[2] Mason was a convert to Catholicism from Methodism and seems to have been responding to a four part anti-Roman Catholic catechism then circulating in Stourbridge.

Several interesting themes are discussed by both authors. Gilbert suggests that the use of the word 'Papist' is really an insult and is discriminatory. Roman Catholics do not normally call Methodists by their nicknames of 'Enthusiasts', 'Canorums' (as in Cornwall) or 'Swaddlers' (as in Ireland). Mason thinks that Wesley's attempt to create a Roman Catholic catechism, and then to answer it, is to make his own man of snow who can then be easily knocked down. Both authors are concerned with the refuting of calumnies against the Catholics and suggest that false witness has been borne against them.

The Church of Christ had always existed down the centuries;

if it had not survived, of what value would have been the promises of Christ to Peter that the gates of hell should not prevail against it (Matt. 16:18), or the promise of Christ to be with his people to the end of time (Matt. 28:20)? The errors which Wesley saw had crept into the Church down the centuries were never opposed by the saints of the Church, who, if any, could have resisted false innovations and doctrines. On the other hand, if the Catholic Church can claim 1800 years of continuous history, the Methodists are new and only began in the eighteenth century. Further, their first bishop and priests, far from tracing descent from the Apostles, date from a mere 30 years ago and are named Coke, Whatcoat and Vesey (sic). As to the head of the Church, Mr Wesley objected to a Papacy descended from Peter but was himself a visible head of his own people. Mason is sure that the primacy of the Pope can be traced in the Scriptures and in the Fathers, specifically in Irenaeus, Dionysius, Ambrose, Tertullian, Origen, Hippolytus and others.

On Scripture and Tradition, Mason has some strong points against Wesley. Wesley claims to be a man of the Scriptures and yet these same Scriptures were defined by a Council of the Church; the authority for the canon is the authority of Tradition. Why, too, does Wesley allow into his canon only those books of the Old Testament allowed into the canon by the Jews; does he think the Jews more likely to be infallible than the Council of Trent? Further, Protestants believe things not in the Scriptures and practise ceremonies not listed there. Mason offers as examples the practice of infant baptism, the turning to the East at the creed, the use of gown and surplice in the Church of England. The idea that Catholics have not been allowed the use of Scripture in the vernacular is refuted by Mason; they have a vernacular Bible in their houses, but it is not an heretical one that they read. Wesley had objected in his *A Roman Catechism* to the use of 'legends' in the Breviary. Mason points to the bulk of the Breviary being scriptural, with very little pious legend. The only exception he makes is the admission of material concerning the lives of the saints, but this material is only analogous to the use of such material in Methodist publications such as the *Arminian Magazine*.

Wesley had been extremely critical of the Catholic understanding of the seven sacraments. Mason notes that although
Wesley had used Augustine to defend the Protestant position of
two dominical sacraments, elsewhere Augustine defends all the
other sacraments of the Catholic Church, all of which baptism
and Eucharist bind together. Wesley had objected to lay baptism in cases of emergency and yet had allowed in his lifetime
laymen, whom he had himself ordained, to celebrate the sacraments of baptism and Eucharist, a strange inconsistency. Concerning the Eucharist, why did the people of Wesley's
communion kneel at the distribution if only bread and wine
were being offered? And why, if only bread and wine were the
issue, did he insist that an ordained priest should be the
officiant? All this merely pointed to the 'something more' that
Catholics had always insisted on as being present in the Eucharist. As to communication in one kind only, Gilbert says that the
early Christians broke bread, there being in Acts 2:42 no reference to wine, and even the Reformers at times allowed communion only in one kind, for example in the first year of Edward
VI and in the French synods of 1560 and 1571. In any case,
the Protestants have mistranslated 1 Corinthians 11:27 to read,
'Whosoever shall eat this bread *and* drink this cup . . .' where it
should read 'Whosoever shall eat this bread *or* drink this
cup . . .'. Gilbert was presumably less interested in the context
than in making his polemical point. Gilbert is on firmer ground
where he discusses penance and absolution. He reminds his
Protestant reader that in the Book of Common Prayer there are
two different perspectives. There is the section where ministers
'declare and pronounce' the forgiveness of sins to those who are
penitent (Morning and Evening Prayer). But in the 'Visitation of
the Sick' in the Book of Common Prayer it gives ministers
authority to 'absolve all sinners who truly repent and believe in
him'. It seems that Methodists can apply for absolution but
must not believe in it!

Wesley is most mistaken when he discusses indulgences. He
suggested that one main branch of the Pope's spiritual power
was his ability to grant pardon for all sins, 'past, present and to
come' by means of papal indulgences.[3] Gilbert offers the official

view; that an indulgence is a relaxation of temporal punishment after sins have been washed away, and that the monetary factor arises only where alms are prescribed as a condition for gaining the indulgence. Indulgences are never sold for money. More importantly, popes cannot grant pardon for sins past, present and future. Sins past are taken away by the absolution of a priest, and no pope could ever grant such a licence to sin as would be implied in a pardon for sins to come. It is a pity that, having made these important points, Gilbert aims a blow at Luther for his vexation at not being appointed a preacher of the indulgence in 1517, and for his indulgence to Philip of Hesse to have two wives. The historical reality is a bit less simplistic. On the anointing of the sick, Gilbert has a useful exegetical point to offer to Wesley. If Wesley is anxious to justify the use of confession 'in band' on the basis of James 5:16 ('Confess your sins to one another . . .'), why does he hesitate to allow anointing when it is clearly set out in the previous verses (James 5:14ff)?

Images, relics and saints are not of course worshipped, Gilbert reminds his readers, they are held in reverence. Wesley is guilty of mistranslation when he offers this rendering of the Council of Trent, session 25, paragraph 2: 'The right use of images is to honour them by bowing down before them.' The correct text reads, 'due reverence and veneration . . . not worship' and 'we adore Christ, and venerate his saints'. Mason, as one with inside information, reminds the Methodists that they respect Wesley enough to make graven images of him; as with Wesley for the Methodists, so with the saints for the Catholics. Gilbert is concerned to correct an impression left by Wesley concerning the Blessed Virgin Mary, that she could in some sense, with a mother's moral influence over her Son, 'command' her Son to have mercy on us. Gilbert protests that he has never found this in any Catholic book and that it is clean contrary to the Catholic faith. If she is called 'Queen of Heaven', she is queen in the sense that an earthly queen sits alongside her husband, in the place of honour, but with no authority over the earthly king. In the same way, she has no authority in heaven over Christ her son.

Three other topics are worth adding here. One is an answer

to Wesley's protest that the vernacular is not used in Catholic worship (Qs 30 and 31 in Wesley's *A Roman Catechism*). Mason replies that in his priestly life he has predominantly used the vernacular in the liturgy, only the canon of the Mass being in Latin. The majority of the service will be found to be in English: the prayer, the sermon, the instructions, the readings.

For Wesley, the Catholic belief that we are justified by faith and works together struck at the heart of Christian faith. Gilbert offers the Catholic belief that there is no merit in man prior to his justification by God. But that cannot mean that all works done prior to justification are sins. Would it be a sin, for example, for a man to work to gain money for his family before his justification? The danger with Wesley's doctrine here is that it leads people to do nothing before justification, to be 'Still Methodists' or even 'Moltherites' (Molther was a Moravian of the Fetter Lane society in London who suggested that nothing should be done before justification, suggesting 'stillness' instead). Surely, even before justification, we are right to seek and knock, and thus do 'works' before justification. Gilbert suggests that even Wesley had to change his mind on this in the *Minutes* of 1770.

Gilbert's final point against Wesley is to hit out against the idea that persecution could ever be 'a favourite doctrine of the Church of Rome'. This is no doctrine of the Church, he says, and any thoughts of coercion belong to more recent ages than those of the ancient Church, and can be said to be owned as much by both sides, Protestant and Catholic. He suggests that the persecution of Catholics during the Gordon Riots of 1780 owed a great deal to John Wesley's inflammatory writings concerning the Protestant Association:

> And so far had he succeeded in infusing his persecutory spirit into the heads and hearts of his followers, and other zealots of all denominations, that, had it not been for the wise measures adopted by the Legislature, and the protection of the magistrates, at the time of the Riots, not a single individual of our communion would be found in the land.[4]

This is one example in many of a tendency in the late eighteenth and early nineteenth centuries to blame John Wesley for the arousal of the mobs in the Gordon Riots. In fact, he cannot be indicted on this count any more than his Methodist followers can be accused of being ringleaders. The indictment, however, appears in several works, including those by Joseph Berington, John Milner, Arthur O'Leary and Robert Petre,[5] as well as in Gilbert.

Father Mason of Stourbridge buries Wesley's Catholic doctrine with these words:

> Mr Wesley's *Catechism* is a small book; yet I never saw so small a book so full of lies.
>
> Any Catholic bookseller can furnish him with books, from the ponderous folio down to the penny tract; and if he cannot purchase them, his Catholic neighbour will lend him sufficient for his instruction.[6]

By the time he wrote these words Wesley had been dead some 37 years. That Mason's efforts bore some fruit can be seen in his account of the conversion of two young Methodist preachers after reading his second stricture.

11

The Papacy

Wesley's opinions on the papal office are clearest in his references to Peter in the *Explanatory Notes on the New Testament*. He has significant things to say about the primacy of the Bishop of Rome. In his comment on Matthew 16:18, Wesley suggests that 'on this rock I will build my church' refers not to Peter but to Jesus, who probably pointed to himself when he said it.[1] We are reminded of Andreas Karlstadt in the sixteenth century who suggested that 'this is my body' was not about the bread but indicated Jesus pointing to his own body. The keys of the kingdom of heaven were not given to Peter alone, says Wesley, although he had the keys of doctrine and discipline in the early years of the Church (Acts 1:5 and Acts 10). The keys were equally given to all the Apostles (John 20:21–3). While Wesley is right about the parallel between John 20 and Matthew 16, in that the keys are given in both passages, he seems reluctant to admit a 'Petrine tradition' in the New Testament at this point in Matthew. When he comments on 1 Peter 5:1, in which the writer describes himself as a fellow-elder, Wesley writes:

> So the first though not the head of the Apostles appositely and modestly styles himself.[2]

When the apostolic decree is sent after the events of Acts 15, the Apostles, elders and brethren salute the Gentiles in Antioch, Syria and Cilicia. The fact that St Peter is not even mentioned in the greeting shows Wesley that the Church had no conception of Peter's primacy nor of his being the chief judge in controversy. The decree was drawn up by St James in the name of the

whole Church.³ Wesley draws equally strong conclusions from
Acts 8:14 when the Apostles sent Peter and John to Samaria:

> He that sends must be either superior, or at least equal to him
> that is sent. It follows, that the college of the Apostles was
> equal, if not superior, to Peter.⁴

When Paul reproves Peter for his vacillation in Galatians 2:11,
Wesley reminds his readers that Paul, who had not received his
teaching from man, was not inferior even to 'the chief of the
Apostles'.⁵ Wesley makes only one reference to the concept of
papal infallibility, in his comment on Acts 11:4. Peter lays before
the Apostles and brethren that the Gentiles have received the
word of God and Wesley writes, somewhat baldly:

> So he did not take ill to be questioned, nor desire to be treated
> as infallible.⁶

He seems to doubt whether Peter was in Rome before St Paul
arrived there, as is recorded in Acts 28. In his comment there
on verse 28, Wesley suggests that no Apostle had been at Rome
before this time.⁷ By implication, Peter came after Paul and so
Paul was the first to bring the apostolic message to Rome. One
wonders how it was that Paul wrote an Epistle to the Romans
some years before if no apostolic messenger had been there
before him to offer the good news to the Romans. Clearly,
Wesley believes that the good news was offered by some figure
outside the apostolic college. He writes on Romans 16:15 that
when Paul saluted the saints in Rome he would have saluted
Peter by name. Obviously then he was not in Rome and so:

> ... the whole Roman tradition, with regard to the succession
> of their bishops, fails in the most fundamental article.⁸

Since Linus and Clemens, the traditional successors of Peter in
the bishopric, are not mentioned, Wesley suggests that they had
not yet arrived in Rome.⁹ While Wesley seems reluctant to accept
Peter's presence in Rome, he readily accepts the story of Peter's
crucifixion, even though the place of crucifixion is not discussed.
In his comments on John 21 he states that Peter lived for some
36 years after the resurrection of Christ, after which he was tied

and then nailed to the cross.[10] The 'follow me' is taken by him to mean 'follow me to crucifixion'. Wesley could at this point have followed Gaius of Rome in the tradition of the Roman crucifixion of Peter, but he is selective with his evidence and does not quote the early Christian writers at all.[11] His attitude, following Bengel, seems to be a rejection of Peter's residence in Rome, and in this he accepts the current polemical stance of eighteenth century Protestantism.

In his tract, *The Advantage of the Members of the Church of England over Those of the Church of Rome*,[12] Wesley states categorically that the Romanists cannot prove the Pope to be the head of the Church from Scripture. He quotes only two texts which they cite:

> (i) 'I will give unto thee the keys of the kingdom of heaven' (Matt. 16:19), and (ii) 'Feed my lambs; feed my sheep' (John 21:15–17). Therefore we answer, these texts by no means prove that Christ made St Peter himself his Vicar; much less that he gave that dominion to the Pope, which he now usurps over the consciences of men.[13]

There is no attempt to justify this statement and it could be argued, on the other side, that they do give some weight to the case for the priority of Peter. For Wesley, it is clear from the New Testament that Christ alone 'is made of God Head over all things to the Church' (Eph. 1:22, 4:15; Col. 1:18). In any case, the way that St Peter and the ancient Bishops of Rome ruled the Church was far different from the manner and doctrine of present Bishops of Rome; the former obeyed the laws of Christ, the latter make laws contrary to the laws of Christ and even exempt people from obeying those laws. Present Bishops of Rome are thus adversaries of Christ rather than his Vicars. Just because a man possesses the see of Rome, it does not mean that he is the true successor of Peter; his claimed right to interpret the Scriptures for himself, and his right to license things which Scripture forbids, prove that.[14]

The early Church knew of no universal head, at least up to the time of the Council of Nicaea, AD 325. Wesley reinforces this point in his *Journal*[15] concerning the period before Nicaea.

Cyprian, in his 74th Letter[16] (to Pompeianus), accuses Pope Stephen of pride and obstinacy, and of defending heretics,[17] against the very Church of God. Wesley wonders why this letter, so damning to papal authority, was ever left out of the *Index Expurgatorius*. The conflict is of interest in that it contained the first polemical use of the 'Thou art Peter' text by Rome. Cyprian responded with 'the twelve were equal'. Wesley sees the conflict as a blow at papal infallibility. 'He that can reconcile this with his believing Stephen the infallible Head of the Church, may reconcile the Gospel with the Koran.' Historically, Wesley was totally misinformed since the outcome of the dispute was the affirmation of Stephen's position (that baptism outside the Church in the name of the Trinity was valid) over that of Cyprian (baptism conveys the Holy Spirit and the Spirit is only in the Church of Christ). Wesley seems to have little knowledge of the growth of the concept of papal primacy in the years after Nicaea.[18] He believes Gregory the Great's contention that the disciples rejected the title of 'universal head', and even Rome had refused the title when offered it at Chalcedon in AD 451.[19] (Gregory here was wrong, the title was in fact introduced into the Latin version of Chalcedon.) In his vehement letter to John of Constantinople, Gregory rejects John's acceptance of the title 'universal bishop' on the grounds that it is a title of pride, unfitting for a follower of Christ.[20] Elsewhere, Gregory is happy to assert the priority of the Roman see, as in his letter to Eulogius of Alexandria:

> Wherefore, though there are many apostles, yet with regard to the principality itself the See of the Prince of the Apostles alone has grown strong in authority ... (*Epistles of Gregory the Great*, Book VII, Epistle XL)

Going on with his theme, Wesley writes that the Emperor Phocas (incidentally, the only original Christian monument in the Forum at Rome is to him) gave the title of 'universal bishop' to Boniface III in AD 606, in return for his absolution of Phocas following the murder of the Emperor Maurice and his family. Succeeding popes increasingly acquired their power after this by fraud and force, many were notoriously wicked men, and sometimes popes reversed the decrees of their predecessors. Yet we are required to believe that they were so enlightened by the Holy Spirit as to be rendered infallible. Members of the Church of England should be glad for their liberation from the dominion of popes such as these.

In 1748 Wesley read a history of St Patrick in Ireland. He saw the whole story as a romance; there was no persecution, no scandal of the cross, only kings and nobles bowing down before Patrick. The Bishop of Tours is supposed to have sent Patrick to Rome on a commission to convert Ireland. Wesley states that the Bishop of Tours had as much authority at that time in Ireland as the Bishop of Rome:

> The Bishop of Rome had no such power in the beginning of the fifth century as this account supposes.[21]

In 1772 a correspondence began between Rowland Hill, a Calvinist, and Wesley on the interpretation of Wesley's doctrines.[22] By March 1773 Wesley was forced to respond to Hill's *Farrago Double-Distilled* which contained a fascinating exchange about whether Hill's tenets or Wesley's were nearer those of Rome. Hill claimed that the principles of the Pope and John Calvin were quite opposite and cited ten propositions. Wesley believed that since many popes were Benedictines and Dominicans, they were as firmly in favour of predestination as Calvin himself. The popes also were said by Hill to believe in a twofold justification, one now, another at the last day; so do all Protestants. The popes hold to sinless perfection, wrote Hill, but Wesley was not sure he could prove this. A fascinating dialogue was opened out but was too short for any reasonable discussion. Suffice it to say that at the end Wesley presumed that Calvinists were closer to Papists than they were to Methodists.[23]

There are two passages in the *Explanatory Notes on the New Testament* where the Papacy is compared very unfavourably with the historical Peter. In his comments on Acts 3:6 Wesley contrasts Peter with his successor:

> Then said Peter, Silver and gold have I none – How unlike his

supposed successor! Can the Bishop of Rome either say or do the same?[24]

These words were probably written around 1753 when Benedict XIV sat on the papal throne. As Renée Haynes has shown, Benedict was by no means the worst of popes,[25] and it is clear that we are once again in the area of conventional Protestant polemic. When he writes of Acts 15:29, and the apostolic prohibition of the eating of blood, Wesley remarks that the decree comes from the Holy Ghost and was not repealed before the middle of the eighth century by the Bishop of Rome, when eating blood became an indifferent matter. He concludes his comment on the verse by noting the contrast between the affectionate greetings at the first apostolic council with the anathemas hurled by many episcopal councils since the first century.[26] In a letter of 1777 to Joseph Benson he discusses Bishop Newton's book on prophecy and disagrees with Newton's understanding of the Papacy. Newton seems to have suggested that the Roman Anti-Christ was raising its head again and that papal tyranny was about to return. Wesley offers his contrary view:

> I believe that the Romish Anti-Christ is already so fallen that he will not again lift up his head in any considerable degree. The Bishop of Rome has little more power now than any other of the Italian Princes. I therefore concur with you in believing that his tyranny is past never to return.[27]

Wesley was writing not long after the dissolution of the Jesuits in 1773, an act which indicated the impotence of the Papacy in the face of pressure from the Catholic states. Within a few years of Wesley's death the Papacy would be subjected to the vagaries of Napoleon Bonaparte's rule, Pius VI would die exiled from Rome, while Pius VII would be a prisoner of the French. Wesley's polemical words seem to be prophetic of the immediate future in 1777, while the nineteenth century saw a real change in papal fortunes. In any case, as we shall see, Wesley did not expect the Papacy to last beyond 1836.

A few other small quotations on the Papacy are worth mentioning. The first concerns Leo X, the Medici Pope, the one who excommunicated Luther. Wesley does not think much of him, but not because of the Luther affair. His objection to Leo X is that he was responsible for allowing harmony into the music of the Church. The winding together of different voices caused the words to be lost and the listener to have more interest in the music than in the words, which were of course often biblical words.[28] Another comment is aimed at Sixtus V, one of those remarkable figures that are suddenly thrown up in history and contradict all expectations. He came to the Papacy in 1585 from the Spiritual Franciscans and set about being as contradictory to Franciscan ideals as he could be. In his five years in the see of St Peter he changed the face of the city of Rome. He was primarily responsible for the major road systems of Rome and for the erection of the obelisks that are so much a part of its scenery today. Wesley read his life in 1773 and his remarks are fascinating:

> In this journey I read over that strange book, *The Life of Sextus Quintus*; a hog-driver at first, then a monk, a priest, a bishop, a cardinal, a pope. He was certainly as great a genius, in his way, as any that ever lived. He did great things, and designed far greater; but death prevented the execution. And he had many excellent qualities; but was full as far from being a Christian as Henry VIII or Oliver Cromwell.[29]

No doubt even a visit to Rome would have failed to change Wesley's estimate. A further Wesley anecdote of a pope presumably concerns Clement XIV, another Franciscan. Wesley writes in 1786 of 'the late Pope' and gives this account of him.[30] One day he was being transported to St Peter's in a carriage from St John-in-Lateran when torrential rain stopped everything. When the storm was over, the grooms returned to the carriage only to find the Pope had made his own way through the water and mud and was in the Basilica saying his prayers. Wesley praises this extraordinary humility, an example of a member of the Church of Rome who was highly favoured by God, despite his wrong opinions.[31]

Wesley left his oddest thoughts on the Papacy to the final

part of the *Explanatory Notes on the New Testament* of 1755, the section on Revelation.[32] Most of the notes were lifted straight from Bengel's *Gnomon*, first printed in Germany in 1742.[33] Bengel has some fascinating arithmetic in his comments on Revelation and this led Wesley to believe that the 'third woe' in Revelation 11:14 was the time of the Papacy from 947 to 1836. At the appointed time in 1836 the Papacy would come to an end. Wesley's interpretation of the Papacy in Revelation, mainly following Bengel, can be briefly summarized. The prediction of the suffering of the saints in Revelation 6:11 was fulfilled in papal Rome when the Papacy was in the vanguard of the persecutors from AD 98 until AD 1209, from the period of Trajan to the first crusade against the Waldensians (a magical figure of 1111 years, of great significance to Bengel).[34] Writing on Revelation 9:12 Wesley declares, in some contradiction to what he writes elsewhere, that the first woe began in AD 606 when the Emperor Phocas declared Boniface III Universal Bishop and Rome the Head of all Churches.[35] In Revelation 11:14 the end of the second woe is the breaking of Saracen power by the forces of the French around AD 847.[36] The prelude to the third woe occurred when the Papacy began to enlarge its grandeur, as in the year 755 when Pepin made the Bishop of Rome a secular prince by granting him the exarchate of Lombardy.

With Revelation 13:1 we come to the crux of Wesley's discussion of the decline of the Papacy. Here Bengel is considerably expanded. 'This beast is the Romish Papacy, as it came to a point 600 years since, stands now and will for some time longer.'[37] Wesley's evidence for the identification is as follows: the beast is spiritual and secular; he is connected with Rome; he still exists; the papal kingdom began in its present form with Gregory VII in 1073. Wesley gives his own dates for the rise and decline of the beast of which we gather just a few examples:

AD 1033 Benedict the Ninth, a child aged eleven, is Bishop of Rome, and occasions grievous disorders for above twenty years.

AD 1048   Damasus II introduces the use of the triple crown.

AD 1073   Hildebrand, or Gregory VII, comes to the throne.

AD 1076   He deposes and excommunicates the emperor.

AD 1095   Urban II holds the first Popish council, at Clermont, and gives rise to the Crusades.

AD 1123   The first Western general council is held in the Lateran. The marriage of priests is forbidden.

AD 1143   Celestine II is, by an important innovation, chosen to the Popedom without the suffrage of the people; the right of choosing the Pope is taken from the people, and afterward from the clergy, and lodged in the Cardinals alone.

AD 1204   Innocent III sets up the Inquisition against the Vaudois.

AD 1208   He proclaims a crusade against them.

AD 1300   Boniface VIII introduces the Year of Jubilee.

AD 1305   The Pope's residence is removed to Avignon.

AD 1377   It is removed back to Rome.

AD 1378   The 50 years' schism begins.

AD 1564   Pius IV confirms the Council of Trent.

AD 1682   Doctrines highly derogatory to the papal authority are openly taught in France.

AD 1713   The constitution, *Unigenitus*.

AD 1721   Pope Gregory VII canonized anew.[38]

The list is interesting in that it is selective and severely antipapal. The full list can be found in the *Notes*. One could argue that Innocent III should be remembered less for the Inquisition than for the promotion of the Franciscans and Dominicans, that the removal of the franchise from the people and clergy of Rome in 1143 would help to make the Papacy more universal in outlook, that the papal schism lasted not for 50 but for 39 years. However, Wesley's sole purpose here is to prove that the beast ascending from the sea must be fixed between Gregory VII and Alexander III, with a preference for Gregory VII as the beast.

His piece on Gregory VII extends to several pages of the commentary on Revelation 13:1–3.[39] Among Gregory's maxims were: the Bishop of Rome alone is universal bishop; all princes ought to kiss his foot; he can depose emperors; he alone can convene a general synod; he is subject to no human judgement; the Roman Church never did, nor ever can, err; the Roman bishop is immediately made holy on his election by the merits of St Peter; he can absolve subjects from their allegiance. This is a weighty list of maxims. Wesley later was to use at least two of them again in his opposition to the claims of the Catholic Church; the power to depose emperors, and the power to absolve subjects from their allegiance. Wesley goes on in his account of Gregory VII to discuss the controversy with the Emperor Henry IV. This history shows that the Papacy, from at least 1073, is the wild beast with seven horns which came up out of the sea.[40] Later popes, far from disclaiming the power of the Papacy, have canonized it in some sense by elevating Gregory VII to the status of *beatus*, and *sanctus*, after this extending his feast to the whole Church, in the reigns of Clement VIII, Paul V and Benedict XIII. That the beast is the Roman Papacy is then 'proved' by Wesley in some 23 observations. The wounds of the beast were inflicted by the emperors in their continuing conflict with the Papacy. The popes before the Reformation spoke 'great things and blasphemy' (Rev. 13:5) and made war against the saints (Rev. 13:7), principally the Waldensians and Albigensians (Bengel, interestingly, does not include the Albigensians). The Pope is thus shown to be the Anti-Christ and the name of the beast is 'Papa' or 'Pope':

> Whosoever, therefore, receives the mark of the beast does as much as if he said expressly, 'I acknowledge the present Papacy, as proceeding from God'; or, 'I acknowledge that what St Gregory VII has done, according to his legend, (authorized by Benedict XIII), and what has been maintained in virtue thereof, by his successors to this day, is from God'.
>
> In a word, to have *the name of the beast* is, to acknowledge His papal Holiness; to have *the number of his name* is, to acknowledge the papal succession.[41]

Further references follow to Rome as 'the slaughter house of the martyrs' (Rev. 17:6), which are picked up again in Revelation 18:24 where Rome is guilty of spilling the blood of the saints; innumerable martyrs have followed elsewhere, 15 million between 1518 and 1548 at the hands of the Inquisition, and many in Bohemia, Germany, Holland, France, England, Ireland and other parts of Europe, Africa and Asia.[42] But Babylon will fall one day. Wesley reverses the appeal of Benedict XIII to all Catholics to come to the Jubilee of 1725 in Rome and applies it to Babylon.[43] Eventually there will be papal residences on all the seven hills of Rome (Rev. 17:10), while at present there have only been four. When that comes to pass, the Papacy will end. At this point Wesley follows Bengel's chronology:

'1836. The beast is finally overthrown.'

The last Pope will be pre-eminently the Anti-Christ, adding to the wickedness of his predecessors 'a peculiar degree of wickedness from the bottomless pit'. On the whole, Wesley's strictures on the Papacy in the *Explanatory Notes on the New Testament* are directly quoted from Bengel. Here and there Wesley adds his own extra pieces of historical knowledge, as when he amplifies the history of Gregory VII. The results are far from edifying and one wonders how he could square it with the positive remarks quoted above on Clement XIV. Perhaps again we have a situation in which Wesley is using material that he has barely had time to consider in all its implications. He was writing 200 years before Vatican II and its Constitution on the Church, *Lumen Gentium*. The *Notes* are still part of the doctrinal standards of the Methodist Church, but few Methodists would accept any of this today; nor are they expected to do so, for, as the Deed of Union states: 'The *Notes on the New Testament* ... are not intended to impose a system of formal or speculative theology on Methodist preachers, but to set up standards of preaching and belief which should secure loyalty to the fundamental truths of the gospel of redemption and ensure the continued witness of the Church to the realities of the Christian experience of salvation.' The objective history of the Papacy is safe with the Methodists of the twentieth century in a way it was not with Wesley.

12

Catholic Saints

It has often been suggested in this century, as indeed in the eighteenth, that John Wesley had an instinctive sympathy with Catholic saints that caused him to be entirely uncritical of them. How wrong this is can be seen by looking at Wesley's writings, since just at this point he is a true son of the Reformed tradition in his criticism of the Catholic saints. His major criticism, as in his other controversial discussions concerning Catholicism, is that the Catholic saints are holders of wrong 'opinions'. These opinions are usually catalogued as those 'extras' brought into the doctrinal deposit of the Church at the infamous Council of Trent. Most of his negative comments about the saints concern these opinions which have given rise to credulity, superstition and idolatry.

There is an early reference to a phrase of St Francis of Assisi in the *Journal* for March 1736: '*Nudus nudum Christum sequens*', naked following the naked Christ.[1] Although the saying is usually attributed to Francis it appears also in Jerome, in Bernard of Clairvaux, and in the life of Francis Borgia, Duke of Gandia. Wesley quoted the phrase in a positive sense when a young man was turned out of doors by his friends for becoming a Methodist.[2] The same phrase appears later in a letter from Josiah Tucker quoted in the *Journal*.[3]

In 1742, riding between Evesham and Bristol, he read over the life of Ignatius Loyola, one of the chief instruments of what Wesley perceived to be the changes in faith brought about by the Council of Trent. He offers this assessment of Ignatius: 'Surely one of the greatest men that ever was engaged in the support of so bad a cause!'[4] It was consistency with his own principles, says Wesley, that caused Ignatius, like Zinzendorf, to use guile to promote his cause and the interest of the Church. The observation ought to be made here that sixteenth century Rome and its ways were not the ways of an eighteenth century English parson, and the context in which sanctity has to be formed must always be taken into account. Methodists and Catholics celebrated in London 1991 with a visit from the Methodist President and Archbishop Bowen on behalf of the Cardinal to the Methodist/Roman Catholic Committee to celebrate the two hundredth anniversary of Wesley's death which coincided with the five hundredth anniversary of Ignatius' birth. They had a lot more in common than Wesley believed, not least their main principle, which was to save souls. Wesley was even more critical of Francis Xavier, the Jesuit missionary, than he was of Loyola. He accuses him of failing to teach true religion to his converts.[5] Xavier and the other Jesuits spent their time teaching 'opinions' and externals to their converts, but not the religion of the heart:

> Allowing then, that the Paraguay converts have peace and plenty, allowing that they have moral honesty, allowing they have an outward form of religion (and thus far I know not but their guides may bring them), I cannot believe they have gone one step farther, or that they know what True Religion is.

The question is whether their instructors have the inward experience of the righteousness, peace and joy in the Holy Ghost. If they do not have it themselves, they cannot convey heart religion to others. When he remembers the death of Francis Xavier he is more generous:

> I was never more struck than with a picture of a man lying upon straw with this inscription, 'The true effigy of Francis Xavier, the apostle of the Indies, forsaken of all men, and dying in a cottage'. Here was a martyrdom, I had almost said, more glorious than that of St Paul or St Peter![6]

In 1747, Wesley was obliged to make a response to Bishop Lavington's *Enthusiasm of Methodists and Papists Compared*. Lavington had accused the Methodists of carrying on the work of Popery in England. One method by which this had been done was by the recommending of Popish books, in particular the life of de Renty and the work of Francis de Sales. We shall look at de Renty below and comment first on Wesley's remarks concerning St Francis de Sales. Wesley admits to having read the *Introduction to the Devout Life*, though whether with profit he does not say.[7] One would have thought that it would have appealed to his spiritual understanding with its severe practicality. His remark on Francis de Sales is interesting: 'I believe he is in Abraham's bosom; but he is no bosom friend of the Methodists. I question whether one in five hundred of them has so much as heard his name.' Wesley's lack of contact with St Francis de Sales is a pity in many respects, not least because one might have found here a spiritual link between the eighteenth century Methodist movement and the English Roman Catholic Church, as it has been shown how deeply affected was that Church by the Salesian tradition.[8] In this same year, Wesley read some account of the deaths of monks of the Order of de la Trappe, the Order that owed its foundation to the abbot Armand de Rancé.[9] The quotation shows his appreciation of the life of God in those with whom theologically he has little affinity:

> I am amazed at the allowance which God makes for invincible ignorance. Notwithstanding the mixture of superstition which appears in every one of them, yet what a strong view of piety runs through all! What deep experience of the inward work of God; of righteousness, peace, and joy in the Holy Ghost![10]

It is somewhat ironic that the phrase 'invincible ignorance' that he uses is the very term used in Catholic theology for people, like Wesley, who do not know the Catholic Church to be the true Church founded by Christ![11]

Early in December 1761 he read the life of Catherine of Genoa.[12] He describes her as 'a fool of a saint', unless it was her biographer who perhaps made her into an idiot. Catherine had been canonized in 1737 and no doubt Wesley was reading a popular life. We are fortunate in having the two massive tomes of Baron Friedrich von Hügel on Catherine against which to measure his eighteenth century assessment.[13] The hardest thing to decide is why he calls her an idiot. It could be because of her desire to live in celibate union with her husband, though this is hardly likely as Wesley might well by 1761 have opted for this in his own marriage. It is even less likely to be because of her work among the poor in the hospitals of Genoa, after all corporal works of mercy were very much part of Wesley's teaching. The most likely explanation is that she added to the central doctrines of the faith her thoughts on purgatory. As we saw in his examination of the Roman Catechism, Wesley is vehemently against even the sniff of this belief. In the next century he would have been equally unhappy with John Henry Newman's *Dream of Gerontius*, based as it is on Catherine's view of purgatory.

In 1785 Wesley's designated successor John Fletcher died at Madeley. The next year Wesley wrote an account of the life of this man, whom even his wife regarded as having been a saint.[14] John Wesley had despaired for many years of finding anyone in Great Britain who could stand comparison with two men, Gregory Lopez and Monsieur de Renty. Both these men had been Catholics and it seemed to indicate some failure on the part of Protestantism that, for all its truth, it could not provide an example of Christian sanctity to compare with these two. Here, at last, in the Swiss-born Fletcher, was one not inferior to them. But what of Lopez and de Renty? The writings of Wesley are full of references to them, and Wesley prepared short lives of them both, even though neither had been canonized by their Church. He believed that such Papists were yet children of God and were indeed now in heaven:

> Is not a Papist a child of God? Is Thomas à Kempis, Mr de Renty, Gregory Lopez gone to hell? Believe it who can. Yet still of such (though Papists) the same is my brother and sister and mother.[15]

Yet even these exemplary men had their Catholic warts. Gregory Lopez, the hermit of Mexico, lived his life in an uninterrupted communion with his God, even while writing or performing other tasks. He lived in great simplicity and one day, after Wesley had dined in luxury in Bath, he asks, 'What would Gregory Lopez have called it?'[16] This good and wise man was yet much mistaken, writes Wesley, since his life was full of Catholic superstition, with the idolatrous practices of worship of images and invocation of the saints. At the apex of his superstition was the worship of the Virgin Mary and the way in which Lopez ascribed all his virtues to the merits and mediation of the Queen of Heaven, instead of to God.[17]

Wesley had edited the life of another holy man, the Marquis de Renty, a Frenchman who had at one time been councillor to King Louis XIII. Despite his careful editing, Bishop Lavington assumed that Wesley had left unaltered the offensively Catholic parts in the life. Wesley replied that he had pared away the trash, but was forced to leave some bits of Popery in, to show that de Renty was really a Catholic.[18] Wesley felt so strongly about de Renty as a good example, though a Catholic, that he recommended him, and Thomas à Kempis, to 'men of reason and religion' in 1745.[19] He started abridging de Renty's *Life*, from an English translation of 1658, in about 1729 and in January 1738, on his way home from America, the revision was still in progress. (The final abridgement, finished in 1741, reduced the work from 358 pages to just 67.) The original author had, in Wesley's view, left far too many weak things in the book, particularly casting 'the shade of superstition and folly over one of the brightest patterns of heavenly wisdom'.[20]

In his brief note, *A Disavowal of Persecuting Papists*,[21] he offers a positive appreciation of some Catholic saints, agreeing that many Papists in former ages were good men, and he lists the names of Thomas à Kempis, Francis de Sales and the Marquis de Renty. The problem today, he says, is that the majority of Roman Catholics are not good men, and most would willingly fall into the persecuting habits of their forebears. But some have been, and some are, saints in whom is a strong view of piety, righteousness, peace, and joy in the Holy Spirit. Francis de Sales is, Wesley suggests again, surely in the bosom of Abraham.[22] Even those saints accused by Bishop Lavington of 'enthusiasm' for avoiding uttering idle words, to the extent of putting stones in their mouths, are obeying Christian precepts from the letter of James.[23] Mechtildis tortured herself for having spoken idle words, Katherine of Sienna never uttered a word which was not religious and holy, while Magdalen di Pazzi's lips were never open but to chant the praises of God. If these were Catholic enthusiasts, would that the Methodists could be the same in their speaking! Another passage concerning Magdalen di Pazzi and other saints was written after Wesley had read her life.[24]

> I could not but observe (1) that many things related therein are highly improbable. I fear the relators did not scruple lying for the Church, or for the credit of their Order; (2) that many of their reputed virtues were really no virtues at all; being no fruits of the love of God or man, and no part of the mind which was in Christ Jesus; (3) that many of their applauded actions were neither commendable nor imitable; (4) that what was really good in their tempers or lives was so deeply tinctured with enthusiasm that most readers would be far more likely to receive hurt than good from these accounts of them.

Wesley's most surprising quotation comes from that champion of Tridentine theology, St Robert Bellarmine, who was asked on his deathbed to which of the saints he would turn. To this Bellarmine replied, '*Fidere meritis Christi tutissimum*' – 'It is safest to trust in the merits of Christ.' Can we assume, says Wesley, that he had no share in Christ's righteousness?[25] In the recent edition of *The Works of John Wesley*, Albert Outler suggests that the story of Bellarmine had no basis in fact but was a piece of widely believed Protestant propaganda against Catholics, possibly having its origin in a book published in 1679 by Christopher Nesse, called *A Protestant Antidote Against the Poyson of Popery*.

We end this section with one of Wesley's questions which is still being asked, even in Catholic circles, at a time when cardinals, popes, and founders of religious orders are more easily canonized than laity and parish priests. Speaking as it were on behalf of à Kempis, Lopez, de Renty and others, he asks simply, Why is it that we seldom find God's saints made saints by the Bishop of Rome?[26]

13

Catholic Spirituality

It has been claimed that John Wesley was able to combine successfully the 'Catholic' elements of his theology and spirituality with the 'Protestant' elements.[1] While he spoke the language of evangelical Protestantism, he commended to his people the use of Catholic writers and, with certain reservations, the examples of Catholic lives such as Gregory Lopez and the Marquis de Renty. In addition, he advocated a form of Christian perfection, carefully qualified it is true, but this suggested to many a dangerous leaning to Catholicism which was inconsistent with the evangelical position. Here we shall try to put in brief compass four topics: Wesley's doctrine of the end of all spirituality, namely the way of Christian perfection; his use of Catholic sources up to the events of 1738; his use of Catholic writers after 1738; his arguments against some of the wilder views of the Catholic mystical writers.

Wesley's *A Plain Account of Christian Perfection, as believed and taught by the Rev. Mr John Wesley from the year 1725 to the Year 1765* was first published in 1766. The account underwent only minimal alterations until its last revision in 1777. It is not a systematic theology of perfection but an almost polemical account of the steps by which Wesley was led to embrace the doctrine. Wesley attempts to answer false interpretations of the doctrine which had been offered by others. He claims to have held essentially the same beliefs from 1725 to 1765 (and later 1777). The main argument is that Christian perfection is demanded and expected in the New Testament and therefore cannot be disregarded. Wesley calls as evidence the lives of several notable individuals who could claim to be free from all sin. He guards himself from misinterpretation by saying in some detail what perfection is not; indeed he prefers to use such terms as 'perfect love' or 'entire sanctification' rather than 'sinless perfection'. At the risk of over-simplification, we offer Wesley's 'brief thoughts' at the end of the 1767 book.[2]

1. By perfection I mean the humble, gentle, patient love of God and our neighbour, ruling our tempers, words and actions. I do not include an impossibility of falling from it, either in part or in whole. Therefore, I extract several expressions in our hymns, which partly express, partly imply, such an impossibility.

   And I do not contend for the term sinless, though I do not object against it.

2. As to the manner. I believe this perfection is always wrought in the soul by a simple act of faith; consequently in an instant. But I believe in a gradual work both preceding and following the instant.

3. As to the time. I believe this instant generally is the instant of death, the moment before the soul leaves the body. But I believe it may be ten, twenty or 40 years before. I believe it is usually many years after justification; but that it may be within five years or five months after it, I know no conclusive argument to the contrary.

   If it must be many years after justification, I would be glad to know how many.

Here are Wesley's main points in brief compass: perfection as perfect love rather than sinless perfection; the possibility of an instantaneous change as well as a gradual; the change comes before death, perhaps several years before; and though it comes after justification, it could be close to it in time. Wesley's principal appeal is to the biblical witness where he finds 'Scripture perfection'; pure love which fills the heart and governs all words and actions. Although Wesley was first attracted to the dedication of his whole self to God by reading Jeremy Taylor, Thomas à Kempis and then William Law, the Bible quickly became 'the only standard of truth, and the only model of pure religion'.[3] Not till August 1738 did he meet one who gave him an account of an experience of perfect love, the German Arvid Gradin. Later in the *Plain Account*, he names the Catholic Marquis de Renty as a prime example of his understanding of Christian perfection. In 1758 Wesley claimed that de Renty's *Life* was his favourite book; certainly it was the one that he quoted from most in his later life. Other 'Catholic' elements quoted in the *Plain Account* are very difficult to find. There are passages which read like Jean-Pierre de Caussade's *Self-abandonment to Divine Providence*:

> Whether in ease of pain, whether in life or death, he giveth thanks from the ground of the heart to Him who orders it for good; into whose hands he hath wholly committed his body, and soul, 'as into the hands of a faithful Creator'.[4]

Sadly, though de Caussade was an older contemporary of Wesley, dying in 1751, his work was not published till 1861, so dependence cannot be suggested. We are on safer ground with the thoughts of Brother Lawrence which Wesley may be remembering when he writes:

> Whether he 'sit in the house, or walk by the way', whether he lie down or rise up, he is promoting, in all he speaks, or does, the one business of his life.

Wesley had read Brother Lawrence sometime before 1754 for in that year he included some of Lawrence's letters in his *Christian Library*. The understanding of the 'practice of the presence of God' has a parallel in Wesley's use of Brother Lawrence's *Conversation IV*, November 25, 1667:

> Being questioned by one of his own society . . . by what means he had obtained such an habitual sense of God? He told him, that since his first coming to the monastery, he had considered God as the end of all his thoughts and desires, as the mark to which they should tend, and in which they should terminate.[5]

Towards the end of the *Plain Account*, Wesley offers reinforcement of what he has written with a series of quotations or reflections, which he recommends as being next in value to the Scriptures.[6] Massa has suggested that the tracing of these quotations to their sources would enable us to have deeper knowledge of the Catholic sources of Wesley's doctrine of perfect love.[7] Some of them clearly come from authors such as Jeremy Taylor and Thomas à Kempis, but some look like reflections of later Catholic teachings. Thus, one quotation reads like the quietism of Molinos:

> In the greatest affliction which can befall the just, either from heaven or earth, they remain immovable in peace, and perfectly submissive to God by an inward, loving regard to Him, uniting in one all the powers of their souls.[8]

Another passage, though it reads like the work of Brother Lawrence, is traceable to the French *Christian Reflections:*

> We ought to be in the Church as the saints are in heaven, and in the house as the holiest men are in the Church: doing our work in the house as we pray in the Church; worshipping God from the ground of the heart.[9]

The tracing of all these final reflections in the *Plain Account* to their sources, both Catholic and Protestant, would be an invaluable piece of work which would enhance Wesley studies and indicate connections with Catholic spirituality.

From 1725 up to the experience of 1738 at Aldersgate Street, Wesley read widely in the spiritual classics. Thomas à Kempis is one of the most frequently quoted authors and in 1735 Wesley, being dissatisfied with the current English edition of Dean Stanhope, dating from 1698, published what he hoped would be a better translation of *The Christian's Pattern*. There is a suggestion in Denis Gwynn's biography of Richard Challoner that Wesley's translation so led the field in England that Challoner was forced to produce his own translation of *The Pattern* or *Imitation*.[10] One of Wesley's quotations from à Kempis is interesting in that he uses it as an appeal for humility:

> '*Nihil est quod hactenus feci*' (what I have hitherto done is nothing).[11]

The early diaries and the later journals and letters abound with the name of à Kempis.[12] Initially, as in a letter to his mother in 1725, he was drawn to differ a little from the great writer:

> I think he must have been a person of great piety and devotion, but it is my misfortune to differ from him in some of his main points. I can't think that when God sent us into the world He had irreversibly decreed that we should be perpetually miserable in it. If it be so, the very endeavour after happiness in this life is a sin; as it is acting in direct contradiction to the very design of our creation. What are become of all the innocent comforts and pleasures of life, if it is the intent of our Creator that we should never taste them?[13]

Nevertheless, despite this youthful criticism, he constantly quoted à Kempis throughout his life and recommends *The Christian's Pattern* in his letters.[14]

In 1736 he first read about those two authors which were so influential in the life of Luther: John Tauler and the author of the *Theologia Germanica*.[15] Tauler he later dismissed as an unhelpful mystic and he elsewhere accused both Tauler and Luther of being opposed to reason.[16] The *Theologia Germanica* he read to the company on board the 'Simmonds' on the journey to America, though later he wondered why he had admired the obscurity of this writer. 'Glory be to God,' he writes, 'that I now prefer the plain Apostles before him and all his mystic followers.'[17]

Two better exemplars of the Catholic spiritual tradition John Wesley found, as we have seen, in Gregory Lopez and the Marquis de Renty. Lopez seems to have been his own discovery and he read his life as early as 1735 just before setting foot on the 'Simmonds'. The original life of the Mexican hermit had been translated from the Spanish of his follower Francisco do Losa in 1675. References to Lopez and his holiness abound throughout the *Journal* and the *Letters*, so much so that one might wish that he had investigated the spiritual writings, rather than just the lives, of other Catholic saints of the Counter Reformation. He remarked of de Renty:

> O that such a life should be related by such an historian! Who,

by inserting all, if not more than all, the weak things that holy man ever said or did, by his commendation of almost every action or word which either deserved or needed it not, and by his injudicious manner of relating many others which were indeed highly commendable, has cast the shade of superstition and folly over one of the brightest patterns of heavenly wisdom.[19]

Eamon Duffy has indicated the reasons for Wesley's love of de Renty: his charitable work for the poor; his promotion of religious societies in Paris and Toulouse; his constant experience of the plentitude of the Holy Trinity; his non-reliance on outward visions; his amateur medical practice; his personal austerity; his conversing while standing. Duffy also reminds us of what Wesley left out of the abridgement: de Renty's attempt to become a Carthusian; his dislike of Protestantism; his devotion to the saints; his devotion to the Infancy of Jesus.[20]

In the period before Aldersgate Street 1738, Wesley also read at least two other Catholic writers, Quesnel and Gother. On Christmas Day 1735, whilst in Georgia, Wesley spent four hours with Quesnel and à Kempis.[21] Quesnel was the most important writer of the second generation of the Jansenist movement. This movement, named after Cornelius Jansen, sought to recover the theology of St Augustine for the Catholic Church, and its supporters were suspected of introducing Calvinism into the Church. It would be fascinating to know which work he was reading. If it were the one usually called *Reflexions Morales* it would have pleased Wesley with its emphasis on the devotional use of the Scriptures rather than the 'manual' spirituality in vogue in late seventeenth century France. Wesley would have had sympathy with this French Jansenist who was condemned by Clement XI in his bull *Unigenitus* of 1713. There are in fact several references in Wesley to the injustice of the condemnation of the Jansenists.

Of even greater interest to the historian is the tantalizingly brief mention of John Gother's book, *Sinner's Complaint to God*.[22] Gother was a Catholic missionary priest working in England from 1682 to 1704, who wrote many spiritual and polemical works for Catholics. Through Gother we have a direct link to eighteenth century English Catholicism since it was Gother who received Richard Challoner into the Roman Catholic Church. It was Gother who was the chief apologist for the Roman Catholic faith, producing his most famous work, *A Papist Misrepresented and Presented*, in the reign of James II. The work elicited an enormous number of responses from Anglican divines and was still very much alive in the time of Wesley, as Challoner had the work reprinted. One wonders if, in using Gother's work, Wesley knew the reputation of the one he recommended to the sinners of Georgia. Did Wesley even know that he was recommending a Catholic author?

Moore, in his *Life of Wesley*,[23] quotes a particularly interesting paragraph from this period at the beginning of 1738. Wesley had become acquainted with mystical writers who made their description of internal religion so vivid that all else seemed mean, flat and insipid. But it was nothing like the religion of the Apostles. Love was the primary motivation of these mystics and a plenary dispensation seemed to be offered by them from all the commands of God. When Wesley had turned from this delusion he recognized that the mystical writers were the most dangerous enemies of Christianity:

> – all the other enemies of Christianity are triflers; the Mystics are the most dangerous of its enemies. They stab it in the vitals; and its most serious professors are most likely to fall by them. May I praise Him who hath snatched me out of this fire likewise by warning all others that it is set on fire of hell.[24]

As early as 1736 he had written in a letter to his brother Samuel that the mystical writers were the rock on which he nearly made shipwreck of the faith.[25] By 1738 he had begun a correspondence with William Law, his former mentor, accusing him by his mystical teaching of laying a foundation other than that of Jesus Christ.[26] Later, Wesley claimed in a response to Sir Richard Hill that he was 'never in the way of Mysticism',[27] and in a later reply to the same author he accuses the mystics of leaving off the outward means of grace.[28]

The rejection of mystical writers was not wholesale after 1738

as Wesley needed some aspects of their teaching to back up his
own thought. Thus, as we shall see, although he was often forced
to make strong reservations about the teaching of Madame
Guyon (1648–1717), he needed her plan of a simple route to
perfection and her description of the state of perfect love as
well.[29] He contradicted Madame Guyon's quietism, the understanding of 'pure love' that meant to her the abandonment of
the search for one's salvation in favour of stillness before God.
How could her *Short and Easy Method of Prayer* teach indifference to eternal salvation and still be sensibly Christian? Wesley
also regarded Fénelon, the Archbishop of Cambrai (1651–1715),
the defender of Madame Guyon, as equally misguided in his
doctrine. When Wesley read *Telemachus* in 1760, he found the
work sensible but far too long and over-involved, 'drawn into
mere French wire'.[30] Yet he quoted one of Fénelon's maxims on
some four occasions: 'true simplicity', Fénelon says, 'is that
grace whereby the soul is delivered from all profitable reflections
upon itself.'[31] Here, says Wesley, is the meaning of the single
eye. Fénelon also appears in the *Christian Library* in extracts
from two letters to the Duke of Burgundy on the love of God.
Here Fénelon speaks of loving our friends:

> When we love our friends for our own sakes, self-love is
> impatient, delicate, jealous, full of wants, and void of merit,
> always suspicious both of itself and its friends; it grows weary
> and disgusted; it soon sees an end of what it entertained the
> highest thoughts of; it meets with disappointments every-
> where; it would always have perfection, but can never find it;
> it grows angry, it changes, it can rest in nothing. But the love
> of God loves its friends without views of self-interest, and so
> loves them patiently with all their faults; it seeks no more but
> what God has given them; it looks to nothing in them but God
> and his gifts; it is pleased with everything, because it loves
> what God has made and bears with what he has not made,
> but permitted, and would have us to permit likewise, in com-
> pliance with his designs.[32]

Wesley, with his two imperatives of love for God and love for
our neighbour, would have appreciated this.

That he also used the works of Miguel de Molinos (c. 1640–97), the Spanish Quietist, in his *Christian Library* perhaps should not surprise us since the Pietist circles of Halle and elsewhere were greatly influenced by the Spaniard. The Pietist leader August Hermann Francke (1663–1727), professor at Halle, was a strong defender of Molinos yet said of the mystical writers generally: 'They do not describe one common Christianity but everyone has a religion of his own.'[33] Wesley offers in the *Christian Library* part of Molinos' *Spiritual Guide* written in 1675:

> Finally, Be not afflicted nor discouraged, he returns to quiet thee: this divine Lord will be alone with thee, to rest in thy soul, and from therein a rich throne of peace: within thine own heart, with his heavenly grace, then mayest look for silence in tumult, solitude in company, light in darkness, vigour in despondency, courage in fear, resistance in temptation, peace in war, and quiet in tribulation.[34]

That Wesley should have used the *Pensées* of Blaise Pascal (1623–62) should also not surprise us. Pascal was of course a follower of the Jansenist beliefs that Wesley felt were so unreasonably condemned by Pope Clement XI.[35] That he held traditional Catholic beliefs and that therefore the reader must be cautious was clear to Wesley. When Pascal writes of the concealment of God:

> ... He chose a concealment more strange and obscure than either of the former (hidden as divine, hidden as human), under the species of the Eucharist.

Wesley adds an editorial footnote:

> The judicious reader will easily trace, in some parts of this Paragraph, the peculiarities of that school of Roman-Catholic theology to which the excellent Author belonged; and will exercise a suitable discrimination.[36]

By 'school of Roman-Catholic theology' Wesley does not mean only the doctrines of Jansenism as a deviant form of Catholicism, but the post-Tridentine Catholic theology of the whole Church of Rome. Despite this caveat, Wesley used far more of Pascal's writing in his *Christian Library* than that of any other post-Tridentine Catholic author. He includes Pascal's cynical wager: bet on there being a God; if there isn't, you lose nothing, if there is, you gain everything. But it was the rational Pascal that one suspects he liked the most, as seen in the inclusion of this passage:

> If we bring down all things to Reason, our Religion will have nothing in it mysterious or supernatural. If we stifle the principles of Reason, our Religion will be absurd and ridiculous.[37]

The works of Madame Bourignon form the second largest group of post-Tridentine Catholic works in the *Christian Library*, which perhaps calls for comment, for Wesley had some very strong things to say about her mystic way, thinking her to be very many degrees below de Renty and Gregory Lopez. The preface to *A Treatise of Solid Virtue* has her name at the end, but Wesley does not include her name either in the list of contents of the book or in the frontispiece. His reservations were thus clear even in 1754 when this volume appeared. Most of Bourignon's 25 letters are addressed to 'my dear child', though others are addressed 'dear son' and 'dear daughter'. Wesley used the work of the Flemish mystic in order to cement in his people the fact that solid virtue depended mainly on the love of God, as in this extract from Bourignon:

> God bestows sweetness and consolations on those who begin, to take them off the more easily from earthly affections, and to draw them to his love: but we must not rest on them or on any thing that is not God. But our whole heart ought to be taken up in the love of God only.[38]

In Volume 38 of the *Christian Library* Wesley uses abridgements of the work of Brother Lawrence and Mary Henrics, in addition to those of Fénelon and Molinos. Again, in Brother Lawrence, the aim is the love of God:

> I have no pain or difficulty about my state, because I have no will but that of God, which I endeavour to accomplish in all

things, and to which I am so resigned, that I would not take up a straw from the ground against his order, or from any other motive but purely that of love to him.[39]

The love of God seems to be paramount in Wesley's use of Mary Henric's *Pious Reflections:*

> When we say to God, that we love him with all our heart, it is often a mere form of words, without truth or meaning. Men learn it when they are young, and they continue to use it when they are grown up, without thinking of what they say. To love God, is to have no other will but his; to keep faithfully his law, and have in abhorrence all violations of it.[40]

George Hickes (1642–1715) was a non-juror and titular Bishop of Thetford, later becoming the leader of the non-juring movement in England. Wesley abbreviated Hickes's *Reformed Devotions* for his *Christian Library* and although he reduced it to about a quarter of its original length, most of Volume 42 is taken up by it. Green, in his Bibliography of the works of the Wesleys,[41] states that the original work first published in 1672 was by John Austin (1613–69), a Roman Catholic, and was considerably revised by Mrs Susannah Hopton and then given a preface by Dr George Hickes. Green rightly describes it as a buried gem within the 50 volumes of the *Christian Library*. Austin has composed special psalms for each day of the week which breathe a rare spirit of devotion, perhaps imitated in our day only by the prayers of Eric Milner-White.[42] We offer just three examples. The first reminds us how easy are the Lord's commands and how little we work to fulfil them. By comparison a worker is a slave to his job and people expose themselves to a thousand difficulties to gain a few pence or a petty honour:

> O bounteous Lord, how easy are thy commands; how cheap hast thou made the purchase of heaven.
> Half these pains will make us saints; half these sufferings canonize us for martyrs;
> Were they devoutly undertaken for thee, and the higher enjoyment of thy glorious promises.

Thou dost not bid us freeze under the Polar Star, or burn
in the hearts of the Torrid Zone;
But proposest a sweet and gentle rule, and such as our
nature itself would choose,
Did not our passions strongly mislead us, and the world
about us distract our reason.[43]

For the Friday office, Austin bids us consider the crucifixion:

The Lord is sold, that the slave may go free; the innocent
condemned, that the guilty may be saved.
The physician is sick, that the patient may be cured; and
God himself dies, that man may live.
Tell me, who ever wished us so much good? Who ever loved
us with so much tenderness?
What have our nearest friends done for us, or even our
parents in comparison of this love?
No less than the Son of God came down to redeem us; no
less than his own life was the price paid for us.
What can the favour of the whole world promise us,
compared to his miraculous bounty?[44]

In Austin's office for Thursday we have a reference to the
Eucharist which leaves us wondering what the unexpurgated
version was:

Enter the palace of his glorious evidence, the place where
his honour dwelleth.
There we shall see the Eternal Word, who descended from
heaven to become man for us;
There we shall see the Prince of Peace sacrifice himself to
reconcile us with his Father;
There we shall see, O stupendous mercy! the Son of God
with food entertaining the sons of men . . .
Can we acknowledge thy supreme veracity, and not believe
this wonder of thy love?
What, though our eyes see nothing but bread and wine! our

faith, yea experience too, assure us, that thou art there
also . . .
Let us not then refuse to believe our God, because his
mercies transcend our capacities.
No, no, it is thy very self, O blessed Jesu; and it is thine
own light by which we see thee.[45]

It is interesting that Wesley included a passage such as this in
part of the library for his preachers. It is highly likely that
Bishop Richard Challoner would have believed that he and
Wesley shared the same eucharistic faith, had Wesley presented
his own eucharistic faith in words like Austin's.

Juan d'Avila (1500–67), the confessor of St Teresa of Avila, is
represented in Volume 46 of the *Christian Library* by some
fourteen letters of spiritual direction. The letters remind their
readers of the need for all persons to draw closer to God and
to see themselves in the light of God. To his spiritual children
at Ezija he wrote:

> Who ever looked after Christ, and was deceived? Infallibly
> there was never any. Let us therefore never take our eyes off
> from him. He died for this, that we, by looking at him, might
> die to our sins. Let us approach his wounds; for by his, ours
> shall be cured. And if we think it a heavy thing to part from
> our sins, it was much more hard and heavy for his soul to part
> from his body, when he died that we might live.[46]

To the life and example of Gregory Lopez (1542–96) Wesley
continued to turn to again and again after 1738. His abridged
life appears in the final volume of the *Christian Library*,[47] later
in the *Arminian Magazine* for 1780. Lopez was born in Madrid
but spent his last 34 years in Mexico, almost all of which were
as a solitary. Wesley reverenced the biography of one he knew
to have spent life in union with God, an example of Christian
perfection, as Lopez himself said:

> When those whom God has enabled to love him with all their
> soul, do with his assistance all that is in their power, and that
> with deep humility, it is possible for them to remain without

committing sin; as clearly appears, in that our Lord, who commanded nothing which was impossible to be performed, commanded this: 'Thou shalt love the Lord they God, with all thy heart, mind, soul, and strength.' But he who does this, not only does not sin, but grows daily in all holiness.[48]

These sentences could have been culled straight from *A Plain Account of Christian Perfection*, so reminiscent are they of Wesley's teaching. The Spanish biographer felt that Lopez was a real portrait of Jesus Christ, 'having no affection but for a life wholly divine'. Another example from Lopez' life which was much quoted by Wesley concerned the prayer that he lived in constantly, as in his biographer's words:

> That from the time he came to court, he prayed continually, and went through his business with the same inward peace, as he could have done twenty years after: And that neither the noblemen he met in the way, nor the noise and distractions of the court, any more interrupted his inward prayer, than if he had been in a cavern.[49]

One who was never interrupted in his constant love for God and neighbour could truly be said to be living in perfect love.

For Wesley, who published his abridged *Life* in 1741, the Marquis de Renty's perfect love was shown most clearly in two incidents: the first is the remarkable reaction of the Marquis to the death of his wife, concerning which Wesley has at least five references in the *Journal* and the *Letters*.[50] He quotes de Renty as follows:

> I feel my pains in all *their extremity*. But by the grace of God I give myself up to Him and not to them.

> I cannot say but my soul is *deeply grieved* at the sense of so great a loss; yet I feel such joy in that the will of the Lord is done, not that of a poor sinner, that, were it not for giving offence, I could dance and sing.[51]

Wesley boldly asked two of his female correspondents whether they had an experience parallel to that related by de Renty:

I bear about with me an experimental verity, and a plenitude of the presence of the ever-blessed Trinity.[52]

This constant sense of the presence of God with de Renty was for Wesley a proof of his perfect love. Whether modern pastoral tutors would agree with Wesley and de Renty on their grieving techniques is debatable, but perhaps few of them have had to deal with students in a state of perfect love. Could it be that a state of perfect love to God and neighbour might allow the saints to deviate even from the prescribed paths?

In Volume XXIV of the 1771 edition of Wesley's *Works* printed by William Pine, there are three Catholic works. The first is called *Instructions for Christians*, a translation from the French of the Abbé Fleury by M. Poiret.[53] The original had been published by Wesley in 1745 under the title *Instructions for Children* and was later translated into Latin for the boys at Kingswood School. Some of it is catechetical in form and some of it proverbial wisdom. As an example of the catechesis, here is part of the section on the means of grace:

3. Which are the chief means of grace?
   The Lord's supper, prayer, searching the Scriptures, and fasting.
4. How often did the first Christians receive the Lord's Supper?
   Every day; it was their daily bread.
5. How often did they join in public prayer?
   Twice a day, as many of them as could . . .
8. How long is ever Christian to use all these means of grace?
   To his life's end.[54]

As an example of the wisdom and proverbial material:

In a word: with regard to God, always live and act, as being in the presence of God.
Remember he is continually looking upon you.
And he will bring into judgement, all that you have done, said, or thought, whether it be good or evil.[55]

The second Catholic source in Volume XXIV is called *Christian Reflections*, a translation from the French of some 336 reflections on how the Christian should live. Here are four of them that Wesley might have appreciated above some of the others:

> 19. Whether we think, or speak to God, whether we act or suffer for him, all is prayer, when we have no other object than his love and the desire of pleasing him.
>
> 57. Nothing is so capable of destroying the grace of God, even in retirement, as idleness.
>
> 116. The way to advance more and more in love, is to practise it to the uttermost.
>
> 291. We ought to desire the Lord's Supper with the same earnestness as we desire to preserve the health we enjoy, or to recover that we have lost.

Some of the reflections escaped Wesley's critical eye: the assistance expected from the saints (29); the mention of penance (293); the role of the guide of souls (312) which guide Wesley probably mistakenly thought to be the minister.

Instructions for Members of Religious Societies, translated from the French, is a very short pamphlet and contains directions 'to preserve fervency of spirit'. Wesley made the translation in 1768 and made the classic remark in the *Journal:* 'What a multitude of wrong opinions are embraced by all the members of the Church of Rome! Yet how highly favoured have many of them been.'[56] The 'wrong opinions' mentioned must in this context have included the necessity of the conventual life since these *Instructions* were written for a community of nuns. The author, in paragraph 12 of the first part, advises his readers against the desire to please others:

> All the imperfections of religious societies, all their irregularities, flow from this poisoned fountain. Where discipline is wanting, it produces gross evils. It produces evils no less dangerous, though spiritual, wherever true piety is not sufficiently known, and where the depth of human misery is covered, not healed, by superficial remedies.[57]

Wesley would have added his 'amen' to this as he attempted to maintain discipline within his Methodist societies. It would, as the author suggests, have been easier to please others than to insist on discipline. In the second part, again in paragraph 12, there is a hint of 'the sacrament of the present moment', Wesley's 'never be triflingly employed'.

12. When you are doing a thing, never depend on doing it better another time; but at this time give it all possible attention. When you are doing one thing, do not think on another that is to follow it. Always limit yourself to the present moment, and distrust projects which cause you to slight the present work, by promising wonders in time to come.[58]

The amount of Catholic literature recommended by Wesley is fairly small, but perhaps substantial for its time by the standards of the eighteenth century. It has also to be judged by the paucity of such literature available at the time. For example, although Richard Challoner was writing and abridging almost as copiously as Wesley, the only books that Wesley is known to have read by Challoner are *The Grounds of the Old Religion* in 1743[59] and *A Caveat Against the Methodists* in 1760.[60] If Wesley did read other works by Challoner there is no account of it in the *Journal* or *Letters*. There is no doubt that he would have appreciated the Salesian traditions of the eighteenth century Catholics, as he had shown by his appreciation of the place of St Francis de Sales in Abraham's bosom.[61] If the amount of Catholic spirituality is somewhat selective, it is still reasonably substantial. About five per cent of the *Christian Library*, recommended by Wesley to his preachers, consists of Catholic authors. If we allow John Austin's contribution to count in the total, in all 835 pages of the 30 volume edition of 1819–27 are devoted to Catholic authors.

Wesley's critique of forms of Catholic spirituality seems to be confirmed to a false mysticism which he discovered principally in Madame Guyon. When he wrote the Preface to his abridgment of her life in 1776, he was careful to extract the wheat from the chaff.[62] Her mistake, he writes, was in not being guided

by the written word of Scripture; inward impressions, inspir-
ations, were the rule that she followed. The capital mistake
followed: that God could not purify her soul but by inward
and outward suffering. This led her into taking voluntary sufferings on herself, into giving way her estates to ungrateful relatives
and finally into going to Geneva to convert Protestant heretics
to the Catholic faith. All this was because the scriptural way
was not followed. As he wrote to Ann Bolton in 1772: '. . . keep
in the plain, open Bible way. Aim at nothing higher, nothing
deeper, then the religion described at large in our Lord's Sermon
upon the Mount and briefly summed up by St Paul in the 13th
Chapter to the Corinthians.'[63] The mystics, such as Madame
Guyon, refine religion too much. When they speak of desertion
by God[64] and the need for self-emptying,[65] they are indulging
in their own speculations. Yet even if there is, as Wesley baldly
put it, no ecstasy in Methodism,[66] the Methodist people should
still, in contradiction of the mystics, let their light shine before
men. The mystics have indeed been highly favoured by God,
possessing, as did Madame Guyon, the mind that was in Christ
Jesus. Most significantly of all, the really profitable part of
Christian history is that which deals with souls:

> . . . it is certain no part of Christian history is so profitable as
> that which relates to great changes wrought in our souls: these,
> therefore, should be carefully noticed and treasured up for the
> encouragement of our brethren.[67]

14

Catholic Practices

The question at issue here is the one: what difference does your religion make to the way you live? Here Wesley has some very harsh things to say about Catholics. 'The mystery of iniquity' still works in the Church since only a third of the Western Church was affected by the Reformation.[1] 'Yet two-thirds of them are still involved in the corruptions of the Church of Rome; and most of these are entirely unacquainted with either the theory or practice of religion.'[2] In his tract *Popery Calmly Considered*,[3] written in 1779, Wesley argues that the principles of Popery destroy the love of God, the love of our neighbour, and then all justice, mercy and truth. This is an extremely serious accusation and Wesley, despite admitting that there have been holy men in the Church of Rome, states clearly that their goodness has been seen in them *despite* their principles. To support the charge of destroying the love of God, Wesley brings the charge of idolatry. This he sees in many forms, but especially in the cult of images, in what he perceives to be the worship of the Virgin Mary, and in the offering of prayer to the saints. The offering of worship to a consecrated wafer is 'flat, palpable idolatry', the paying of worship to the creature which is due to God alone. Idolatry destroys the love of God.

Rome destroys the love of neighbour by her belief that the bulk of humankind (non-Catholics) are despised and hated by God. Bitter anathemas forecasting everlasting destruction on non-Catholics, the description of them as 'vessels of wrath, fitted for destruction', show that Catholics do not love their neighbours. The anathemas hinder, even destroy, the love we must have for our neighbours. In the same way, natural justice is destroyed by the doctrine of the Church of Rome that 'all but those of their own Church are accursed'.[4] Wesley refers to the horrible 'opinions' propagated by Rome as of the essence of the faith:

> How many thousand lives have been cast away by those who were zealous for the Romish opinions! How many of the excellent ones of the earth have been cut off by zealots for the senseless opinion of transubstantiation.

Mercy has also been destroyed, as can be proved from history. Wesley sets forth the records of the Crusades, the crusade against the Albigensians, the wars in the wake of the Reformation, the dungeons, the racks and the Inquisition. How ironical, writes Wesley, that the house of the Inquisition (which he locates in another source in Lisbon) is called 'The House of Mercy'. It is mercy such as the natives of Ireland, the Roman Catholics, showed to their Protestant countrymen in the last century. It is the mercy shown to Protestants by Philip II of Spain and by his wife, 'bloody Queen Mary' of England in the sixteenth century. It was zeal that caused the Catholics to kindle fires in the reign of Mary and that made France a field of blood during the massacres of Paris.[5] Wesley does not remember that Elizabeth and James I burned any heretics; bad as they were, they were not as bad as Queen Mary![6] Presumably, the process of being hanged, drawn and quartered was preferable to burning!

Perhaps even more significantly, the doctrine of the Church of Rome tends to destroy truth from off the earth. Here Wesley raises his customary argument that in 1415 Rome said that no faith should be kept with heretics. Wesley does not believe that this has ever been renounced, despite the affirmations by apologists for Rome that it has. It is easy to show that Wesley was wrong on the whole about Constance in 1415 (see Chapter 6 above), but he believes himself to be right and that Rome is habituated to lying and dissimulation. Habits of lying will not be confined merely to religion but will spread into common life. Some of the Roman casuists have said that officious lies, lies told in order to do good, are innocent and meritorious. This opens the floodgates for all kinds of falsehood and in his sermon *An Israelite Indeed*, Wesley condemns officious lies as an abomination of the God of truth.[7]

Wesley ends his consideration of Popery with a sledgehammer blow against absolution by priests. This practice not only destroys justice, mercy and truth. It drives all virtue out of the world. Men of corrupt minds with the power of absolution can forgive even the most heinous sins on easy terms. If a problem remains, there are always papal indulgences to be had, even plenary indulgences to be bought. Wesley's final sentence in the tract *Popery Calmly Considered* reads:

> And were the Church of Rome ever so faultless in all other respects, yet till this power of forgiving sins, whether by priestly absolution or papal indulgences, is openly and absolutely disclaimed, and till these practices are totally abolished, there can be no security in that Church for any morality, any religion, any justice, or mercy, or truth.[8]

This is why Wesley did not believe that Catholics should be tolerated and in his notorious letter to the *Public Advertiser* written the year after this, 1780, he set out his reasons for intolerance.[9]

Elsewhere, he offers the examples he knows of intolerance on the part of the Papists. During his visit to Germany, immediately after his Aldersgate experience, Wesley visited Cologne cathedral.[10] He described it as 'mere heaps upon heaps; a huge, mis-shapen thing, which has no more of symmetry than of neatness belonging to it'. (It did not reach its present glory till 1880.) Outside the cathedral, a procession had begun, presumably of the Blessed Sacrament, and one of Wesley's company deliberately failed to remove his hat. A zealous Catholic called out, 'Knock down the Lutheran dog', but the company retired quickly into the church to prevent further problems. This piece of intolerance was compensated for by the observed behaviour of Catholics on the boat in the Rhine who offered prayers each morning for their journey and by the Catholic boatmen who, unlike the English, were never heard to take the name of God in vain or laugh at matters of religion. Other acts of intolerance are occasionally mentioned in the *Journal*. There are the Catholic priests who cast Catholics out of Church for hearing the Methodist preaching,[11] the parents who turn their daughter out of the house for becoming a Methodist convert though later her father said she was right,[12] and the Irish Catholics who would still like to cut the throats of all Protestants, as they did in the previous century.[13] Persecution of non-Catholics has become less widespread in the Church of Rome, says Wesley, but the fact is that Romanists have not yet renounced the doctrine of the Council of Constance. Persecuting their brothers, even to death, is the ultimate intolerance. Till the Romanists renounce the doctrine of Constance they will be charged with the blood of Jerome of Prague, and many thousands besides, in the sight of God and of man.[14] There is a solitary passage in the *Journal* where Wesley has something like grudging praise for Papists. The Seceders of Northern Ireland, he writes, are much more uncharitable than the Papists, since the Papists do not kill heretics.[15] Wesley had been told by a Seceding Minister that, were it in his power, he would cut the throats of all Methodists. Here the Papists are shown to be more tolerant in Ulster. Wesley notes in a letter of 1787 an increase in tolerance among the Papists: 'And even in the Romish countries scarce any are now called to resist unto blood.'[16] The reference is of course to Protestants in Catholic countries.

As to the moral behaviour of Papists, all their problems begin with their failure to observe the second Commandment concerning the worship of images. None of the Romish idols were known in the early Church and even St John, in Revelations 22:9, is prevented by the angel from worshipping the creature, with a strong reproof.[17] This form of idolatry leads easily into other idolatries, as Wesley shows in his sermon *Spiritual Idolatry*. Also, he writes, the Papists are guilty of vain repetitions in their prayers, saying over and over the same string of prayers without ever feeling what they speak.[18] Worst of all for an evangelical Protestant, Christianity as the antidote of sin has become so adulterated in Catholic countries that it retains no part of its original virtue.[19] Papists also have a very bad record in some areas of morality. Take the notorious cases of murder that have taken place in Catholic countries. Wesley cites the example of an Englishman in Brescia who was told he would be murdered by a fellow guest. The host sent another to murder his would-be assassin, and in the morning the Englishman was presented with a dead body outside his window, and a man demanding payment for the murder. The murderer, says Wesley, was a Catholic man of honour! Wesley cannot resist the example of two Catholic soldiers of the Duke of Alva who murdered a family in Flanders and then sat down to eat. In the middle of the meal, the conscience of one of them pricked him. He realized his salvation was at risk; he was eating meat in Lent![20]

Wesley acknowledges that the vices of those who belong to the Church of Rome are probably little different from those who belong to the Church of England. Members of both Churches agree in condemning profanity, drunkenness, adultery, theft, disobedience to parents, and other like sins. Unhappily Catholics, like Anglicans, practise the very things that they condemn. So much is this so that Wesley likens the modern Church of Rome to the ancient Church of Carthage at the time of Cyprian, when such abominations occurred that God poured out his fury in the blood persecution of Decius.[21] They agree with denying themselves and the daily taking up of the cross, with the value of good works, yet they live at ease and fare sumptuously every day, with the result that the hungry are not fed, the strangers not entertained, the prisoners not visited. Wesley recommends that Catholics should read not pious Prot- estant writers, whom they account heretics, for their instruction on true religion but their own holy men, à Kempis and de Renty, who show love and self-denial in all their writing.[22] The problem, says Wesley, generalizing from the few people he had known from Portugal, Spain, Italy, France and Germany, is that the bulk of the members of the Church of Rome know very little of scriptural Christianity. In general, they are totally ignorant as to the theory and practice of Christianity; they are perishing by the thousand for lack of knowledge.[23] For example, Catholics, like some Protestants, are convinced that works of piety and mercy are more important than faith in supplying qualifications for heaven.[24]

Wesley was all his life concerned to protect against what he considered to be noxious Christian practices, particularly when clergymen, who should have been exemplary in conduct and advice, suggested them. That is why he becomes vexed when he relates in the *Journal* a particular instance of a Catholic priest's advice to his people. First, he commends the Irish priest at Athlone for being a true shepherd of the souls of the Catholics. He had given them strict orders not to work on the Lord's day, orders that Wesley with his deep Puritan foundations would have found heartening in a Papist environment. Sadly, instead of suggesting they employ their time in pious reading or in hymn singing, he had allowed them to play instead, even at cards, saying it was their duty to refresh both their bodies and minds. Wesley's judgement is: 'Alas, for the blind leader of the blind! Has not he the greater sin?'[25] The problem is that the Romanists carry obedience to their pastors to an extravagant height, even though these same pastors are nearly as bad as they were before the Reformation.[26]

Finally, there is the political question about the loyalty of the Catholics in England, the matter addressed in Wesley's 1780 letter to the *Public Advertiser* (see Chapter 6). The dilemma, and Wesley's fear of the Catholic Church, are neatly summed up in the story of a Romish priest and a woman of his acquaintance, with which he ends the 'Letter'. The priest claimed, after a long conversation, 'You are no heretic; you have the experience of a real Christian!' 'And would you,' she asked, 'burn me alive?' He said, 'God forbid – unless it were for the good of the Church!' The woman could have no security for her life:

> The *good of the Church* would have burst all the ties of truth, justice, and mercy; especially when seconded by the absolution of a Priest, or (if need were) a Papal pardon.[27]

15

Other Works

Several other works written by Wesley have importance in describing the relationship between Methodists and Catholics in the eighteenth century. We shall take these in chronological order. The first of them dates from October 1745 and was written at the beginning of 'the late rebellion' when 'open Papists' were 'on the very point of swallowing up the pretended Protestants'.[1] It is entitled *A Word in Season*, or *Advice to an Englishman*. In paragraph 2 Wesley asks what might happen if French forces should conquer England:

> If they prevail, what but Popery and slavery? Do you know what the spirit of Popery is?[2]

Wesley suggests that the spirit of Popery was seen in Mary's reign when holy men were burned alive by the Papists because they would not worship angels and saints, pray to the Virgin Mary, and bow down to images. If a new king were to come in of this spirit, would anyone be safe? Either a man would have to go into the fire for his beliefs, or into the fire that would never be quenched. The solution would be found only in personal and national repentance.

In the same year Wesley wrote *A Word to a Protestant*, a pamphlet of just four pages.[3] Again the context was the 1745 rebellion. In it Wesley asks whether the reader knows the difference between a Papist and a Protestant. A Papist is he who holds the Pope to be the head of the whole Christian Church, and the Church of Rome to be the only Christian Church. A Protestant is he who protests against the fundamental errors of Popery: the doctrine of merit; the doctrine of praying to the saints and worshipping images; the doctrine of persecution. The errors of the Church of Rome crept into that Church gradually over many years but the Council which met in the German (sic) town of Trent did not amend these errors but established them in the law of the Church. These errors include: the doctrine of the seven sacraments; transubstantiation; communion in one kind only; purgatory and prayer for the dead therein; veneration of relics; and indulgences, granted by the Pope, to be bought for money. The doctrine of merit strikes at the very root of Christian faith, which is that man can merit nothing of God but is justified freely through the grace of Jesus Christ. The doctrine of praying to the saints and to Mary, and of worshipping images, strikes at the root of the great commandment not to bow down in worship to any image whatever. This gross, open idolatry cannot be denied or excused. The doctrine of persecution has been for ages a favourite doctrine of the Church of Rome and Papists maintain that heretics ought to be either forced into the Church or out of the world by death. At the heart of the religion of the true Protestant should be the love of God and love of neighbour. Wesley ended the pamphlet by appending three of his brother Charles' *Hymns of a Protestant*, of which the following verses illustrate his thoughts:

Hymn I (Against the Popish doctrine of Merit)

2. O how shall I presume,
      Jesus, to call on thee,
    Sunk in the lowest dregs of Rome,
      The worst idolatry!

3. A stranger to they grace,
      Long have I laboured, Lord,
    To 'stablish my own righteousness,
      And been what I abhorr'd.

4. Foe to the Popish boast,
      No merit was in me!

Yet in my works I put my trust,
    And not alone in thee.

5. For works that I had wrought
    I looked to be forgiven,
    And by my virtuous tempers thought
    At last to purchase heaven.

6. Or if I needed still
    The help of grace divine,
    Thy merits should come in to fill
    The small defects of mine.

Hymn II (Against the idolatry of the Papists)

2. My body I disdain'd to incline,
    Or worship at an idol's shrine,
      With gross idolatry:
    But O! my soul hath baser proved,
    Honour'd, and fear'd, and served, and loved
      The creatures more than thee.

3. Let the blind sons of Rome bow down
    To images of wood and stone;
      But I, with subtler art,
    Safe from the letter of thy word,
    My idols secretly adored,
      Set up within my heart.

Hymn III (Against the persecuting Papists)

3. The servants most unlike their Lord,
      How oft did I condemn!
    The persecuting Church abhorr'd,
      Nor saw myself in them!

4. The spirit of my foes I caught,
      The angry, bitter zeal;

And fierce for my own party fought,
And breathed the fire of hell.

9. How vainly then the zealots blind
Of Rome did I disclaim!
Still to the church of Satan join'd,
And differing but in name.

12. A murderer convict, I come
My vileness to bewail;
By nature born a son of Rome,
A child of wrath and hell.

13. Lord, I at last recant, reject,
The fiery spirit unclean,
The persecuting zeal impure,
The sin-opposing sin.

18. Heathens, and Jews, and Turks, may I,
And heretics embrace:
Nor e'en to Rome the love deny
I owe to all the race.

It may be significant that none of these verses was printed again after 1745.

One of the most curious pieces of work that Wesley produced was *A Short Method of Converting all the Roman Catholics in the Kingdom of Ireland, Humbly Proposed to the Bishops and Clergy of that Kingdom* in 1752:

> It is a melancholy consideration to those who love the Protestant interest, that so small a part of this nation is yet reformed from Popery. They cannot but observe without a very sensible concern, that, in many parts of the kingdom, there are still ten, nay, fifteen, perhaps upwards of twenty, Papists to one Protestant.[4]

The reason why Catholics may not be coming over to Protestantism is that they are 'bigoted to their clergy', believing that their own Catholic clergy are the holiest and wisest of men. How can the clergy of the Church of Ireland turn this around? By noting that the Papists believe that only one set of clergy have been better than their own, namely the Apostles themselves:

> Here, therefore, is the short and sure method. Let all the clergy of the Church of Ireland only *live* like the Apostles, and *preach* like the Apostles, and the thing is done.[5]

The Catholics will be convinced in their hundreds, and eventually there will not be a single Roman left in the whole kingdom of Ireland. The clergy of the Church of Ireland only have to live with the mind of Christ totally taken into themselves, only have to preach with sincerity the doctrines of Justification, rebirth and sinlessness, and 'every Papist within these four seas will soon acknowledge the truth as it is in Jesus'.[6] The naivety of this final paragraph matches the naivety of the pamphlet as a whole.

Wesley's next work against the Catholics was the same size as *A Short Method* but theologically much fuller. It came out in 1753 and was called *The Advantage of the Members of the Church of England over Those of the Church of Rome*.[7] While it is less substantial than *A Roman Catechism* published in 1756, it appears like this to be dependent upon John Williams' response to the Catholic Catechism published in 1686. Wesley begins with the 'undoubted truth' that the more the doctrine of any Church agrees with Scripture, the more readily it ought to be received. Thus the Church of England, as a Church which is based theologically on Scripture and what can be inferred from Scripture, has an immediate advantage over the Church of Rome. The latter Church began at the Reformation to oppose the principle that articles of faith must be proved from Scripture, and added to Holy Scripture tradition, with the decrees of popes. The Council of Trent then decided that the Scriptures and the traditions had to be received *pari pietatis affectu ac reverentia*, with equal piety and reverence. Wesley adds, 'it suffices for laymen if they believe and practise what the Church believes and requires, whether they understand the ground of that doctrine and practice or not'. Although he states that this last sentence comes from Trent Session 4, the reader of the acts of that Council will not find it there. One has to assume that he found it from some popular anti-Catholic tract of his time. Wesley suggests that many of the Roman practices, doctrines and ceremonies were not provable by Scripture, and even contradicted it. The Fathers and Councils in a hundred instances contradicted one another, thus showing that tradition is a very fragile thing. Much of the criticism of the Church of Rome found here is also found in *A Roman Catechism* and in more detail (see Chapter 9). Perhaps it will suffice to summarize briefly Wesley's remaining criticisms:

1. The Church of Rome has taken away the Scripture from the people, and denied them the use of it. The controversies with the Jansenists in France are a recent instance of this.
2. The Church of Rome flatly contradicts the written word of God: in not allowing concupiscence to be understood as sin (Trent Session 5); in condemning the proposition that the grace of Christ is necessary for every good work (in the bull, *Unigenitus* of 1713); adding traditions into the Mass and imposing them upon the consciences of men; taking away the cup from the laity; in proposing that seven sacraments are dominical and work *ex opere operato*.
3. That in the rite of baptism the 'intention' of the minister to do the appropriate thing is essential. That confirmation is a true and proper sacrament.
4. That in the Eucharist the bread and wine are converted into the natural body and blood of Christ; that the elements should be worshipped; that the laity ought not to receive the cup.
5. That full confession to a priest is necessary for absolution; that penances imposed and performed co-operate in our reception of forgiveness; that the merits and intercession of the Blessed Virgin Mary and other saints help us obtain forgiveness.
6. That extreme unction is a sacrament instituted by Christ.
7. That ordination gives an indelible character; that seven orders were in the Church from the first – Priest, Deacon, Sub-Deacon, Acolyte, Exorcist, Reader and Door-keeper; that the

priest's work is to consecrate and offer the body and blood
of Christ, and to remit sins in the confessional.

8. That marriage is a sacrament instituted by Christ; that it can
   be dissolved by either party entering into a convent even
   against the consent of the other; that the marriage of clergy is
   unlawful.

After this long list of criticisms, Wesley concludes that on doctrine the Church of England has an immense advantage over the
Church of Rome, since her doctrines are founded on the written
word of God.

He continues with the advantages of the Church of England
over the Church of Rome with respect to public worship:

1. The worship of the Roman Church is far from the simplicity
   of the first Christians, with its magnificent buildings, altars,
   images, ornaments and habits, splendid ceremonies, processions, pilgrimages, prayer in an unknown tongue, constant
   repetition of the Creed, the Lord's Prayer and the Ave Maria,
   with the use of beads.
2. They do not worship God 'in spirit and in truth' as a beloved
   Father, nor praise him with psalms, hymns and spiritual songs.
   They are not edified by sermons and catechesis from the word
   of God, as the Scriptures are rarely cited in sermons and then
   only allegorically. The people are not encouraged to search
   the Scriptures for themselves and are by this means kept in
   ignorance and superstition.
3. They are kept in doubt about their salvation by the doctrine
   of purgatory, pardon of sins, redemption from purgatory
   bought by Masses and indulgences, the latter being sold daily
   for money.
4. Their trust in Christ alone is hindered by the doctrine of the
   merits and intercession of the Blessed Virgin and saints. The
   images and relics of the saints teach them to place considerable
   trust in these means of devotion to help them in their troubles.

Wesley next turns his spotlight on the Papacy. The Anglican

Reformers of the sixteenth century doubted whether the traditional doctrine of the Papacy could be proved by Holy Writ. The main reasons against it were:

1. Neither St Peter nor the ancient bishops had the same doctrine or manner of governing as the Pope now has. Christ alone is the head of the Church in Scripture (Eph. 1:22; Eph. 4:15; Col. 1:18).
2. The kingdom of Christ bears no resemblance to the hierarchy and monarchy of the papal kingdom. The possession of the See of Rome does not by itself prove the Pope to be St Peter's successor.
3. Even if the Pope were the Vicar of Christ, that would not enable him to change the laws of his Lord and King; that popes have made laws against Christ and exempted people from obeying Christ's laws shows that the Pope has been an adversary of Christ.
4. The idea of a universal head only became reality in AD 606 when Boniface III received the title 'Universal Bishop' from the tyrant Phocas.
5. Many of the popes have been notoriously wicked men, and yet we are asked to believe that they are enlightened by the Holy Spirit with the gift of infallibility. In fact popes have contradicted each other and reversed the solemn decrees of their predecessors.
6. The 'papal texts' of Matthew 16 and John 21 by no means prove that Christ made Peter his Vicar, much less that he gave dominion to the Pope over the consciences of men.

Wesley finishes his tract with a blessing to God who has caused the Church of England to be excluded from the communion of the Church of Rome. Thus members of the Church of England have liberty of conscience in which, by the grace of God, they shall remain. This liberty is a liberty to be guided by the written word of God as revealed by the Holy Spirit, to pray in the spirit of adoption, to be assured of justification through faith in Christ while the Spirit bears witness with our spirits that we are children of God. Wesley closes with these words:

> He may freely enjoy every blessing which God hath bestowed upon our own Church; and may take advantage of whatever good the providence of God has still preserved in the Church of Rome: He may cheerfully look for a happy death, and a blessed eternity; and at length, by resting on Christ alone, and patiently partaking of his sufferings, he may, with certain hope of resurrection to eternal life, without any fear of either purgatory or hell, resign his spirit into the hand of God, and so be ever with the Lord.[8]

The sermon on *Catholic Spirit*[9] is an exposition of the non-dogmatic strain in Anglicanism, an expression of the understanding of *adiaphora* or 'things indifferent' within Wesley's thought. The sermon is based on a sentence from 2 Kings 10:15, a question from Jehu to Jehonadab:

> And when he departed thence, he lighted on Jehonadab the son of Rechab coming to meet him. And he saluted him and said, 'Is thine heart right, as my heart is with thy heart?' And Jehonadab answered, 'It is.' 'If it be, give me thine hand.'

Wesley's aim in the sermon is to concentrate on the irreducible minimum agreement needed between professing Christians in order for them to live, love and work together. The hope is that the debate can be transferred from disagreement about 'opinions' to agreement about the practical way in which we love God and each other.

At the beginning of the sermon he makes it clear that we owe a particular love to those who love God. We may not think the same things that others do but we may still love them as Christ loves us. All men will not see things alike. This same point is made in Sermon 20, *The Lord our Righteousness*:

> But still, though their opinions as well as expressions may be confused and inaccurate, their hearts may cleave to God through the Son of his love, and be truly interested in his righteousness.[10]

Wesley goes on in the *Catholic Spirit* to say that amongst Christians there will be various ways of worshipping God and no person can be obliged to prefer one congregation or one manner of worship against his conscience. Wesley quotes the rule that place of birth determines our religion, a rule proposed by John Locke, which he then strenuously opposes:

> Not the least of which is that if this rule had took place, there could have been no Reformation from Popery, seeing it entirely destroys the right of private judgement on which that whole Reformation stands.[11]

Wesley continues with what amounts to a minimum credal statement, though the emphasis is less on orthodox doctrine than upon 'experimental religion':

> Is God the centre of thy soul? The sum of all thy desires? Art thou accordingly 'laying up' the 'treasure in heaven' and 'counting all things else dung and dross'? . . . Is 'thine eye single' in all things? Always fixed on him? Always 'looking unto Jesus'?

In the second section of the sermon Wesley works out what 'give me thine hand' means. It does not mean 'be of my opinion', nor 'embrace my modes of worship'. It does mean love me as a friend who is closer than a brother, 'a fellow citizen of the new Jerusalem, a fellow soldier engaged in the same warfare, under the same Captain of our salvation'. It means, commend me to God in all your prayers, provoke me to love and good works by telling me of my faults and making me more fit for the Master's use. It means, finally, join with me in the work of God, as far as you can in conscience. This early expression of the 'Lund principle' of 1952 is unusual in ecumenical history before the twentieth century. It will be remembered that the World Council of Churches Conference on Faith and Order asked this question of the Churches:

> Should not our Churches ask themselves whether they are showing sufficient eagerness to enter into conversation with other Churches and whether they should not act together in

all matters except those in which deep differences of conviction compel them to act separately?[12]

Wesley had clearly posed the Lund question as early as 1755.

Having made his main points about the catholic spirit, Wesley had to guard against its misinterpretation. It does not imply 'speculative latitudinarianism', by which he means having no fixed doctrines and halting between two opinions. Nor does it imply 'practical latitudinarianism', an indifference to public worship and its performance. The man of catholic spirit is fixed in his congregation and not indifferent to congregations. Wesley would presumably have been unhappy with modern 'ecumenical' Christians who seem to belong to no particular denomination or worshipping community but float indifferently between congregations. The person with a truly catholic spirit is a firm adherent to the form of worship he believes to be most acceptable to God, he is united to one particular congregation, and yet his love goes out to all people, neighbours and strangers, friends and enemies. This is true catholic love, this is a true catholic spirit.

It is tempting to ask whether Wesley would have included Roman Catholics within this description of those with a catholic spirit. There are indications that he might not have done so. After all, he says in his *Popery Calmly Considered* of 1779 that, although members of that Church have been holy, their very principles undermine holiness. Idolatry destroys the love of God, persecution of others destroys the love of neighbour, officious lies and the possibility of absolution destroy the love of truth. However, earlier in 1770 he had expressed himself somewhat differently. He was preaching on the death of George Whitefield, claiming that Whitefield was a man of truly catholic spirit. He suggests that his hearers might take a lesson from their dead brother:

> 'O yes', says one, 'I have all this love for those I believe to be children of God. But I will never believe he is a child of God who belongs to that *vile congregation!* Can he, do you think, be a child of God who holds such *detestable opinions?* Or he that joins in such senseless and superstitious, if not idolatrous

worship?' So we justify ourselves in one sin by adding a second
to it! We excuse our want of love in ourselves by laying
the blame on others. To colour our own devilish temper we
pronounce our brethren children of the devil ... Go and learn
that truly catholic love which 'is not rash or hasty' in judg-
ing; that love which 'thinketh no evil', which 'believeth and
hopeth all things'; which makes all the allowances for others
which we desire others should make for us. Then we shall
take knowledge of the grace of God which is in every man,
whatever be his opinion or mode of worship.[13]

The use of the words 'superstitious' and 'idolatrous' seemed to
indicate that even Roman Catholics must be within the company
of those possessing the true catholic spirit. Wesley thought that
Fénelon, the Archbishop of Cambrai, clearly had it:

We have not much more to do with the members of the
Church of Rome [than with heathens, Mahometans and Jews].
But we cannot doubt that many of them, like the excellent
Archbishop of Cambrai, still retain, (notwithstanding many
mistakes) that faith that worketh by love.[14]

Two further quotations from his sermons may help to
reinforce the conclusion that Wesley was on the whole positive
about members of the Church of Rome and their catholic spirit.
The first is from the sermon *Of the Church*:

I dare not exclude from the church catholic all those congregations in which any unscriptural doctrines which cannot be
affirmed to be 'the pure word of God' are sometimes, yea
frequently, preached. Neither all those congregations in which
the sacraments are not 'duly administered'. Certainly if these
things are so the Church of Rome is not so much a part of
the catholic church; seeing therein neither is 'the pure word
of God' preached nor the sacraments 'duly administered'.
Whoever they are that have 'one Spirit, one hope, one Lord,
one faith, one God and Father of all', I can easily bear with
their holding wrong opinions, yea, and superstitious modes of
worship. Nor would I on these accounts scruple to include
them within the pale of the catholic church.

Wesley adds the following, which will certainly raise a smile in another period than his:

> Neither would I have any objection to receive them, if they desired it, as members of the Church of England.[15]

The second source is the sermon *On Faith* where Wesley, speaking of Catholics, says:

> If most of these are volunteers in faith, believing more than God has revealed, it cannot be denied that they believe all which God has revealed as necessary for salvation. In this we rejoice on their behalf: we are glad that none of these new articles which were added at the Council of Trent to 'the faith once delivered to the saints' does so materially contradict any of the ancient articles as to render them of no effect.[16]

In a letter to Rev. Mr Clarke written on 3 July 1756,[17] Wesley replies to a letter he had received concerning the *Catholic Spirit*. Orthodoxy, he writes, is a slender part of religion. Even a child of the Devil could be orthodox! The essential point is scriptural Christianity, all 'opinions' being 'things indifferent' for Wesley. In the letter to Clarke Wesley makes a point that we have already mentioned: 'heresy' in the New Testament does not mean 'an error in fundamentals' but something like 'opinions'. Therefore, the anathemas and excommunications in the history of the Church for 'heresy' are really a blot on that history.[18]

In a letter to a Gentleman at Bristol on 6 January 1758 Wesley enters the realm of controversy over 'opinions' again.[19] The letter was meant to guard against salvation by works on the one hand and Antinomianism on the other.[20] Wesley is responding to *A Seasonable Antidote Against Popery*, presumably a tract written against the Bristol Methodists, though there are few details offered in Wesley's letter. Wesley begins by accepting the principles of the Church of England: justification through faith in Christ; the evidence of conversion in our lives; the fruits that show that we have been justified. The letter is of interest to us when Wesley objects that justification by works is not the fundamental doctrine of Popery. The fundamental doctrine is the universality of the Roman Church and the supremacy of the

Bishop of Rome. The place of works in the scheme of salvation is one that would create much discussion in Methodism later on. Wesley was anxious in this letter not to concede too much to the ultra-Protestants by giving no place to works in this theology.

The other works of Wesley described here conform by and large to the pattern of his views described elsewhere in this book. We see again the abhorrence of the system of seven sacraments as being against the teaching of Scripture, the rejection of transubstantiation, the difficulties raised by the Catholic doctrine of merit, the practice in Catholicism of idolatry and persecution. But alongside the rejection of such things as the Papacy and purgatory there is the desire not to unchurch all catholics and the plea that 'opinions' need not divide Christians. It is small wonder that those concerned with ecumenism in our century have been more interested in the Wesley of the *Catholic Spirit* rather than the Wesley of the letter to the *Public Advertiser.*

16

Catholics and Other Methodists

There is little evidence that the early Methodists in the British Isles knew much about the Roman Catholic Church, with the notable exception of their knowledge of Ireland where, as Crookshank suggests, some eight-elevenths of the people were Catholic.[1] If the contacts of the Methodists with the Catholics were meagre in England and Wales yet frequent in Ireland that does not mean that many of their contacts there were fruitful in conversions. Charles Wesley in 1748 suggests a possible reason for the paucity of conversions: 'A few of these lost sheep we pick up, but seldom speak of it, lest our own good Protestants should stir up the Papists to tear us to pieces.'[2] The converts from Roman Catholicism remained small in number and even dialogue with local priests was minimal, as Thomas Walsh's biographer complains: 'I do not find that from the time of his leaving their communion he had ever any settled, personal interviews with them, although, for the sake of their poor, ignorant people, for whom he had the tenderest compassion, he has frequently desired it; sometimes even in public.'[3] There are hints in the literature that some Irish priests may have been as poor and ignorant as their flocks and therefore incapable of dialogue even with the unordained Methodist itinerants.

In Ireland the early preachers experienced many hostile reactions to their preaching. Henry Moore's preaching in Cappoquin in 1783 to a large congregation, most of whom were Romanists, caused the local priest to take to his pulpit for the first time in twelve months. His sermon, which does not seem to have done much to inspire the local Catholics against Moore, included the line: 'O you brute beasts, you ought to be the greatest people in the world, as you are the only Church: and yet you are nothing but beasts.' The congregation were threatened with excommunication if they attended Moore's preaching: 'I will put out the candle upon everyone of you.'[4] Some two years earlier Moore had the temerity to preach at one of the annual celebrations in Downpatrick 'when he saw the infatuated multitude who loitered about the town when Mass was over'.[5] Moore had other interesting altercations with Catholics including one at Dublin in 1787 when he decided that open air preaching would be more persuasive than confining himself to local chapels. His attempt to preach to a large crowd of Romanists in Lower Abbey Street had the usual consequences; clods of dirt and rotten eggs were thrown, the preacher's chair was attacked and taken over by a drunken sailor who began to preach in his own way. The moral stories at the end of the day were two: the services were continued in that neighbourhood with great success, and the sailor was drowned attempting to reach his ship from the quay. After the prayers and the Lord's Prayer, a Catholic woman was heard to shout out, in exasperation at being short-changed, 'Where is the Hail Mary?'[6] The violence in this account was repeated on many occasions. George Story gives an account of a Popish gentleman who hired some men to pull him out of his pulpit.[7] Crookshank gives an account of a preacher, probably Thomas Halliday, who was waylaid by eight ruffians in the pay of a local magistrate, knocked down with sticks, his clothes cut to pieces. Naked, he was dragged by the hair to a pond and left to die.[8] Charles Graham was struck on the side of the head by a leading Papist in Sligo, egged on by the denunciations of the Methodists by the priests. Graham turned the other cheek and prophesied his assailant's early death. When he died eight days later, it is hardly surprising that 'from that time forward preachers and leaders passed to their appointments unmolested'.[9] Stories of this type abound in the literature of the early Methodist preachers and perhaps one from the life of George Whitefield can exemplify them all. Whitefield had decided to preach outside Dublin at Oxminton Green in July 1757. Having preached 'without much molestation; only now and then a few stones and clods of dirt were thrown at me',

Whitefield had to make his way through hundreds of Papists who barred his way. 'Vollies of hard stones came from all quarters, and every step I took a fresh stone struck, and made me reel backwards and forwards, till I was almost breathless, and all over a gore of blood.' Eventually he reached a minister's house whence a coach arrived to carry him through the mob in which he 'rid in Gospel triumph through all the oaths, curses and imprecations of whole streets of Papists unhurt, though threatened every step of the ground'.[10]

Catholics who listened to the Methodist preaching were sometimes made to do penance for having listened to 'a mad heretic', as in the case of those who heard Rev. James Creighton.[11] Charles Wesley had several brushes with Catholic priests in Ireland, most notably a priest at Athlone called Father Ferril. Ferril had organized a mob to murder the Methodists in an ambush outside Athlone on 11 February 1748. One of the Methodist company, John Healy, would have been killed but for the intervention of a poor woman who later died from her injuries. Charles and his group later visited the ground stained with blood and sang a hymn of triumph which included the following reference to Father Ferril:

> The idolatrous priest
> Their purpose had bless'd;
> And, armed with his zeal,
> And inspired with the tenderest mercies of hell,
> They rush'd on their prey,
> The victims to slay,
> And accomplish their doom,
> And offer us up to the Moloch of Rome.[12]

At Cork not only the Catholic clergy but even the Anglican clergy prevented their people from hearing Charles Wesley.[13] In the same place in August 1748 he was set upon in the street by a Romish priest for words that the priest said one of the preachers had spoken against him. Wesley's comment is interesting:

I tried to undeceive him; but he was too loud, and too fond of showing his learning, (as far as Latin went,) to hear reason. However, we parted without coming to blows.[14]

At Passage in the same month a local justice sent word to the resident priest that if he forbade his people from hearing Charles Wesley, he would shut up his Mass-house and send him to jail for a year at least. At Rathcormuck the Papists flocked to hear Wesley and the priest was so intimidated by the great people of that place that he did not dare to prevent his people hearing.[15] Wesley's normal attitude was to point out the hypocrisy of priests who prevented their people from hearing by using the threat of excommunication and yet themselves heard the Methodist preaching by stealth.[16]

> Cast up, cast up an iron road,
>   The stumbling-block remove,
> The sin that keeps them back from God,
>   And from Thy redeeming love.
> The hinderer of the world restrain,
>   The Babylonish beast,
> The men who sell poor souls for gain,
>   Or curse whom Thou has bless'd.[17]

Not all contacts with Catholics were as negative. When Walter Griffith preached at his parents' village of Clogheen he was listened to with great attention by the local Roman Catholics who suggested that he should preach in the Catholic chapel. Later on their priest declared war against the Methodists although this did not deter the people from coming again to hear Griffith.[18] At Kinsale all denominations claimed Charles Wesley, the Catholics in particular being his firm friends: 'The Presbyterians say I am a Presbyterian; the church goers, that I am a Minister of theirs; and the Catholics are sure that I am a good Catholic in my heart.'[19] In Dublin in 1747 he preached repentance to Catholics in their own terms using 'their own Kempis, and their own Liturgy . . . I advised them to go to their respective places of worship.'[20] Clearly here there is a positive view of the Roman Church since Charles does not suggest that Papists should leave their Church after coming to repentance. In the next year he met an intelligent Roman Catholic who was satisfied with the answers Wesley gave to his objections and was credited as being not far from the kingdom of heaven.[21] There is a marvellous cameo in the *Journal* for February 1748 where a Papist lad whistling a Methodist hymn is overtaken by Charles and later joins the Methodist people.[22] The ambiguity of the relationship between Catholics and Methodists in this period is probably best caught in the words of Christopher Hopper who, with several companions, found himself landed in 1756 some twenty miles from Cork. They were put up by a Papist farmer: 'We lodged that night in the midst of our enemies; but the Lord suffered no man to hurt us.'[23]

It might be expected that in England John Fletcher (1729–85), with his background in continental Protestantism, would have been one of the more antagonistic to the claims of Rome in his parish of Madeley. This indeed was the case and in 1762 he was forced to bring an action against Mr Haughton, a Papist, who had been at the head of a mob who threatened a small assembly at Madeley Wood. His reasons for bringing the action included the accusation that Haughton had been drunk, had cursed, disturbed Fletcher in his discharge of the labours of his ministry and shown disregard for the liturgy of the established Church.[24] Fletcher in late 1769 was forced to take a stand against the opening of a Mass-house in Madeley when even two of his 'poor ignorant Churchmen' were deluded into joining the Papists. His remarks are instructive: 'The priest at Madeley is going to open his Mass-house, and I declared war on that account last Sunday, and propose to strip the whore of Babylon and expose her nakedness tomorrow.' Benson's biography of Fletcher in 1804 remarked that because of his endeavours not a dozen Popish families were then to be found in the parish.[25] During a visit to France and Italy in 1770 Fletcher attended the sermons of the clergy and conversed with the most serious of them 'in order that he might know their sentiments concerning spiritual religion'. As late as 1781 we find him contemplating a visit to the South of France in order to convert the Papists.[26]

In *The Lives of the Early Methodist Preachers* there are
accounts of 41 itinerants in John Wesley's connection. Of these
just three are converts from Roman Catholicism: John Valton,
Matthias Joyce and Thomas Walsh, while a fourth, John Pritchard, had a Catholic mother. Matthias Joyce was born in Dublin
and was baptized and brought up as a Catholic. In 1773 he
heard Wesley preach and then read an account of the conversion
of Anthony Egan, a Popish priest, in which he discovered some
'abominable tricks made use of by the priests'.[27] John Valton
was born in London of French Catholic parents and was regular
in attendance at Popish chapels as he grew up, being for some
time an assistant at the altar. 'In this school I remained six
months, bowing to images of wood, and stone, and wax, and
imbibing the baneful potions of idolatry and superstition.'[28] At
Purfleet he met one of Mr Wesley's followers who taught him
the true way and eventually he sought the advice of John Wesley
himself. After his conversion he spent many hours in dialogue
with his own Catholic family in an attempt to bring them to
the truth. Thomas Walsh's biography is the longest of the 41
Lives, occupying most of the third volume. After a strong
grounding in Catholicism Walsh grew dissatisfied with some of
the answers offered to his questions, and began to read the
Bible. Charles Wesley captures this initial Catholic period:

> ... Thy grace had first prepared his heart,
>   Dispell'd the Babylonish gloom,
> And bid his early youth depart
>   The camp of Anti-Christian Rome.
>
> Drawn by a secret power, he flew,
>   (Nor stay'd to prop the Papal throne,)
> The truth determined to pursue,
>   And panting for a God unknown:
> By works of legal righteousness
>   He blindly sought the grace to obtain,
> But could not find the paths of peace,
>   But labour'd through the fire in vain.[29]

After his conversion he began to preach in 1750, when he was just twenty, often using the Irish tongue for the sake of his listeners. Walsh died at the early age of 28 and was celebrated in verse by Charles Wesley.

There are several other examples of conversions from Catholicism, none perhaps more amusing than one that took place during a Methodist meeting in the county of Wexford in Ireland. The society there had been pestered by a Popish mob who wanted to know what they did at their meetings. A Catholic contrived to get into a sack in the barn where the Methodists met in the hope that he would unlock the door to let the mob in. He was so charmed by the hymns and convicted by the prayers that the sack became a centre of bawling and screaming. His cries for mercy were the beginnings of the work of God in his soul.[30] Conversions were not always as quick as this one. Anne Devlin was converted to the Methodist cause in Fermanagh and then went again to Mass. Her ensuing melancholy was treated somewhat lightly by the local priest and bishop, but Anne's anguish only became worse. After hearing a Methodist sermon in 1711 she began a long haul back to set her soul at liberty. By 1774 she had decided to renounce Popery and was predictably told by her priest that none could be saved outside the Catholic Church. Her family's efforts to get her back to the true Church and even to have her married by force only led to her leaving home and wandering from place to place, until a Methodist woman gave her a home.[31]

The most famous convert in this period did not move from Catholicism to Methodism but from Methodism to Catholicism. Charles Wesley's son Samuel and his conversion to the Roman Catholic Church has already been discussed in relation to John Wesley. The reaction of Charles to the move seems to have been much less rational. That Samuel was already contemplating the leap is clear from a reference in a letter from Charles to his wife of 1778: 'Make him a living Christian, and he will never wish to be a dead Papist.'[32] Jackson suggests that the interest in Popery came from Mary Freeman Shepherd who invited Samuel to make an open avowal of his new allegiance. The blandishments of papal worship gave Samuel more scope and possibly greater remuneration for his music than he had within his own tradition.[33] It was suggested that Father O'Leary, John Wesley's correspondent, should inform Charles of his son's decision but this was not felt to be appropriate because of his priestly office. In the end the Duchess of Norfolk told Charles the news, to which he is said to have replied, in great agitation, no doubt with the thought of the financial implications for Samuel: 'Say, "the loaves and fishes," Madam! say, "the loaves and fishes!" ' Charles thoughts on the matter are best expressed in his poetry and he wrote many stanzas on the loss of his son to the Catholic Church. Here we offer three stanzas out of many that can be found in his complete works:

> 4. That poison of the *Romish* sect,
>   O let it not his soul infect,
>   With close serpentine art,
>   With bitter persecuting zeal;
>   But from those mysteries of hell
>   Preserve his simple heart.[34]

> 2. Thy power be in his weakness seen,
>   Nor let him the commands of men
>   Rashly mistake for thine,
>   Nor heed to lying wonders give,
>   Or legendary tales receive
>   As oracles divine.

> 3. Preserve, that he may never know
>   Those doctrines of the hellish foe
>   Which contradict thy word,
>   Subvert the truth of holiness,
>   Or supersede the work of grace,
>   The presence of his Lord.[35]

As we have indicated above, it is likely that Samuel returned to his father's beliefs and is said by Telford in consequence to have scorned the threat of excommunication.[36] During his Catholic period he composed a Mass setting for Pius VI for which he received the thanks of the Pope by the agency of the Vicar-

Apostolic of the London District, James Talbot. It is of interest
that in all his vicissitudes Charles could write:

> 2. Against the instrument of ill
>   O may I no resentment find,
>   No wrong, vindictive temper feel,
>   Unfriendly wish, or thought unkind;
>   But put the yearning bowels on,
>   The tender mercies of Thy Son.[37]

Thus the catholic spirit of his brother found itself also in
Charles.

The accusation of being Papists in disguise was often levelled
against the Methodists, specifically that they were intent on
remaining within the Church of England to destroy it from
within:

> They with the Church establish'd join,
> Its Pow'r the more to undermine.
> By Rule they eat, by Rule they drink,
> Do all things else by Rule but think.
> Accuse their Priests of loose Behaviour,
> To get more in the Laymens Favour,
> Method alone must guide 'em all,
> Whence METHODIST, themselves, they call,
> Here I [Satan] my Triumphs fix to come,
> And here shall thou fix thine, O Rome![38]

John Wesley was often accused of being a Jesuit yet there are
not many references to his followers being accused of the same.
One of the few is in Charles Wesley's *Journal* where John Healey
confessed that he had been a Jacobite before he had heard the
Wesleys. He was then accused by a Nottingham alderman of
being an old Jesuit.[39] In a satire of 1778 called *The Fanatic Saints;
or Bedlamites Inspired* the Methodist leaders were described as
'Sons of Loyola' and 'Bedlam-Popes' who used the confessional
of the Class Meeting to discover willing penitents and to keep
Jesuit-like control over Methodist members.[40]

During the long period of rumour before the Jacobite rebellion and during the rebellion itself the Methodists came under
heavy fire. As has been seen, Charles Wesley wrote to John
arguing against the formulation of a loyal address to George II,
against the Stuart succession, on behalf of the Methodists on
the grounds that such a document would seem to constitute the
Methodists as a sect rather than as a movement within the
Church of England.[41] Nevertheless, they were often linked with
the rebellion and thought to be on the side of the Pretender.
John Nelson was brought before an alderman at Nottingham
who accused Wesley and his followers of being the cause of all
the commotions in the land. Nelson simply asked in response,
'Sir, can you prove that one man who is joined to us did assist
the Pretender with either men, money, or arms?'[42] Charles
Wesley heard that a warrant was being drawn up which accused
him of being a Jacobite. The warrant called for 'information
against one Wesley, or any other of the Methodist speakers, for
speaking any treasonable words or exhortations, as praying
for the banished, or for the Pretender, etc.' Charles had to face
his accusers and as a result of his attack on their veracity the
charges melted away. His prayer 'for the banished' he pointed
out had not meant the Stuart usurper of the throne but all those
who were strangers and pilgrims on this earth who sought a
better country.[43] His hymns in this period speak of the difficulties of the time, 'Hymns for Times of Trouble', 'Hymns in Time
of Persecution' and 'Hymns to be Sung in a Tumult'. How
Charles felt about the rights of the Pretender can be readily seen
from a verse which celebrates God's past goodness to Protestant
England and then prays for an end of the invasion:

> 2. Thou in danger's darkest hour
>   Didst on our side appear,
>   Snatch us from the wasting power
>   Of *Rome* and Satan near:
>   Whom the winds and sea obey,
> Thou, Lord, Thy mighty arm didst show,
>   Chase the alien hosts away,
>   And stop the' invading foe.

But even if the worst should happen and the Stuart kings should reign again in England:

2. Destruction may come, The scourge may o'erflow,
   And bloodthirsty *Rome* Our country o'erthrow;
   May torture and burn us, But never can shock,
   But never o'erturn us Who stand on *the Rock*.

3. The waster of *Rome* Is now on his way,
   The lion is come To scatter and slay:
   Beyond his fierce power We run to the Lamb,
   And rest in the tower Of Jesus's name.[44]

Charles' hope was that the Romish Anti-Christ might never finally prevail in the kingdoms.[45] Yet even as late as July 1746 he was accused of bringing in the Pretender in the guise of James Waller and £100 was set upon his head.[46] For the Public Thanksgiving Day in October 1746 he wrote several hymns, including this one which exonerates him from any interest in the Catholic and Stuart succession:

Hymn III

1. Still let us in our rising song
   Pursue the wild rebellious throng,
   With tenfold rage and fury fired,
   With all the zeal of hell inspired,
   The sons of *Rome* and Satan see,
   And trace them to their destiny.

2. Bold they return to sure success,
   Whom all *the saints* conspire to bless,
   Supported by their friends *beneath*,
   In covenant with hell and death;
   And *Spanish* gold, and *Gallic* pride,
   And *Holy Church* is on their side.

3. See how they fly to set us free

From all our *northern heresy,*
Our feuds and grievances to heal,
And purge the land with northern steel,
Bring back to *their* infernal god,
And re-baptize us in our blood.

5. Lo! the audacious hopes of *Rome*
Rush headlong to their instant doom,
Slaughter and threats the aliens breathe,
Nor see the Lord of life and death,
Till struck with lightning from His eye,
They fear, they turn, they fall, they die!

6. How are the mighty fallen! dead!
Who fill'd our conscious land with dread;
Perish'd the keenest tools of war,
The crafty caught in their own snare,
And Anti-Christ robb'd of his plea,
His blind infallibility![47]

Other Methodists trod similar paths to that of Charles Wesley. William Grimshaw of Howarth aided the recruiting officers of King George II in 1745.[48] George Whitefield preached a patriotic sermon in Philadelphia at the end of the rebellion in August 1746 called *Britain's Mercies and Britain's Duty* which was published as a pamphlet in both America and Britain.[49]

The Class Meeting of the Methodists often gathered to it the accusation of being a kind of Catholic confessional. Thomas Taylor, an early itinerant, recognized that the people of Scotland were conservative in their Presbyterianism and would not take kindly to the confessionalism of the Class Meeting which reminded them of Catholicism.[50] In the same way, Thomas Walsh was insistent in his refusal to acknowledge any parallels between the Methodist Class Meeting and the Popish practice of auricular confession, a practice which had failed Walsh in his early years.[51] The Class Meeting was a spiritual conversation between fellow Christians and was not meant to extend to every thought, word, and action as Popish confession did.[52]

Methodism was not a device whereby the believer might sin, repent, be converted, sin again, and follow the same pattern over and over again as did the Catholics. Perhaps few clergymen of the Church of England went as far as the evangelical William Grimshaw in his restoration of the ancient rite of public penance. In the 1746 returns for the archdiocese of York only 171 out of 836 parishes recorded any acts of public penance and only three parishes were in double figures. One of these was Howarth where Grimshaw was incumbent with twelve public acts of penance for only 326 families. Baker reproduces some indications of the record of adultery and fornication which Grimshaw brought publicly against members of his flock.[53] Public penance in church was a great deal more than a confession in a Class Meeting and there is no doubt that Grimshaw would have been accused of being a crypto-Papist by many observers.

Charles Wesley was accused of being a 'fiddling priest'.[54] This reference is to the musical evenings his sons gave during which Wesley acted as not only the host but as the evangelical who enquired after the spiritual health of his guests. That his son Samuel was already associated with the Catholic Church could have given the air of crypto-Papism to the musical gatherings. Papism was also the cry when some of the ordained preachers associated with Mr Wesley gave out the communion bread and wine. They used only the words, 'The Body of our Lord Jesus Christ' and 'The Blood of our Lord Jesus Christ', missing out the rest of the qualifying words. This was an attempt to introduce a belief in transubstantiation said an author.[55]

There are several references to the Cork Riots of 1749 in the sources, specifically in Charles Wesley, though they hardly do other than repeat what is in John Wesley's *Journal*. Of more interest is the eirenical spirit of the *Letter to a Roman Catholic* and the question of the place of the catholic spirit in Wesley's followers. There is no doubt that something of it was there in the Wesleys' grandfather, Samuel Annesley. Newton quotes Daniel Williams' tribute to Annesley as one whose life was a rebuke to 'a narrow Sectarian Spirit', 'a Spirit that confineth Charity to a Sect distinguished from other Christians, by Customs or Opinions that are not essential to true Godliness, and is

embittered and enraged against all who differ from such Usages
and Opinions'.[56] Something of the same spirit lived on in grand-
son Charles whose hymn on 'Catholic Love' was appended to
his brother John's sermon on the *Catholic Spirit*:

> Forth from the midst of Babel brought,
>   Parties and sects I cast behind,
> Enlarged my heart, and free my thought,
>   Where'er the latent truth I find,
> The latent truth with joy to own,
>   And bow to Jesu's name alone.
>
> My brethren, friends, and kinsmen, these,
>   Who do my heavenly Father's will;
> Who aim at perfect holiness,
>   And all thy counsels to fulfil;
> Athirst to be whate'er thou art,
>   And love their God with all their heart.[57]

William Grimshaw also had a similar catholic disposition: 'I
assure you the partition wall of party and religious denominations are long ago utterly fallen down in me. I love all
denominations, and so far as I find them endued with the Holy
Spirit, to be taught of God, and worshipping Him inwardly and
outwardly, in spirit and in truth, adorning every circumstance
of life with all holy conversation and godliness.'[58] Even Pantycelyn of Wales is less than severe on the Catholics as he writes at
the end of *A View of Christ's Kingdom*:

> God will not judge the Indians, the Turks or the Chinese
> By standards unexpected of infidels like these,
> Nor Papists, whose strange Gospel is all they've ever heard,
> Like Protestants accustomed to hear God's Holy Word.[59]

A similar spirit is found in the Irishman, Thomas Walsh, who
had left the Church of Rome and yet could write:

> And now that I have left the Church of Rome, I nevertheless

declare, that I think there are many sincere souls among them. For I bear them witness that they have a zeal for God, though not according to knowledge. Many of them have justice, mercy, and truth; and may, (notwithstanding many errors in sentiment, and therefore in practice, through invincible ignorance,) since as is God's majesty, so is His mercy, be dealt with accordingly.

There have been, doubtless, and still are, amongst them, some burning and shining lights; persons who whatever their particular sentiments may be, are devoted to the service of Jesus Christ, according as their light and opportunities admit. And, in reality, whatever opinions people may hold, they are most approved of God, whose temper and behaviour correspond most with the model of His holy word.[60]

It is fascinating to find, firstly, the sentiments of John Wesley reproduced here, and, secondly, also the Catholic view of 'invincible ignorance' often used by the theologians from whose company Walsh had severed himself. John Wesley found the same 'catholic spirit' in George Whitefield and in his sermon on the death of his former friend preached in 1770 at the Tabernacle in Tottenham Court Road said:

He is a man of truly catholic spirit who bears all these continually upon his heart; who having an unspeakable tenderness for their persons, and an earnest desire of their welfare, does not cease to commend them to God in prayer, as well as to plead their cause before men; who speaks comfortably to them, and labours by all his words to strengthen their hands in God.[61]

Objections to Popish doctrines are found in many places in the early Methodists' works. Pantycelyn finds the true faith only in the line of the Reformation and its morning stars: John Hus, Jerome of Prague, Luther and Calvin. Disappointingly, there is no reference to early Catholic Christianity in Wales.[62] Benson in his *Life of Fletcher* offers the main themes of Fletcher's anti-popery sermon of late 1769: Tradition is added to the Scriptures; Papists worship the host and the saints; believe in many mediators; have a doctrine of merit; hold the Virgin Mary to be a source of grace; openly break the second commandment; pervert prayer by offering it to the saints, and corrupt the sacraments and marriage.[63] It is a comprehensive list of errors and is reproduced in many of the other early Methodist writings. Thomas Walsh complains that the Romish clergy have taken away the key of knowledge from their people by replacing the Scriptures with the traditions of men.[64] John Valton in the same way writes: 'But it is hard to convince the Papists. They always fly off from the Bible to the Church.'[65] Another main complaint of the Methodists against the Catholics concerned their doctrine of merit. John Valton discovered through the agency of a woman who had lent him Baxter's *Saints' Rest*, Rutherford's *Letters* and Law's *Serious Call* the papistical notions of merit that still floated in his mind, and that salvation was the free, unmerited gift of God. Until this time he had considered that leaving off grosser sins, acts of self-denial and 'some little charities' would be highly meritorious and blot out the handwriting that stood against him in the book of God.[66] Thomas Walsh, ruminating on the arguments against the Church of Rome urged on him by his friends, came to his own conclusion in September 1748 when these words of St Paul made a deep impression upon him that made him renounce the Catholic Church: 'If righteousness came by the law, then surely Christ is dead in vain' (Gal. 2:21). The doctrines of merit and works of supererogation were contrary both to reason and Scripture.[67]

The idea that personal confession to a priest could be a saving grace no longer held true for Valton. He had made a good confession as a boy at school in France and could only thank God that it had not stamped him forever as a Papist:

> Here I can once remember with pain and praise making auricular confession, and receiving the absolution and benediction of my confessor. What a mercy that all this had not irrevocably grounded me in the errors and principles of the Romish Church, and indelibly stamped me a Papist![68]

In a conversation with his father Valton observed the way in which the older man used the names of God and Christ in vain. How could he be assured of salvation while living in such gross sin; surely not because he belonged to the true Church.[69] At a hanging in Kilkenny Duncan Wright is amazed that Papists could die declaring their innocence. The secret is, he writes, because they have confessed their crimes to the priest and so received absolution, hence they believed themselves guiltless.[70] Thomas Walsh, in dialogue with a Catholic man in the Irish tongue, asked the man how he hoped to be saved. 'I have saved some money, to leave to some priest or friar, when I die, in order to procure for me the forgiveness of my sins . . .'. Walsh responded that no man could forgive his sins and that the gift of God could not be purchased with money.[71] There are several references in the literature where the doctrine of purgatory is attacked as a belief that makes people avoid the search for holiness without which no one will see the Lord (Heb. 12:14). Fletcher believes that the Romish purgatory is at least more severe than the Calvinistic notion that a sinful believer's last breath can blow away all the inward corruption that twenty to 40 years of faith, prayer, and sacraments could not remove. Purgatory is at least an awesome prospect: 'Those half-damned or a quarter-damned creatures must go through a severe discipline, and fiery salvation in the very suburbs of hell, before they can be perfectly purified.'[72] When John Nelson preached on the need to be holy on earth so that we might not be damned eternally, a lusty, red-faced gentlewoman exclaimed, 'I am a Papist, and believe I shall be cleansed in Purgatory'.[73] Walsh pointed out the contradiction in the doctrine of being cleansed beyond the grave when the means were all provided this side of the grave. Did not Scripture say, 'The blood of Christ cleanseth from all sin' (1 John 1:7)? If so, then there can be no need for purgatory; all sin is taken away, and there can be none remaining to be cleansed. Why do people defer the present opportunities for deliverance from sin and death under the pretence of some future means of purgation in the invisible world; the business of salvation is a *now* affair.[74]

John Fletcher was on the way to Rome with a friend in 1770 when they came to the celebrated Appian Way. Fletcher stopped the carriage as the ancient road into Rome began, refusing to ride over the ground where the apostle Paul had walked, chained to a soldier. He walked towards Rome with his hat off and his eyes raised towards heaven, thanking God for the truths which Paul had preached and praying for the revival of these truths in Italy.[75] Some eight years later he was once again in Rome going through the streets in a coach when he was informed that the Pope was coming. Fletcher was told that he would be required to kneel and that if he did not do so the crowd would probably assault him. He refused to kneel, regarding it as idolatrous. The coachman was terrified and turned aside into a side road. As the Pope passed, Fletcher felt constrained to bear a public testimony against the Anti-Christ, even though he could not speak Italian. Wesley comments, 'He could hardly refrain from doing it in Latin, till he considered that only the priests could understand him.'[76] It can only be speculated as to what Fletcher's comments might have been today if he could have seen the statue of the same Pope, Pius VI, now the nearest papal monument to the grave of St Peter. There are few other references to the Papacy in the literature, apart from the usual references to the 'Romish Anti-Christ'[77] and the interesting speculation in Thomas Coke that the Papacy would come to an end in 1866 (some 30 years after Wesley's suggested date of 1836).[78]

One of the very few references to Catholic saints comes again from Thomas Walsh when he resolves no longer to allow anybody to beguile him into worshipping saints and angels since he can find no authority in the Bible for invoking any saint or Apostle.[79] His biographer, James Morgan, remarks at the opening of his work that Walsh, if he had supported the interests of Rome rather than those of Jesus Christ, would have stood fair to be made a saint himself.[80] The general view of the Methodists towards the saints and the Virgin Mary was probably that of George Whitefield who in 1754 had the opportunity to see Catholicism in Lisbon: '... what engaged my attention most, was the number of crucifixes, and little images of the Virgin Mary, and of other real or reputed saints, which were placed almost in every street, or fixed against the walls of the house almost at every turning, with lamps hanging before them.' And his comment, 'every day I have seen or heard something, that hath had a native tendency to make me thankful for the glorious reformation'.[81]

Perfect love or sanctification was one of the main tenets of early Methodist preaching and it seems clear from the accounts that several Methodists attained the grace of Christian perfection. In the year 1759 Thomas Walsh and John Wesley examined the London Society on their profession of being fully sanctified. If the number of 652 in London seems to be an exaggeration, it has to be remembered that Walsh and Wesley were by no means the most lenient of examiners.[82] Walsh himself was regarded as truly perfected by many of the Methodists and even by Robert Southey. John Fletcher was another who had reached such a state that even his own wife had no reservations about it.

Evidence for the use of Catholic spirituality amongst the early Methodists is somewhat limited. Susanna Wesley we know to have used Lorenzo Scupoli's *Spiritual Combat* in the version by Castaniza. The Wesley brothers knew the book and it was certainly used by George Whitefield along with à Kempis and the Greek New Testament: 'Every day God made me willing to renew the combat . . .'.[83] Though Charles Wesley is often claimed as sympathetic to the Catholic mystical writers,[84] there is also better evidence that he was critical of them, perhaps even more so than his brother, as is indicated in the preface to *Hymns and Sacred Poems* of 1739:

> Some verses, it may be observed, in the following Collection, were wrote upon the Scheme of the Mystick Divines. And these, 'tis owned, we had once in great Veneration, as the best Explainers of the Gospel of CHRIST. But we are now convinced that we therein greatly err'd: not knowing the Scriptures, neither the Power of GOD.[85]

The errors of the mystical writers were, that they used their inward righteousness as a ground for acceptance by God, and chose solitude and not the congregation, rather than the foundation of Jesus Christ. The writers that appear to have been most quoted by the Methodists from the Catholic sources are Blaise Pascal and de Renty. Charles Wesley for example uses Pascal's prayer for conversion on behalf of his sister Kezia in

1737 and his mother Susanna uses Pascal's language: 'To know God only as a philosopher; to have the most sublime and curious speculations concerning his essence, his attributes, his providence . . . will avail us nothing, unless at the same time we know him experimentally . . .'.[86] The life of de Renty was probably read by Hester Ann Rogers and there is a letter in her biography asking whether she has experienced what Mr de Renty called 'an experimental verity, and a plenitude of the presence of the ever blessed Trinity'. Mrs Rogers indicates that she can answer the question in the affirmative.[87] Mrs Mary Tatham, an early Methodist in Nottingham, wrote that she had read an original life of the Marquis de Renty.[88] Although there is little doubt that Wesley's early itinerants and society members read widely, there are very few accounts of them having read the *Christian Library* and the Catholic authors there.

Thomas Coke was not one to flinch from using what he considered improper Popish practices at his parish of South Petherton in 1776. He used an 'ancient and rusty weapon', a section of canon law intended for the protection of Popish priests in the reign of Mary I, to replace the Psalms for congregational singing with Wesley's hymns.[89] William Grimshaw was brought up in Brindle, an area that had known Catholic practices for several centuries, including a visit from Edmund Campion in 1581, the work of consecutive priests of some worth, and the survival of much Catholic lore such as the ancient crosses used as resting places along the way to St Helen's Well.[90] Charles Wesley suffered greatly from the practices of Father Ferril, as has been noted above, and wrote against the practices of hermits and monks:

> Not in the tombs we pine to dwell,
> Not in the dark monastic cell,
> By vows and grates confined;
> Freely to all ourselves we give,
> Constrain'd by Jesus' love to live
> The servants of mankind.[91]

George Story had read the Bible through several times by his sixth year and had also read the *History of the Sufferings of the Protestants in the Valleys of Piedmont*. How much a six-year old would understand of this is debatable, yet he states that this reading 'fixed in me an aversion to the principles of the Church of Rome'.[92] George Whitefield, on his way to America, was in Lisbon for Holy Week in 1754 and was able to see some Catholic practices at first hand which he set down in *A Brief Account of some Lent and Other Extraordinary Processions and Ecclesiastical Entertainments Seen at Lisbon*. He described a procession of some two hundred penitents in white linen with holes for their eyes, bare footed and some with chains on their ankles, others with stones on their backs and with skulls and bones in their hands, some with large heavy crosses on their shoulders and some flagellating themselves as they went along. His response to this display was: 'Never did civil and religious liberty appear to me in so amiable a light as now. What a spirit must Martin Luther and the first Reformers be endued with, which dared to appear as they did for God!' After a service in the cathedral at which a statue of Christ was venerated he remarked that he was 'not a little affected, to see so many thousands led away from the simplicity of the gospel, by such a mixture of human artifice and blind superstition, of which indeed I could have formed no idea, had I not been an eye-witness'.[93]

John Nelson had an interesting confrontation with a Roman Catholic who had suggested to him that all other sects and parties should be condemned as there was but one true Church, the Church of Rome. Nelson argued that the Catholic did not belong to the true Church but the synagogue of Satan because he continued to curse, swear and break the Sabbath. A little later he had a similar argument with a Catholic whom he accused of damning his soul with cursing and swearing.[94] When a gentleman Papist some time later brought a group to mob Nelson with the cry, 'Knock out the brains of that mad dog', the Methodist preacher was confirmed in his attitude to Catholics.[95] On the other hand we set a positive experience when John Nelson describes an incident at Easingwold in Yorkshire when the head man of the town, a professed Papist of good character, asked him many questions and was shown the fruits of justifying faith that are needed if people are to escape the damnation of hell. Nelson was amazed to find such an honest and God-fearing man among the Papists.[96] Thomas Walsh, as a convert from Roman Catholicism, had a prayerful comment about Catholic practices which sums up the problems that the Methodists saw in all that Catholics did and thought: 'I beseech Thee, therefore, eternal God, show Thy tender mercies upon those poor souls who have been long deluded by "the god of this world", the Pope, and his clergy.'[97]

That many of Wesley's contemporaries and helpers lived in the faith of a deliverance here on earth is not to be doubted. Perhaps just one might serve for all the rest, although he died in 1802, a little beyond our period. As Christopher Hopper lay dying he was visited by a fellow itinerant Charles Atmore to whom he said these words:

> You and I often met; and this will be our last meeting on earth. But we shall meet in our Father's house above ... I have not a doubt, – no, not the shadow of a doubt; and as for the enemy, I know not what is become of him. I have neither seen him, nor heard of him, for some time. I think he has quitted the field.[98]

But what of the Papists who were constantly criticized for their false doctrines and wicked practices by the early Methodists? It might be thought that the Methodists would be content to leave them to go to hell, yet in the hell of the Gordon Riots of 1780 they found a friend in Charles Wesley. Charles had refused to sign the petition of the Protestant Association against the 1778 Catholic Relief Act. This had caused him to be proscribed as a Popish priest. Yet his concern and the concern of the London Methodists was clear:

> Imagine the terror of the poor Papists ... I preached peace and charity, the one true religion, and prayed earnestly for the trembling, persecuted Catholics. Never have I found such love for them as on this occasion; and I believe most of the society are like-minded.[99]

Conclusion

Some kind of apologia is needed for the title of this book. Both the terms 'Papist' and 'Methodist' are of course polemical words used in the context of the eighteenth century. But even in our own day we still have many instances of them being used without real understanding. My wife's Uncle Ben was a very old Anglican minister from the south of Ireland, living in retirement in Sussex with his daughter. We went to see him after I had come back from a year in Rome looking at the theology of the two Vatican Councils. When Uncle Ben asked me where I had been I told him in all innocence. From the depths of his two inch clerical collar he spat out 'Ugh, Papists!'. I didn't think that our dialogue that afternoon would have been very fruitful. I have on my desk at the moment a letter from a Roman Catholic in Eire complaining about a pamphlet drawn up by Michael Jackson and myself on the Roman Catholic/Methodist international dialogues. My correspondent seems to know all that Methodists believe and how far away they are from the true Church. Methodists I am informed do not believe in the Eucharist except in the sense of a bare memorial. I replied with a couple of lines from a Charles Wesley hymn that we had recently sung at a Eucharist in our college chapel, words that appear at the end of the hymn 'Victim divine, Thy grace we claim':

> To every faithful soul appear
> And show Thy real presence here.

That there still exist prejudices on both sides of the Protestant–Catholic divide is one of the reasons why this book was written.

In the eighteenth century there were some who believed that the Methodists were in fact very close to the Catholics. Bishop Lavington of Exeter produced a curious book in 1747 called *The Enthusiasm of Methodists and Papists Considered* (Wesley in his response called it *The Enthusiasm of Methodists and Papists Compar'd*). John Wesley wrote several letters about this book disclaiming any similarities, but the accusations show that the two nicknames were often associated. The term 'Methodist' has of course stuck while the term 'Papist' has been relegated on the whole to the polemical past.

It is embarrassing to realize just how wrong John Wesley was on the subject of Roman Catholicism and how prejudiced he was when he met it. Historical knowledge concerning the condemnation of Hus was not well understood in his day and O'Leary's comments on the matter were relevant. Wesley's understanding of Catholic doctrine was by and large taken from Bishop John Williams' work of the previous century, when polemic against Catholics was part of the atmosphere of the reign of James II. It is a pity that Wesley's misrepresentations were not fully answered until the next generation, principally by Gilbert and Mason. The death of the Papacy predicted for 1836 by Bengel and lifted by Wesley into his *Explanatory Notes on the New Testament* is another embarrassment, especially when the *Notes* are meant to be a standard of preaching and belief within the Methodist Church of Great Britain.

So many of the misunderstandings came about because Wesley and his followers hardly met Catholics and even when they did found that confrontation rather than dialogue was the order of the day. It is tempting to compose a dialogue between Challoner and Wesley on the matters that divided them. That they might well have had some major agreements on the doctrine of Justification was for me an important discovery in this work. The parallels between Challoner and Wesley are illustrative of what might have been. I have often wondered why Challoner made a new translation of *The Christian's Pattern* or *The Imitation of Christ* by Thomas à Kempis in order to prevent his people from reading Wesley's translation produced in 1735. When I found a copy of the 1735 work I realized why it was that ordinary Catholics thought it to be a sound work: the frontis-piece is an engraving which shows a crucifixion scene that could have been taken from any Catholic work of the same period. Challoner's people probably did not see from the appearance of the book any need to beware of the author.

Wesley's views on Catholics have perhaps too often been classified in terms of the eirenical *Letter to a Roman Catholic* of 1749 in the wake of the Cork Riots. Alongside this can be set his sermon on the *Catholic Spirit* and his use of Catholic authors in the *Christian Library*. As this book has shown, the eirenical Wesley is more often replaced by the polemical Wesley. His followers were similar and if anything show a slightly more combative spirit against anything or anybody Catholic. Even Charles Wesley's eirenical disposition is put severely to the test when his son Samuel is received into the Catholic Church. John's letters to Samuel are the work of a wise uncle but of course Samuel was not his son. His remarks to Samuel about the validity of Christian experience whether from the Rome of Bellarmine or the Wittenberg of Luther are worthy of placarding as an ecumenical contribution of the highest order.

A recent publication from the Protestant Truth Society, edited by Oliver Beckerlegge, has extracts from the writings of John Wesley on Catholicism. The extracts make depressing reading when taken together, since when viewed as a whole his writings are anti-Catholic and this has to be accepted as typical of a non-ecumenical age. What makes his writings interesting for our time is his interest in the core of the Christian experience. When 'heart speaks to heart' (the motto of John Henry Newman and the title of a recent book by John Newton) the Christian faith can be found even in those areas where doctrine seems to be totally divisive. So Gregory Lopez and the Marquis de Renty seem to Wesley to have the core of the Christian experience. Archbishop Fénelon, Madame Guyon, Blaise Pascal and Brother Lawrence can show us the way to heaven as well as Richard Baxter, Jeremy Taylor and William Law. I like to think that when John Wesley died in 1791 he found himself in the same heaven as Richard Challoner who had gone there some ten years before. As polite men they will have initially regretted that they never met and apologized for their misrepresentations of each other's positions. But it will be bliss for them to be speaking the same language and uttering the same praises of the God who was utterly real for both of them on earth and is now seen face to face.

Appendix A

Penal Laws Against the English Catholics

Copy of Eighteenth Century Manuscript of the Penal Laws Against the English Catholics, from the Archive of the Venerable English College in Rome

By the 5th of Eliz. Cap 1°: whoever shall maintain the Jurisdiction of the Bishop or See of Rome within the Queen's Dominion, Incurrs a Praemunire.

By the 13th of Eliz. Cap 2°: whoever shall Sue for, obtaine or put in Use Bulls of Absolucon or Reconciliacion from the Bishop of Rome, or absolve or be absolved thereby They and their Accessaryes before the fact, shall be adjudged guilty of High Treason.

By 23d of Eliz Cap 1°: Any person having or pretending to have power or to put in practice to absolve perswade or withdraw any from their Obedience to her Majesty or withdraw them for that Intent from the Religion Established to the Romish Religion, and persons who shall be soe withdrawn their procurers and counsellors guilty of High Treason.

A person saying Mass, forfeits two hundred Marks, and shall suffer one years Imprisonment and untill the Fine be paid.

A person hearing Mass forfeits 100 Marks and one years Imprisonment.

One not Repairing to Church according to 1° of Eliz Cap 2° forfeits £20 for every Month he is absent.

By 27th Eliz Cap 2°: Jesuits, Seminary Priests and other Ecclesiasticall persons borne in these Realms and Ordained by the pretended Authority of the See of Rome coming into or remaining in the Queen's Dominions are Guilty of High Treason.

The Receivers Aiders and Maintainers knowing them to be such Guilty of felony without benefitt of Clergy.

All persons brought up in Seminarys beyond Sea and not in Orders not returning within Six Months after Proclamacon in London, and within two days after their return not Submitting and not taking the Oath of Supremacy Guilty of High Treason.

Giving Carrying or Sending Relief to any Ecclesiasticall person or Seminary beyond sea Guilty of a praemunire.

By the 29th of Eliz: Recusant Charging or Incumbring his Estate to prevent Seizures or forfeitures

Such Charges and Incumbrances as against the Crown are void.

Ever Recusant absenting from Church in such of the Terms of Easter and Michas as shall first happen next after Conviction. The Crown may Seize all his goods and two thirds of his Lands and Leases for the fforfeitures of the £20 per month then due, and afterwards halfe yearly for the fforfeitures of £20 per month, without any fresh conviction untill he comes to Church.

By 35th Eliz Cap 1°: If anyone above sixteen years of age shall be convicted of absenting himselfe from Church one Month without lawfull Excuse and Impugn the Queens authority in Causes Ecclesiasticall He shall be Committed to prison, and there remaine until he Conforms himselfe.

By 35th Eliz Cap 2°: A Popish Recusant above Sixteen years of age who does not within 40 days after his convicion Repair to his Dwelling and remain there (not going 5 miles from thence)

fforfeits all his goods absolutely, His Lands and Annuityes during his life.

If such convict, have not Lands of 20 Marks per annum shall abjure the Realm And not departing this Realm within the time Limitted by the Justices or the Coroner, or returning without Licence

Adjudged a ffelon without Benefitt of the Clergy.

Marryed Women are Included in this Act Save in the Clause relating to Abjuring the Realm.

By 1st Jac 1st Cap 4th: If the Heir of a Recusant who shall be under 16 at the death of his Ancestor shall after the age of 16 become a Recusant

His Lands shall not be freed till he Conforme and take the Oath of Supremacy

And whosoever shall send a child or other person under their government beyond sea to the Intent to Enter into or be Resident in any popish Colledge or Seminary or to repair to the Same to be Instructed in popery, fforfeits £100.

Every person so passing or being sent in respect of him or herself only, and not in respect of his Heirs or posterity is disabled to Inherit purcase take, Have, or Enjoy any Mannors Lands Tenements Annuityes profitts Commodityes Hereditaments Goods Chattles Debts Diityos Legacyes or Summes of money within this Realm of England or any of his Majestyes Dominions.

Whoever shall keep a School out of the Universityes, Except a ffree School, or in some persons House that is noe Recusant, or by Licence of the Bishop or Ordinary

As well the Schoolmaster as the person retaining him shall forfeit fforty shills a day.

By 3rd Jac 1st Cap 4th: persons absolving or withdrawing any Subject from the Obedience of his Majesty or Reconciling them to the Pope, or moving them to promise Obedience thereto or to any other prince or State and the persons being soe absolved etc

shall be adjudged Guilty of High Treason.

persons not repairing every Sunday to some Church or Chappell forfeit 12d for every neglect

Harbouring such as absent themselves from Church for a month fforfeit £10.

By 3rd of Jac 1st Cap 5°: who ever within 3 days after the offence shall discover to a Justice of peace any one that harbours a popish priest or discovers any that has heard or said Mass

Shall have a Third part of the forfeiture, if it does not exceed £150 and then he shall have but £50.

Recusant Convict coming to court without Commission from the King or warrant from the privy Councill under their hands

Forfeits £100: to be Divided between the King and this discoverer.

If a popish Recusant Convict or Indicted or any other person absenting from Church for 3 months that shall remain in London, or 10 miles of this same shall not depart thence within 10 days after such convicion or Indictment. Such person shall forfeit £100

But this does not Extend to Tradesmen or such as have no other Habitacon but in London or 10 miles distance.

A Recusant Convict practising the Common or Civil Law physick or the Art of an Apothecary or being an Officer in any Court or bearing any Office among Soldiers or in a Ship Castle or Ffortress fforfeits £100 to be decided between King and prosecutor.

A Popish Recusant Convict (or anyone whose wife is such) unless he himself his servants and children of nine years old repair to Church once a month Disabled to executing public Office in the Common Wealth by himself or Deputy.

A marryed woman being a popish Recusant Convict, whose Husband
is not, if she does not Conforme one whole year before his death fforfeits
the issues and profitts of two parts of her Joynture and two parts of her
Dower and is Disabled to be an Executrix or Admatrix to her Husband
or to have any part of his Goods or Chattles.

A popish Recusant after Convicion untill he Submits and Conformes
Disabled as a person Excommunicate, Save that he may Sue for his Interest
in Lands not Seized into ye King's hands.

A popish Recusant patron of a Benefice: Disabled to present but the
University is to present in his Stead.

A popish Recusant Convict Disabled to be Executor Adm^r or Guardian.

Every marry woman being a popish Recusant Convict who shall not
Conforme 3 months after Conviction To be Committed to prison without
Bail till she Conformes unless her Husband will pay £10 per month to ye
King or yield him a third part of his Lands.

By 3rd Carl 1^{mi} Cap 2do: Whoever shall pass or go Convey or Send any
Child or other person beyond Sea to the Intent to Enter into, be Resident
or Trained up in any Convict College School or popish ffamily and shall
be there Instructed in the popish Religion or shall Convey or Send or
Cause to be Conveyed or Sent any Relief to such person or to the Relief
of such College &c

The persons soe Sending or Relieving &c and the persons sent being
thereof Convicted

Disabled to prosecute any Suit in Law or Equity, to be Guardian,
Executor or Admr or Capable of a Legacy or Deed of Gift, or to bear
Office, forfitt all their Goods and Chattles, and forfeit their Lands, Rents
Annuityes &c for life.

By the 25th Carl 2^{di} Cap 2°: Noe person whatsoever shall bear any
Office Civil or Military unless he first take the Oaths of Allegiance and
Supremacy and Receive the Sacrament of the Lord's Supper according to
the Usage of the Church of England & Subscribe the Declaracon following viz

I AB Doe declare that I doe believe that there is not any Transubstantiation in the Sacrament of the Lords Supper or in the Elements of
Bread and Wine at or after the Consecration thereof by any person
whatsoever.

By the 30th of Carl 2^{di} Cap 1ma: Every peer of England and Ireland
being 21 years of age and every of the Members of the House of Commons
who shall not take the Oaths of Allegiance and Supremacy and make and
Subscribe the Declaracon in this Act

To be adjudged a popish Recusant Convict disabled to hold any Office in England Ireland &c to Sitt in parliament or make proxy in the House of Peers, To Sue in any Court to Guardian, Exec^r or Adm^r or take any Legacy or Gift and to forfeit £500 for every offence to him that will Sue for the Same.

The Declaracon is as follows, viz

I AB Doe Solemnly and Sincerely in the presence of God profess Testify and Declare that I Doe believe that in the Sacrament of the Lord's Supper there is not any Transubstantiation of the Elements of Bread and Wine into the Body and Blood of Christ at or after the Consecracon thereof by any person whatsoever, and that the Invocation or Adoration of the Blessed Virgin Mary or any Saint and the Sacrifice of the Mass, as they are now used in the church of Rome, are Superstitious and Idolatrous. And I doe solemnly in the presence of God profess Testify and Declare that I doe make this Declaracon and every part thereof in the plain and Ordinary Sense of the Words, read unto me, as they are Commonly Understood by English Protestants without any Evasion Equivocation or Mentall Reservation whatsoever, and without any Dispensation already granted me for this purpose by the Pope or any Authority or person whatsoever, or without thinking that I am or can be acquitted before God or man or absolved of this Declaracon or any part thereof, altho' the Pope or any other person or persons or power whatsoever should Dispense with or annull the Same, or Declare that it was null and void from the beginning.

By ye 1st of W^m & Mary Sess 1° Cap 8th: Whosoever shall refuse the Oaths prescribed to be taken by this Act when lawfully Tendered To be committed to prison for 3 months, unless he pay down 40s or such lesser sume not under 5s as the persons Tendering them shall Sett.

And if at the End of 3 Months such person shall then again Refuse to take the said Oaths,

To be committed for 6 months, Unless he pay down such a Sume as the persons Tendering then require not Exceeding £10 nor under £5 and the Offender to be bound to his good behaviour & to appear at the next Assizes.

By the 11th & 12th of W^m ye 3^d Cap 4th: whosoever after the 25th of March 1700 shall apprehend a popish Bishop priest or Jesuit and Convict him of saying Mass or Exercising his ffunction within this Realm To receive of the Sheriff of the County for every suit Conviction £100.

Every popish Bishop priest or Jesuit who shall say Mass or Exercise this function, Every papist keeping school Educating or Breeding Youth for that purpose To Suffer perpetuall Imprisonment.

Persons Educated or professing the popish Religion, who shall not within Six Months after they Attaine the age of 18 take the Oaths of Allegiance and Supremacy and make the Declaracon in the 30th Carl 2° (called the Test)

Disabled (but not their Heirs or posterity) To Inherit or take any Lands Tenements or Hereditaments within this Kingdome by Discent Devise or Limitacon, and during such persons Lives, untill they take the Oaths and make the said Declaracon the next of Kin being a protestant to Enjoy his Lands &c without being accountable for the profitts, but shall not Committ Waste.

Every papist or person making profession of the popish Religion after the 10th of Aprill 1700

Disabled to purchase Lands in this Kingdome or any Profitts out of the Same.

N.B. By virtue of this clause papists are disabled to take Mortgages for money Lent or any Just Debt, The wives of papists, if papists Disabled to take Joyntures.

Appendix B

Letter to a Roman Catholic

Dublin
18 July 1749

My Dear Friend,

1. You have heard ten thousand stories of us, who are commonly called Protestants, of which, if you believe only one in a thousand, you must think very hardly of us. But this is quite contrary to our Lord's rule, 'Judge not that ye be not judged'; and has many ill consequences, particularly this – it inclines us to think as hardly of you. Hence we are on both sides less willing to help one another, and more ready to hurt each other. Hence brotherly love is utterly destroyed; and each side looking on the other as monsters, gives way to anger, hatred, malice, to every unkind affection, which have frequently broke out in such inhuman barbarities as are scarce named among the heathens.

2. Now, can nothing be done, even allowing us on both sides to retain our own opinions, for the softening our hearts towards each other, the giving a check to this flood of unkindness, and restoring at least some small degree of love among our neighbours and countrymen? Do not you wish for this? Are you not fully convinced that malice, hatred, revenge, bitterness, whether in us or in you, in our hearts or yours, are an abomination to the Lord? Be our opinions right or be they wrong, these tempers are undeniably wrong. They are the broad road that leads to destruction, to the nethermost hell.

3. I do not suppose that all bitterness is on your side. I know there is too much on our side also. So much, that I fear many Protestants (so called) will be angry at me too for writing to you in this manner, and will say, 'It is showing you too much favour; you deserve no such treatment at our hands'.

4. But I think you do. I think you deserve the tenderest regard I can show, were it only because the same God has raised you and me from the dust of the earth, and has made us both capable of loving and enjoying him to eternity; were it only because the Son of God has brought you and me with his own blood. How much more, if you are a person fearing God

(as without question many of you are) and studying to have a conscience void of offence towards God and towards man?

5. I shall therefore endeavour, as mildly and inoffensively as I can, to remove in some measure the ground of your unkindness, by plainly declaring what our belief and what our practice is; that you may see we are not altogether such monsters as perhaps you imagined us to be.

A true Protestant may express his belief in these or the like words.

6. As I am assured that there is an infinite and independent Being, and that it is impossible there should be more than one, so I believe that this one God is the Father of all things, especially of angels and men; that he is in a peculiar manner the Father of those whom he regenerates by his Spirit, whom he adopts in his Son as co-heirs with him, and crowns with an eternal inheritance; but in a still higher sense the Father of this only Son, whom he hath begotten from eternity.

I believe this Father of all, not only to be able to do whatsoever pleaseth him, but also to have an eternal right of making what and when and how he pleaseth, and of possessing and disposing of all that he has made; and that he of his own goodness created heaven and earth and all that is therein.

7. I believe that Jesus of Nazareth was the Saviour of the world, the Messiah so long foretold; that being anointed with the Holy Ghost, he was a prophet, revealing to us the whole will of God; that he was a priest, who gave himself a sacrifice for sin, and still makes intercession for transgressors; that he is a king, who has all power in heaven and in earth, and will reign till he has subdued all things to himself.

I believe he is the proper, natural Son of God, God of God, very God of very God; and that he is the Lord of all, having absolute, supreme, universal dominion over all things; but more peculiarly our Lord, who believe in him, both by conquest, purchase, and voluntary obligation.

I believe that he was made man, joining the human nature with the divine in one person; being conceived by the singular operation of the Holy Ghost, and born of the blessed Virgin Mary, who, as well after as before she brought him forth, continued a pure and unspotted virgin.

I believe he suffered inexpressible pains both of body and soul, and at last death, even the death of the cross, at the time that Pontius Pilate governed Judaea under the Roman Emperor; that his body was then laid in the grave, and his soul went to the place of separate spirits; that the third day he rose again from the dead; that he ascended into heaven; where he remains in the midst of the throne of God, in the highest power and glory, as mediator till the end of the world, as God to all eternity; that in the end he will come down from heaven to judge every man according to his works, both those who shall then be alive and all who have died before that day.

8. I believe the infinite and eternal Spirit of God, equal with the Father and the Son, to be not only perfectly holy in himself, but the immediate

cause of all holiness in us; enlightening our understandings, rectifying our wills and affections, renewing our natures, uniting our persons to Christ, assuring us of the adoption of sons, leading us in our actions, purifying and sanctifying our souls and bodies, to a full and eternal enjoyment of God.

9. I believe that Christ by his apostles gathered unto himself a Church, to which he has continually added such as shall be saved; that his catholic (that is, universal) Church, extending to all nations and all ages, is holy in all its members, who have fellowship with God the Father, Son and Holy Ghost; that they have fellowship with the holy angels, who constantly minister to these heirs of salvation; and with all the living members of Christ on earth, as well as all who are departed in his faith and fear.

10. I believe God forgives all the sins of them that truly repent and unfeignedly believe his holy gospel; and that at the last day all men shall rise again, every one with his own body.

I believe that, as the unjust shall after their resurrection be tormented in hell for ever, so the just shall enjoy inconceivable happiness in the presence of God to all eternity.

11. Now, is there anything wrong in this? Is there any one point which you do not believe as well as we?

But you think we ought to believe more. We will not now enter into the dispute. Only let me ask, if a man sincerely believes thus much, and practises accordingly, can any one possibly persuade you to think that such a man shall perish everlastingly?

12. 'But does he practice accordingly?' If he does not, we grant all his faith will not save him. And this leads me to show you in few and plain words what the practice of a true Protestant is.

I say, a true Protestant: for I disclaim all common swearers, Sabbath-breakers, drunkards; all whoremongers, liars, cheats, extortioners; in a word, all that live in open sin. These are no Protestants; they are no Christians at all. Give them their own name; they are open heathens. They are the curse of the nation, the bane of society, the shame of mankind, the scum of the earth.

13. A true Protestant believes in God, has a full confidence in his mercy, fears him with a filial fear, and loves him with all his soul. He worships God in spirit and in truth, in everything gives him thanks; calls upon him with his heart as well as his lips at all times and in all places; honours his holy name and his Word, and serves him truly all the days of his life.

Now, do not you yourself approve this? Is there any one point you can condemn? Do not you practise as well as approve of it? Can you ever be happy, if you do not? Can you ever expect true peace in this or glory in the world to come, if you do not believe in God through Christ, if you do not thus fear and love God?

My dear friend, consider: I am not persuading you to leave or change your religion, but to follow after that fear and love of God without which all religion is vain. I say not a word to you about your opinions or outward manner of worship. But I say, all worship is an abomination to the Lord, unless you worship him in spirit and in truth, with your heart as well as your lips, with your spirit and with your understanding also. Be your form of worship what it will, but in everything give him thanks, else it is all but lost labour. Use whatever outward observances you please; but put your whole trust in him, but honour his holy name and his word, and serve him truly all the days of your life.

14. Again, a true Protestant loves his neighbour – that is, every man, friend or enemy, good or bad – as himself, as he loves his own soul, as Christ loved us. And as Christ laid down his life for us, so is he ready to lay down his life for his brethren. He shows this love by doing to all men in all points as he would they should do unto him. He loves, honours, and obeys his father and mother, and helps them to the uttermost of his power. He honours and obeys the King, and all that are put in authority under him. He cheerfully submits to all his governors, teachers, spiritual pastors and masters. He behaves lowly and reverently to all his betters. He hurts nobody by word or deed. He is true and just in all his dealings. He bears no malice or hatred in his heart. He abstains from all evil-speaking, lying and slandering; neither is guile found in his mouth. Knowing his body to be the temple of the Holy Ghost, he keeps it in sobriety, temperance, and chastity. He does not desire other men's goods; but is content with that he hath, labours to get his own living, and to do the whole will of God in that state of life unto which it has pleased God to call him.

15. Have you anything to reprove in this? Are you not herein even as he? If not (tell the truth), are you not condemned both by God and your own conscience? Can you fall short of any one point hereof without falling short of being a Christian?

Come, my brother, and let us reason together. Are you right, if you only love your friend and hate your enemy? Do not even the heathens and publicans so? You are called to love your enemies, to bless them that curse you, and to pray for them that despitefully use you and persecute you. But are you not disobedient to the heavenly calling? Does your tender love to all men – not only the good, but also the evil and unthankful – approve you the child of your Father which is in heaven? Otherwise, whatever you believe and whatever you practise, you are of your father the devil. Are you ready to lay down your life for your brethren? And do you do unto all as you would they should do unto you? If not, do not deceive your own soul: you are but a heathen still. Do you love, honour and obey your father and mother, and help them to the utmost of your power? Do you honour and obey all in authority, all your governors, spiritual pastors and masters? Do you behave lowly and reverently to all your betters? Do you hurt nobody by word or deed? Are you true and just in all your dealings? Do you take care to pay whatever you owe? Do you feel no malice, or envy, or revenge, no hatred or bitterness to any man? If you do, it is plain you are not of God; for all these are the tempers of the devil. Do you speak the truth from your heart to all men, and that in tenderness and love? Are you an Israelite indeed, in whom is no guile? Do you keep your body in sobriety, temperance and chastity, as knowing it is the temple of the Holy Ghost, and that, if any man defile the temple of God, him will God destroy? Have you learned, in every state wherein you are, therewith to be content? Do you labour to get your own living, abhorring idleness as you abhor hell-fire? The devil tempts other men; but an idle man tempts the devil. An idle man's brain is the devil's shop, where is is continually working mischief. Are you not slothful in business? Whatever your hand finds to do, do you do it with your might? And do you do all as unto the Lord, as a sacrifice unto God, acceptable in Christ Jesus?

This, and this alone, is the old religion. This is true, primitive Christianity. Oh, when shall it spread over all the earth? When shall it be found both in us and you? Without waiting for others, let each of us by the grace of God, amend one.

16. Are we not thus far agreed? Let us thank God for this, and receive it as a fresh token of his love. But if God still loveth us, we ought also to love one another. We ought, without this endless jangling about opinions, to provoke one another to love and to good works. Let the points wherein we differ stand aside: here are enough wherein we agree, enough be the ground of every Christian temper and of every Christian action.

O brethren, let us not still fall out by the way. I hope to see you in heaven. And if I practise the religion above described, you dare not say I shall go to hell. You cannot think so. None can persuade you to it. Your own conscience tells you the contrary. Then, if we cannot as yet think alike in all things, at least we may love alike. Herein we cannot possibly do amiss. For of one point none can doubt a moment: God is love; and he that dwelleth in love, dwelleth in God, and God in him.

17. In the name, then, and in the strength of God, let us resolve, first, not to hurt one another; to do nothing unkind or unfriendly to each other, nothing which we would not have done to ourselves. Rather let us endeavour after every instance of a kind, friendly and Christian behaviour towards each other.

Let us resolve, secondly, God being our helper, to speak nothing harsh or unkind of each other. The sure way to avoid this is to say all the good we can, both of and to one another; in all our conversation, either with or concerning each other, to use only the language of love, to speak with all softness and tenderness, with the most endearing expression which is consistent with truth and sincerity.

Let us, thirdly, resolve to harbour no unkind thought, no unfriendly temper towards each other. Let us lay the axe to the root of the tree; let us examine all that rises in our heart, and suffer no disposition there which is contrary to tender affection. Then shall we easily refrain from unkind actions and words, when the very root of bitterness is cut up.

Let us, fourthly, endeavour to help each other on in whatever we are agreed leads to the Kingdom. So far as we can, let us always rejoice to strengthen each other's hands in God. Above all, let us each take heed to himself (since each must give an account of himself to God) that he fall not short of the religion of love, that he be not condemned in that he himself approveth. O let you and I (whatever others do) press on to that prize of our high calling: that, being justified by faith, we may have peace with God through our Lord Jesus Christ; that we may rejoice in God through Jesus Christ, by whom we have received the atonement; that the love of God may be shed abroad in our hearts by the Holy Ghost which is given unto us. Let us count all things but loss for the excellency of the knowledge of Jesus Christ our Lord; being ready for him to suffer the loss of all things, and counting them but dung, that we may win Christ.
I am,
Your affectionate servant, for Christ's sake,

John Wesley

Notes

1. The Roman Catholic Church in England in the Eighteenth Century

1. *Works of John Henry Newman – Sermons Preached on Various Occasions*, Christian Classics edition, 1968, p. 169.
2. *Ibid.*, pp. 171–2.
3. Burton, *The Life and Times of Bishop Challoner 1691–1781*, London 1909, I, p. xvii.
4. *Ibid.*, II, pp. 100ff.
5. *Ibid.*, II, pp. 37ff.
6. *Ibid.*, II, pp. 89ff.
7. JWJ II, 486.
8. JWJ III, 122.
9. Michael Williams, *The Venerable English College in Rome*, London 1979.
10. See *English Historical Documents Vol X, 1714–1783*, ed. Horn & Ransome, London 1957, pp. 406ff.
11. JWL VI, 340f.
12. See J. Bossy, *The English Catholic Community 1570–1850*, London 1975; H. Aveling, *The Handle and the Axe*, London 1976; E. Norman, *Roman Catholicism in England*, Oxford 1986.
13. See references in above note.
14. Hemphill gives the following sees amongst others: Adrumetum, Madaura, Marcopolis, Tiberiopolis.
15. Hemphill, *The Early Vicars Apostolic of England, 1685–1750*, London 1954.
16. See Burton, *op. cit.*, I, pp. 225, 243ff.
17. Hemphill, *op. cit.*, up to 1750.
18. See Anstruther, *The Seminary Priests*, Vol. IV, 1977, p. 6.
19. *Ibid.*, IV, p. 102.
20. *Ibid.*, IV, p. 303.
21. *Ibid.*, IV, p. 127–8.

22. See Burton, *op. cit.*, II, pp. 90ff.
23. Barnard, *Life of Challoner*, p. 156, quoted in Burton.
24. Magee, *The English Recusants*, London 1939. Chapter XI.
25. *Ibid.*, p. 207.
26. Bossy, *The English Catholic Community 1570–1850*, London 1976, pp. 182ff.
27. J. Berington, *The State and Behaviour of English Catholics from the Reformation to the year 1780*, London 1780; Burton op. cit.; Magee op. cit.
28. Bossy, *The English Catholic Community 1570–1850*, pp. 126–7, suggests that of three suggested cases, two will not stand up to investigation (Hazlewood and Carlton in the West Riding) and the other (Stonor in Oxfordshire) 'seems extremely hypothetical'.
29. Berington, *op. cit.*
30. Magee, *op. cit.*, p. 186.
31. Burton, *op. cit.*, II, pp. 252ff.
32. *Ibid.*, II, pp. 243ff.
33. The first three were in what is now W1, and about a third of a mile apart, the other three were in WC1, WC2 and SW1.
34. Burton, *op. cit.*, I, p. 138.
35. *Ibid.*, I, pp. 138ff.
36. *Ibid.*, I, p. 79.
37. *Ibid.*, I, pp. 373ff.
38. See picture published in 1784 by J. W. Coghlan of Duke Street.
39. Berington, *op. cit.*
40. JWL II, 35.
41. JWL VII, 204 note.
42. JWL VI, 340ff.
43. JWJ VI, 182.
44. Burton, *op. cit.*, I, p. 42.
45. Williams, *The Venerable English College in Rome*, London 1979.

2. John Wesley – Meeting Papists

1. See, for example, Ayling, S. E., *John Wesley*, London 1979; Edwards, M. L. in *A History of the Methodist Church in Great Britain Vol I*, ed. Davies and Rupp, London 1965; Green, V. H. H., *John Wesley*, London 1964; Heitzenrater, R. P., *The Elusive Mr Wesley*, Nashville 1984, 2 vols; Rack, H. E., *Reasonable Enthusiast*, London 1989; Schmidt, M., *John Wesley: A theological biography*, London 1962–73 (2 vols in 3); Wood, A. S., *The Burning Heart: John Wesley evangelist*, Exeter 1967.
2. JWJ I, 125. Other references to the Pattersons in JWJ I, 232, 267, 312.

3. JWJ I, 357–8.
4. JWJ II, 391.
5. *Ibid.*, 343.
6. JWJ III, 72.
7. Richard Challoner, *The Grounds of the Old Religion*, London 1810 edition. First edition 1742, anon.
8. JWJ III, 398–9.
9. *Ibid.*, 398.
10. JWJ V, 130.
11. *Ibid.*, 136.
12. *Ibid.*, 151.
13. Works IX, 224.
14. JWJ III, 464.
15. *Ibid.*, 467.
16. JWJ IV, 262.
17. JWJ V, 315.
18. JWJ IV, 262.
19. *Ibid.*, 269.
20. *Ibid*, 269.
21. *Ibid.*, 276.
22. *Ibid.*, 269.
23. *Ibid.*, 268.
24. *Ibid.*, 270.
25. JWJ VII, 274.
26. *Wesleyan Methodist Magazine*, 1828, pp. 741–2.
27. JWJ VI, 303.
28. JWL VII, 230ff.
29. JWL VIII, 218ff.
30. Telford, *Life of Charles Wesley*, London 1900, p. 298.
31. Works VIII, 321.

3. **Accusations of Popery**

1. JWJ VIII, 304f.
2. JWJ III, 122.
3. *Ibid.*, 125.
4. Second letter to Lavington, para. 48. JWL III, 329f.
5. JWJ V, 295ff.
6. *Ibid.*, 89.
7. JWJ III, 46ff, and JWL IV, 360.
8. JWJ II, 487.
9. Wesley, *A Plain Account of the People called Methodists*, WJW Vol. 9, ed. Davies, Abingdon, p. 268. Also *Works*, ed. Jackson, VIII, 259.

10. JWJ III, 190.
11. See R. Green, *Anti-Methodist Publications*, London 1902. Nos 312 and 335.
12. Wesley, Works VIII, 215.
13. Second letter to Lavington, para. 45. JWL III, 327.
14. JWJ III, 427.
15. JWL III, 326.
16. *Ibid.*, 145.
17. Elswhere, twelve – see *Farther Appeal*, Part III. WJW Vol. 11, ed. Cragg, p. 290. Works VIII, 215.
18. Letter to Rev. Mr Church, JWL II, 212ff. On this see also WJW Vol. 1, ed. Outler, p. 445f, for introduction to *The Lord our Righteousness* where the controversy with Hervey is described.
19. Letter to John Downes, JWL IV, 325ff.
20. Some of the martyrdoms of the English Catholic priests are set forth graphically on the gallery walls of the Chapel in the English College in Rome. They are not for the squeamish.
21. JWJ II, 262.
22. JWJ III, 404.
23. *Ibid.*, 390.
24. See R. Green, *Anti-Methodist Publications*, London 1902, Nos 422 and 458.
25. For example, 'Letter to Rev. Mr Baily of Kilcully', JWL III, 272ff.
26. Second letter to Lavington, JWL III, 326.
27. JWL III, 330.
28. Letter to Rev. Mr Fleury, 18 May 1771. *Works*, ed. Jackson, IX, 188.
29. Sermon 4, *Scriptural Christianity*, WJW Vol. 1, ed. Outler, p. 180 and note.
30. JWJ III, 130.
31. *Ibid.*, 129.
32. JWL II, 17; JWJ III, 123–4.
33. JWL II, 40–1; JWJ III, 211.
34. JWJ III, 191.
35. JWL II, 107.
36. JWJ III, 224.
37. *Ibid.*, 266.
38. See Green, *Bibliography*, p. 48.
39. JWL VII, 305.
40. JWJ IV, 14–15.
41. Sermon *Salvation by Faith*, WJW Vol. 1, ed. Outler, pp. 128–9.
42. JWJ II, 262.
43. JWJ V, 295, also JWJ II, 262 but quotation a little different.
44. JWJ V, 295.

4. The Cork Riots and the *Letter to a Roman Catholic*

1. 'Letter to Rev. Mr Baily of Kilcully', JWL III, 272–94, para. 14.
2. E.g., JWJ III, 263.
3. J. Walsh, *Studies in Methodism and the Mob in the Eighteenth Century*, in *Studies in Church History* 8, Cambridge 1972, pp. 213ff.
4. Letter to Baily, para. 19, 'Sir you shall find, the Mayor is King of Cork.'
5. JWJ III, 395–422.
6. *Ibid.*, 409.
7. *Ibid.*, 404.
8. *Ibid.*, 408, note.
9. *Ibid.*, 472.
10. See *A Plain Account of the People Called Methodists*, 1749. WJW Vol. 9, ed. R. Davies, p. 253ff. Works VIII, 248ff.
11. Editions in Wesley's lifetime published in 1749, 1750, 1755, 1773; also ed. Michael Hurley SJ (Geoffrey Chapman/Epworth House 1968). Another edition was published by the organizers of the Catholic/Methodist Conference in 1987 in Belfast.
12. For example, see *Anglicanism*, ed. P. More and F. Cross, London 1935. Francis White, Bishop of Ely (c. 1564–1638) in *A Treatise of the Sabbath Day* gives the perpetual virginity of Mary as a tradition of the Church, p. 132.
13. JWJ III, 464.
14. *Ibid.*, 471.
15. *Ibid.*, 474.
16. *Ibid.*, 477 note.

5. Toleration and The Gordon Riots

1. Quoted in H. Kamen, *The Rise of Toleration*, London 1967, p. 162.
2. Kamen, *op. cit.*, pp. 172–3.
3. *The Works of John Locke*, London 1801, Vol. VI.
4. Locke, *ibid.*, p. 28.
5. *Ibid.* p. 40. For Wesley, see JWJ III, 178ff. and JWJ V, 115 in which religious 'opinions' are discussed.
6. Locke, *op. cit.*, p. 45.
7. Sermon 39, *Catholic Spirit*, WJW 2, 81ff.
8. JWJ III, 180.
9. JWJ V, 116.
10. *Thoughts Upon Liberty*, Works XI, 38ff.
11. Sermon 107, *On God's Vineyard*, WJW 3, 503ff. The quote is also in *Thoughts Upon Liberty* in Works XI, 40.
12. Sermon 107, *On God's Vineyard*, WJW 3, 517.

13. JWJ VII, 389.
14. Sermon 127, *On the Wedding Garment*, WJW 4, 146.
15. N. Abercrombie, 'The First Relief Act' in *Challoner and His Church*, ed. E. Duffy, London 1981, p. 174.
16. Butler, *op. cit.*, p. 6, quoted in Abercrombie, p. 176.
17. Abercrombie, *op. cit*, p. 189, quoting Hansard.
18. See *Documents of British History*, Vol X, ed. Horn & Ramsome, London 1957, pp. 406–8.
19. See Abercrombie, *op. cit.*, p. 193.
20. JWL VI, 370ff.
21. Dickens, *Barnaby Rudge*, ch LXIX.
22. See e.g. JWL V, 351; JWL VII, 235; JWL VIII, 26 and *Word to a Drunkard*, Works XI, 169–71.
23. Dickens, *Barnaby Rudge*, ch XXXV.
24. Stevenson, *Popular Disturbances in England*, London 1979, p. 83.
25. *Dictionary of National Biography*, Vol. VIII, London 1908, pp. 197–8.
26. See Green, *Bibliography*, p. 202–3 for Letter to John Whittingham and refs. to the Gordon rioters and the innocence of the Methodists.
27. JWJ VI, 299–300.
28. Green, *Bibliography*, pp. 213–4.
29. JWJ VI, 301; JWL VII, 46f.
30. JWJ VI, 302.
31. *Arminian Magazine*, 1782, p. 199.

6. Keeping Faith with Heretics

1. JWJ, 18 Jan 1780, VI, 267.
2. See M. Spinka/Mladanovic, *John Hus at the Council of Constance*, New York 1965. M. Spinka, *Hus and the Doctrine of the Church*, New York 1967.
3. Some modern scholars have repudiated the association of Hus with Wycliffe's opinions. See *Unity, Heresy and Reform 1378–1460*, C. M. Crowder, London 1977, p. 87.
4. Twelve of the final list of thirty articles concerned the Papacy.
5. *A Word to a Protestant*, Works IX, 187ff.
6. *Ibid.*, 189.
7. Works VIII, 218.
8. Works X, 106.
9. Almost certainly wrongly dated in JWL VI, 370, as 12 Jan.
10. O'Leary, 'Remarks on Rev. John Wesley's Letters on the Civil Principles of Roman Catholics and his Defence of the Protestant Association' in *Miscellaneous Tracts*, London 1781. It consists of just 26 pages.

11. JWL VII, 4.
12. O'Leary, *Miscellaneous Tracts*, 4, p. 35.
13. *Ibid.*, p. 44.
14. *Ibid.*, p. 83.
15. JWL VII, 9ff.
16. D. Hempton, *Methodism & Politics in British Society 1750–1850*, London 1984, p. 52, note 65.
17. JWJ VI, 302: 'What a shocking insult upon truth and common sense.'
18. O'Leary, *Miscellaneous Tracts*, 5.
19. *Ibid.*, p. 308.
20. There is a copy of this in Wesley's City Road library.
21. Sermon 127, *On the Wedding Garment*, in WJW Vol. 3, ed. Outler, Nashville 1987, p. 145.
22. Address 20 May in 'Letter on Catholic Loyalty', pp. 14–22. Quoted in Joseph Chinnici *The English Catholic Enlightenment*, Shepherdstown 1980, p. 18.

7. John Wesley and Richard Challoner

1. Burton, *The Life and Times of Bishop Challoner*, I, p. 117.
2. JWL VIII, 65, 154, 271.
3. JWJ III, 512. His wife Molly died in 1781.
4. Works XI, 456ff.
5. *Considerations Upon Christian Duties, Digested into Meditations for Every Day in the Year*, Derby 1842, II, p. 261.
6. See e.g. JWL I, 183, 289; IV, 312; VII, 180, 193, 256, 259, 291, 301, 352.
7. JWL I, 136; JWJ II, 257.
8. JWJ IV, 140, 147, 243, 249, 258, 299, 366, 372, 418, 423, 434 Sc.
9. JWJ VII, 360.
10. Burton, *op cit.*, I, p. 299.
11. See Green, *Bibliography*, p. 68.
12. Works XI, 1–13.
13. Green, *Bibliography*, p. 10.
14. *A Christian Library*, 50 Vols, 1749ff.
15. Crichton, 'Richard Challoner, Catechist and Spiritual Writer', *Clergy Review* LXVI, 8.
16. *A Collection of Forms of Prayer for Every Day in the Week*, in *John Wesley's Prayers*, ed. Gill, London 1951.
17. *A Christian Library*, Vol. XXI.
18. See Green, *Bibliography*, p. 160.
19. See Burton, *op. cit.*, for individual works.
20. Works XI, 182ff, 187ff.

21. Works X, 129ff, 133ff, 86ff.
22. *Ibid.*, 140ff, 159ff.
23. *Ibid.*
24. Burton, *op. cit.*, I, p. 99.
25. JWL II, 312–388.
26. *Ibid.*, 388.
27. Burton, *op. cit.*, II, pp. 27–29.
28. Butler in Burton, *op. cit.*, I, pp. 82–83.
29. *The New Testament, with an Analysis of the Several Books and Chapters*, John Wesley, London 1790, p. 424. The book was not reprinted.
30. *Popery Calmly Considered*, Works X, 141.
31. For their work in London, see my 'Good News to the London Poor. A Comparison of the Philanthropy of John Wesley and Richard Challoner, the Vicar Apostolic of the London District', *Epworth Review*, Vol. 20, No. 1, 1994, p. 109ff.
32. J. Milner, *Life of Challoner*, p. 35, quoted in Burton, *op. cit.*, I, pp. 117–8.
33. Archives of the Archdiocese of Westminster, Folio 51.
34. Burton, *op. cit.*, II, p. 273.
35. *Think Well On't*, Richard Challoner.
36. Sermon 17, *The Circumcision of the Heart*, WJW 1, 408, also quoted in *A Plain Account of Christian Perfection*, London 1952, pp. 7–8.

8.   *A Caveat Against the Methodists*

1. Burton, *The Life and Times of Richard Challoner*, 2 vols, London 1909. JWJ IV, 434ff.
2. Burton, *op. cit.*, II, pp. 334–5.
3. JWJ IV, 434ff.
4. Challoner, *Caveat*, 3rd Ed., London 1787, p. 3.
5. Or at least, not many. In JWJ VI, 267, Wesley complains about the increase in Popery. He would have called this phenomenon 'conversion to an opinion', rather than true conversion.
6. *Caveat*, p. 5.
7. For a positive appreciation, see B. and M. Pawley, *Rome & Canterbury through Four Centuries*, London, 1974, pp. 58–60.
8. JWL, 25 June 1746.
9. JWJ, III, 72.
10. Sermon 39, *Catholic Spirit*, WJW Vol. 2, ed. Outler, p. 86.
11. Sermon 11, *The Witness of the Spirit II*, WJW 1, 285.
12. *Caveat*, p. 19.
13. Sermon 5, *Justification by Faith*, WJW 1, 187.

14. *Caveat*, p. 20.
15. See. e.g. Sermon 7, *The Way to the Kingdom*, WJW 1, 229.
16. *Caveat*, p. 21.
17. *Treatise on Baptism*, Works X, 192.
18. *Caveat*, p. 21.
19. Sermon 85, *On Working Out Our Own Salvation*, WJW 3, 207.
20. *Caveat*, p. 22.
21. Sermon 1, *Salvation by Faith*, WJW 1, 125.
22. *Caveat*, p. 22.
23. Sermon 5, *Justification by Faith*, WJW 1, 196.
24. *Caveat*, p. 22–3.
25. Sermon 10, *The Witness of the Spirit I*, WJW 1, 276.
26. JWL II, 70.
27. *Ibid.*, 101–2, 105.
28. *Caveat*, pp. 23–4.
29. Sermon 36, *The Law Established Through Faith II*, WJW 2, 41.
30. *Caveat*, pp. 24–5.
31. Sermon 5, *Justification by Faith*, WJW 1, 187.
32. *Minutes of Conference 1744*, Works VIII, 277.
33. *Caveat*, pp. 25–6.
34. Sermon 13, *On Sin in Believers*, WJW 1, 324.
35. JWL VIII, 159.
36. C. Williams, *John Wesley's Theology Today*, London 1960, p. 123.
37. *Caveat*, pp. 26–7.
38. Sermon 35, *The Origin, Nature, Properties and Use of the Law*, WJW 2, 19.
39. *Caveat*, p. 27.
40. Sermon 106, *On Faith*, WJW 3, 496–7.
41. *Caveat*, pp. 27–9.
42. JWL III, 182.
43. *Caveat*, pp. 29–30.
44. Sermon 13, *On Sin in Believers*, WJW 1, 319.
45. *Caveat*, p. 30.
46. NNT I, 383.
47. *Caveat*, pp. 30–31.
48. *Predestination Calmly Considered*, Works X, 230.
49. *Caveat*, p. 31.
50. *Caveat*, pp. 31–2.
51. Sermon 4, *Scriptural Christianity*, WJW 1, 164.
52. *Caveat*, p. 32.
53. Sermon 58, *On Predestination*, WJW 2, 417.
54. *Caveat*, pp. 32–3.
55. Sermon 110, *Free Grace*, WJW 3, 553.
56. JWL VI, 175.

57. *Minutes of Conference 1770*, Works VIII, 337.
58. *Minutes of Conference 1771*, quoted in Tyerman *The Life and Times of the Rev. John Wesley*, London 1880, p. 100. See JWJ V, 427, for a facsimile of the document.

9. Popish Doctrines

1. Works X, 86ff.
2. *Ibid.*, 140ff.
3. JWL I, 118. See also NNT I, 282, on Luke 22:19–20.
4. Works IX, 56.
5. Father Jim Sullivan at the English College in Rome suggested to me that attrition must include the awakening of a conversion to God. It is not just the fear of hell.
6. The same point is made in NNT II, 357f.
7. See, e.g. JWL II, 55, and JWL III, 232, to illustrate the change in his thought on the ministry. For further discussion, see A. B. Lawson, *John Wesley and the Christian Ministry*, London 1963; A. R. George in *Ordination*, Vol. 2 of *History of the Methodist Church in Great Britain* ed. Davies, George & Rupp, London 1978.
8. NNT II, 287.
9. JWL III, 246.
10. JWJ II, 264.
11. Sermon 106, *On Faith*, para. I, 8, WJW 3, 496.
12. JWJ II, 264.
13. Works VIII, 215.
14. *The Additional Articles in Pope Pius' Creed No Articles of the Christian Faith, Being an Answer to a late Pamphlet, Intituled Pope Pius his proffession of Faith Vindicated from Novelty in Additional Articles (Gother) and the Prospect of Popery ... Defended*, by Mr Altham, London 1688, 87pp.
15. *The Advantage of the Members of the Church of England over Those of the Church of Rome*, para. 3 in Works X, 133ff.
16. Works VI, 199.
17. JWL III, 37.
18. *Decrees of Ecumenical Councils*, ed. N. Tanner, London 1990, p. 136.
19. NNT I, 199.
20. JWL III, 309.
21. NNT I, 305.
22. *Ibid.*, 146.
23. JWL VI, 26.
24. JWL V, 276.
25. Sermon 75, *On Schism*, WJW 3, 67.

26. Sermon 78, *Spiritual Idolatry*, WJW 3, 104. See also NNT II, 471.
27. JWL III, 107–8.
28. NNT II, 82, and JWL III, 370.
29. Epiphanius, *Contra Cath. Haer.*, 59; quoted by Wesley at this point.
30. JWL II, 320. See also WJW 4, 8, sermon on Dives and Lazarus.
31. JWJ II, 62.
32. JWL I, 277ff and JWJ II, 263.

10. Mr Wesley's Misrepresentations Answered

1. Oscott Recusant Archives, No. 1923.
2. Oscott Recusant Archives, Nos 2379, 2380.
3. John Wesley, *Letters*, Vol. VI, p. 372, Letter to Printer of *Public Advertiser*, 12 January 1780.
4. Gilbert, *op. cit.*, Archives 1923, p. 80.
5. Berington, *The State and Behaviour of English Catholics from the Reformation to 1780;* 1790, 2 Volumes. Milner, *Brief Account of Richard Challoner*, 1798. O'Leary, *Remarks on John Wesley's Letters*, 1780. Petre, *Address to the President of the Protestant Association*, 1782.
6. Mason, *op. cit.*, Archives 2379, 2380, p. 31.

11. The Papacy

1. NNT I, 77.
2. NNT II, 374.
3. NNT I, 451.
4. *Ibid.*, 421.
5. NNT II, 171.
6. NNT I, 433.
7. *Ibid.*, 507.
8. NNT II, 70.
9. *Ibid.*, 69.
10. NNT I, 385–6.
11. Gaius of Rome in Eusebius *Ecclesiastical History* II, 25.6–7. The deaths of Peter and Paul are also referred to in 1 Clement 5 (c 95).
12. Works X, 133ff.
13. *Ibid.*, 139.
14. *The Advantage of Members of the Church of England over Those of the Church of Rome*, Works X, 138–9.
15. JWJ II, 263.
16. 74th in Oxford edition, 73rd in *Ante-Nicene Fathers*. The question was whether baptized heretics needed to be rebaptized on their entry

into the Catholic Church. Stephen said no, Cyprian said yes, for only the true Church by baptism could convey the Holy Spirit.

17. *Op. cit.*, 73, para. 1.
18. See B. Kidd, *The Roman Primacy to* AD *461*, London 1936; H. Burn-Murdoch, *The Development of the Papacy*, London 1954; J. Tillard, *The Bishop of Rome*, London 1983.
19. Book VIII, Epistle XXX to Eulogius of Alexandria.
20. Book V, Epistle XVIII to John of Constantinople.
21. JWJ III, 348.
22. Wesley, Works X, 374ff.
23. *Ibid.*, 443ff.
24. NNT I, 452.
25. Renée Haynes, *Philosopher King*, London 1970.
26. NNT I, 399.
27. JWL VI, 291.
28. JWJ V, 290.
29. *Ibid.*, 521–2.
30. Works IV, 343. A slightly differing account is offered in JWJ VII, 191. Wesley's own library now at City Road, London, contains the two-volume *Interesting Letters of Clement XIV (Ganganelli)*, Dublin 1777, but there seems to be no record of this incident in the work. In the account in JWJ VII, 191, Wesley adds that Clement said, 'I am ready to go, not only through water, but through fire also, for my Lord's sake'. Wesley adds that Clement XIV sat only for two years in the papal chair. In fact, he was there for five years.
31. JWJ III, 325.
32. *Explanatory Notes on the New Testament*, London 1831, 2 volumes.
33. J. A. Bengel, *Gnomon*, ed. C. F. Werner, Stuttgart 1970, 2 volumes.
34. NNT II, 456.
35. *Ibid.*, 469.
36. *Ibid.*, 479.
37. *Ibid.*, 488.
38. *Ibid.*, 489–90. The date for Gregory VII is not correct, nor are the facts about him. Gregory VII was declared beatus in 1584 by Clement VIII, made sanctus by Paul V in 1606, and the feast of St Gregory VII was made universal in 1728 by Benedict XIII, thereby causing a crisis in the relations of the Holy See and the Catholic states.
39. NNT II, 491–6.
40. *Ibid.*, 489.
41. *Ibid.*, 500.
42. *Ibid.*, 520.
43. 'To this holy city, famous for the memory of so many holy martyrs, run with religious alacrity', NNT II, 512.

12. Catholic Saints

1. JWJ I, 179.
2. JWL I, 324
3. JWJ II, 305.
4. JWJ III, 40.
5. JWL V, 121–2.
6. *Ibid.*, 320.
7. JWL III, 258ff.
8. E. Duffy, 'Richard Challoner and the English Salesian Tradition' in *Clergy Review*, Vol LXVI, 12, pp. 449ff.
9. See H. Bremond, *The Thundering Abbot*, London 1950.
10. JWJ III, 325.
11. See G. Smith, *The Teaching of the Catholic Church*, London 1948, pp. 27, 71, 677, 708.
12. JWJ IV, 480.
13. Von Hügel, *The Mystical Element of Religion*, 2 Volumes, London 1912.
14. 'A Short Account of the Life and Death of the Reverend John Fletcher', Works VII, 431.
15. JWL IV, 293.
16. JWJ IV, 138.
17. JWJ III, 42.
18. Second letter to Lavington. Works IX, 57.
19. 'A Farther Appeal to Men of Reason and Religion', Works VIII, 46ff.
20. JWJ I, 414ff.
21. Works X, 173.
22. Works IX, 57.
23. JWL III, 262.
24. JWJ IV, 540.
25. Sermon 20, *The Lord our Righteousness*, WJW 1, 455.
26. JWJ IV, 480.

13. Catholic Spirituality

1. Croft Cell's dictum of 1935 in *The Rediscovery of John Wesley* is most often quoted: 'a unique and necessary synthesis of the Protestant ethic of grace with the Catholic ethic of holiness'. But see H. Rack *Reasonable Enthusiast*, p. 400.
2. John Wesley, *A Plain Account of Christian Perfection*, Epworth 1968 edn., pp. 112–3.
3. *A Plain Account*, p. 6.
4. *Ibid.*, p. 12.
5. *A Christian Library*, Vol. 38, pp. 14ff.

6. *A Plain Account*, pp. 97ff.
7. Massa, Mark in *Methodist History*, Vol. XXII, No. 1, Oct 1983, *The Catholic Wesley: A Revisionist Prologomenon*, pp. 38ff.
8. *A Plain Account*, p. 99.
9. *Ibid.*, p. 102.
10. Gwynn, Denis, *Richard Challoner*, Douglas Argan 1946, p. 84.
11. JWJ I, 416: quoting *Imitatio* of Kempis I.19.
12. E.g. JWJ I, 152, 184, 198, 209, 222, 416, 466.
13. JWL I, 16.
14. E.g. JWL I, 263n; III, 398; IV, 83n; VII, 54: JWJ, III, 158; IV, 262; V, 117.
15. JWJ I, 175; JWJ I, 137.
16. JWL III, 332, 370; JWJ II, 467.
17. JWJ II, 515.
18. JWJ I, 219.
19. JWL I, 415.
20. Duffy, Eamon, 'Wesley and the Counter Reformation' in ed. Garnett, Jane and Matthew, Colin, *Revival and Religion since 1700*. Essays for John Walsh. London 1993, pp. 1–19.
21. JWJ I, 133.
22. *Ibid.*, 135–6.
23. *Ibid.*, 420, quoted.
24. *Ibid.*, 420.
25. JWL I, 207.
26. *Ibid.*, 238ff.
27. Works X, 403.
28. *Ibid.*, 438.
29. For reservations see e.g. JWL V, 341–2; VI, 125; VI, 233.
30. JWJ IV, 363–4.
31. JWL V, 193; VI, 8; VI, 128; VI, 281.
32. *A Christian Library*, Vol. 38, pp. 5ff.
33. JWL VI, 43–4.
34. *A Christian Library*, Vol. 38, p. 75.
35. JWJ III, 451 and note.
36. *A Christian Library*, Vol. 23. The editorial footnote is in the later edition of 1817 ff. Vol. 13, p. 164.
37. *A Christian Library*, Vol. 23, p. 54 (part V).
38. *A Christian Library*, 2nd ed., London 1826, Vol. 21, p. 359 (Letter XII).
39. *Ibid.*, Vol. 38, pp. 14f (Letter I).
40. *Ibid.*, Vol. 38, pp. 38ff (para XIV).
41. Richard Green, *The Works of John and Charles Wesley*, London 1896, p. 93.
42. See e.g. *My God, My Glory*, SPCK 1954.

43. *A Christian Library*, 2nd ed., London 1826, Vol. 25, p. 374 (Psalm XIII for Saturday).
44. *Ibid.*, p. 349 (Psalm VI for Friday).
45. *Ibid.*, p. 328 (Psalm VI for Thursday).
46. *A Christian Library*, 2nd ed., London 1826, Vol. 26, p. 415 (Letter XIII).
47. *Ibid.*, Vol. 50, p. 335ff. *Arminian Magazine* 1780, p. 249ff.
48. *Ibid.*, Vol. 50, p. 396 (Ch. XIV).
49. *Ibid.*, Vol. 50, p. 389 (Ch. XIII).
50. JWL VI, 166; VI, 200; VI, 373; VI, 381; VIII, 253.
51. JWL VI, 373, to Ann Bolton.
52. JWL VI, 222–3; VI, 270.
53. *The Works of the Rev. John Wesley*, Vol. XXIV, Bristol 1773.
54. *Ibid.*, p. 127.
55. *Ibid.*, p. 127.
56. JWJ V, 249.
57. Works XXIV, 242.
58. *Ibid.*, 249.
59. JWJ III, 72.
60. JWJ IV, 422.
61. JWJ (1747).
62. *An Extract of the Life of Madame Guion*, London 1776.
63. JWL V, 342.
64. JWL VI, 261.
65. JWL IV, 313.
66. JWL III, 269.
67. JWL V, 237.

14. Catholic Practices

1. Sermon 61, *The Mystery of Iniquity*, WJW Vol. 2, ed. Outler, Nashville 1984, p. 464.
2. Sermon 63, *The General Spread of the Gospel*, WJW 2, 487.
3. *Popery Calmly Considered*, Works X, 155ff.
4. Sermon 92, *On Zeal*, WJW 3, 318.
5. *Op. cit.*, 309.
6. JWL VII, 89.
7. Sermon 90, *An Israelite Indeed*, WJW 3, 284–6.
8. *Popery Calmly Considered*, Works X, 155ff.
9. JWL VI, 370ff.
10. *Journal*, 28 July 1738. This extract is from Jackson's edition of the *Works* and does not appear in the Standard Edition. It was probably

in Cologne that he bought a copy of the Catechism of the Council of Trent.
11. *Journal* (ed. Jackson), 30 May 1750, Works II, 191–2.
12. JWJ IV, 270.
13. *Ibid.*, 268.
14. Sermon 127, *On the Wedding Garment*, WJW 4, 145.
15. *Journal* (ed. Jackson), Works III, 276.
16. JWL VIII, 28.
17. Sermon 78, *Spiritual Idolatry*, WJW 3, 104.
18. Sermon 26, *Sermon on the Mount VI*, WJW 1, 577.
19. Sermon 69, *The Imperfection of Human Knowledge*, WJW 2, 581.
20. *The Doctrine of Original Sin*, Works IX, 217–19.
21. Sermon 102, *Of Former Times*, WJW 3, 450–1.
22. *A Farther Appeal to Men of Reason and Religion*, Works VIII, 190–1.
23. Sermon 122, *Causes of the Inefficacy of Christianity*, WJW 4, 8–9.
24. Sermon 91, *On Charity*, WJW 3, 299.
25. JWJ IV, 503; 13 May 1762.
26. Sermon 97, *On Obedience to Pastors*, WJW 3, 374; Sermon 104, *On Attending the Church Service*, WJW 3, 470.
27. JWL VI, 370f.

15. **Other Works**

1. *A Word to a Protestant*, Works XI, 191.
2. *A Word in Season* or *Advice to an Englishman*, Works XI, 182.
3. Works XI, 187ff.
4. Works X, 129.
5. *Ibid.*, 130.
6. *Ibid.*, 133.
7. *The Advantage of the Members of the Church of England over Those of the Church of Rome*, Works X, 133ff.
8. *Ibid.*, 140.
9. Sermon 39, WJW 2, 79ff.
10. Sermon 20, *The Lord our Righteousness*, WJW 1, 454.
11. *Op. cit.*, 86. See also JWJ III, 72, for Wesley's reaction to Challoner on private judgement.
12. The Report of the Third World Conference on Faith and Order, Lund 1952, p. 34.
13. Sermon 53, *On the Death of George Whitefield*, WJW 2, 345.
14. Sermon 106, *On Faith*, WJW 3, 500.
15. Sermon 74, *Of the Church*, WJW 3, 52.
16. Sermon 106, *On Faith*, WJW 3, 496.
17. *Arminian Magazine*, 1779, p. 598ff.

18. See NNT II, 107, 291.
19. JWL III, 244ff. See also Works X, 306ff.
20. JWJ IV, 247.

16. Catholics and Other Methodists

1. Crookshank, *History of Methodism in Ireland*, Belfast 1885, Vol. I, p. 2.
2. Wesley, Charles, *Journal*, Vol. II, p. 34.
3. *The Lives of Early Methodist Preachers*, ed. Thomas Jackson, London 1866, Vol. III, p. 102.
4. Crookshank, *op. cit.*, Vol. I, p. 378.
5. *Ibid.*, p. 357.
6. *Ibid.*, pp. 436–7.
7. *Lives, op. cit.*, Vol. V, p. 235.
8. Crookshank, *op. cit.*, Vol. I, p. 340.
9. *Ibid.*, p. 319.
10. Whitefield, George, *Works*, Vol. III, pp. 207–9.
11. Crookshank, Vol. I, p. 331.
12. *Ibid.*, I, pp. 27 8; *The Poetical Works of John and Charles Wesley*, ed. G., Osborn, Vol. VIII, p. 395.
13. Wesley, Charles, *Journal*, Vol. II, p. 19.
14. *Ibid.*, p. 22.
15. *Ibid.*, pp. 22–3.
16. *Ibid.*, p. 27.
17. *Poetical Works*, op. cit., Vol. VIII, p. 398.
18. Crookshank, *op. cit.*, Vol. I, p. 415.
19. Wesley, Charles, *Journal*, Vol. II, p. 31.
20. *Ibid.*, Vol. I, p. 460.
21. *Ibid.*, Vol. II, p. 5.
22. *Ibid.*, p. 2.
23. *Lives*, Vol. I, p. 208.
24. Tyreman, Luke, *Wesley's Designated Successor*, London 1882, pp. 76–9.
25. *Ibid.*, pp. 156–7.
26. *Ibid.*, pp. 159, 445.
27. *Lives*, Vol. IV, p. 239.
28. *Ibid.*, VI, p. 6.
29. *Ibid.*, VI, p. 286.
30. *Ibid.*, II, pp. 123–4.
31. Crookshank, *op. cit.*, Vol. I, pp. 287–9.
32. *Journal*, Vol. II, p. 272.

33. Jackson, Thomas, *Life of Charles Wesley*, London 1841, Vol. 2, pp. 359ff.
34. *Poetical Works, op. cit.*, Vol. VIII, p. 424.
35. Kimbrough, S. T. and Beckerlegge, Oliver, *The Unpublished Poetry of Charles Wesley*, Vol. I, p. 310.
36. Telford, John, *Life of Charles Wesley*, London 1900, p. 273.
37. *Unpublished Poetry, op. cit.*, Vol. I, p. 315.
38. 'The Methodists, an Humorous Burlesque Poem: Address'd to the Rev. Mr Whitefield and His Followers', London 1739. Quoted in Lyles, Albert, *Methodism Mocked*, London 1960, p. 152.
39. *Journal*, Vol. I, p. 355.
40. Quoted in Lyles, *op. cit.*, pp. 88–9.
41. *Journal*, Vol. I, pp. 354–5.
42. *Lives*, Vol. I, p. 146.
43. *Journal*, Vol. I, pp. 359–361; Baker, Frank, *London Quarterly and Holborn Review*, 'Methodism and the '45 Rebellion', London, October 1947, pp. 326–7.
44. 'Hymns for Times of Trouble' Hymns I and IV, *Poetical Works*, Vol. IV, pp. 57, 88–9.
45. *Journal*, Vol. I, p. 405.
46. *Ibid.*, p. 421.
47. 'Hymns for the Public Thanksgiving Day', Hymn III, *Poetical Works*, Vol. IV, pp. 97–8.
48. Baker, Frank, *William Grimshaw*, London 1963, p. 192.
49. Whitefield, George, *Seventy-Five Sermons*, Vol. I, London 1812.
50. *Lives*, Vol. V, p. 34.
51. *Lives*, Vol. III, pp. 70, 23.
52. Church, Leslie, *The Early Methodist People*, London 1948, p. 157.
53. Baker, *op. cit.*, p. 208.
54. See Church, *op. cit.*, p. 209.
55. 'An Earnest and Affectionate Address to the People Called Methodists' (1745). Quoted in Lyles, *op. cit.*, p. 94.
56. Newton, *op. cit.*, pp. 38–39.
57. *Poetical Works, op. cit.*, Vol. VI, pp. 71–72.
58. Baker, *op. cit.*, p. 241.
59. Morgan, Derek, *The Great Awakening in Wales*, London 1988, p. 264.
60. *Lives*, Vol. III, pp. 36–7.
61. WJW Vol. 2, ed. Outler, p. 344.
62. Morgan, *op. cit.*, p. 234.
63. Benson, Joseph, *Life of Rev. John W. de la Flechere*, London 1804, pp. 128–130.
64. *Lives*, Vol. III, p. 37.
65. *Ibid.*, Vol. VI, p. 86.
66. *Ibid.*, Vol. VI, p. 11.

67. *Ibid.*, Vol. III, pp. 32–3, 40.
68. *Ibid.*, Vol. VI, p. 7.
69. *Ibid.*, Vol. VI, p. 39.
70. *Ibid.*, Vol. II, p. 125.
71. *Ibid.*, Vol. III, p. 105.
72. Tyreman, *op. cit.*, p. 323.
73. *Lives*, Vol. I, p. 71.
74. *Ibid.*, Vol. III, p. 40.
75. Tyreman, *op. cit.*, p. 162.
76. *Ibid.*, p. 411.
77. E.g. Charles Wesley, *Journal*, Vol. I, p. 405.
78. In 'Appendix to Commentary on the Apocalypse', quoted in Vickers, John, *Thomas Coke*, London 1969, p. 330.
79. *Lives*, Vol. III, p. 34.
80. *Ibid.*, Vol. III, p. 4.
81. Whitefield, *Works*, Vol. III, pp. 73, 70.
82. *Works of John Wesley*, ed. Thomas Jackson, Vol. VI, p. 464.
83. Quoted in Dallimore, Arnold, *George Whitefield*, Edinburgh 1960, p. 56.
84. E.g. Orcibal, Jean, 'The Theological Originality of John Wesley', in *History of the Methodist Church in Great Britain*, ed. Rupert Davies and Gordon Rupp, Vol. I, p. 141.
85. Wesley, John and Charles, *Hymns and Sacred Poems*, London 1739, III–X.
86. Newton, John, *Susanna Wesley and the Puritan Tradition in Methodism*, London 1968, p. 155.
87. *A Short Account of the Experience of Mrs H. A. Rogers*, London 1793, p. 41.
88. Quoted in Church, Leslie, *More About the Early Methodist People*, London 1949, p. 49.
89. *Ibid.*, p. 34.
90. Baker, *op. cit.*, p. 18.
91. *Poetical Works*, Vol. VII, p. 43.
92. *Lives*, Vol. V, p. 218.
93. Whitefield, *Works*, Vol. III, pp. 78–9, 68, 76.
94. *Lives*, Vol. I, pp. 154–8.
95. *Ibid.*, p. 160.
96. *Ibid.*, p. 124.
97. *Ibid.*, Vol. III, p. 38.
98. *Ibid.*, Vol. I, p. 227.
99. Jackson, *op. cit.*, Vol. II, p. 320.

Index